CREATIVITY
and
SPIRITUALITY

CREATIVITY and SPIRITUALITY

Bonds between Art and Religion

Earle J. Coleman

STATE UNIVERSITY OF NEW YORK PRESS

Cover illustration: *Bare Willows and Distant Mountains* by Ma Yuan (active 1190–1235; Southern Song Dynasty). Round fan mounted as album leaf; ink and light color on silk (23.8 × 24.2 cm). Chinese and Japanese Special Fund. Courtesy, Museum of Fine Arts, Boston

Production by Ruth Fisher
Marketing by Anne M. Valentine

Published by
State University of New York Press, Albany

For information, address the State University of New York Press,
State University Plaza, Albany, NY 12246

Library of Congress Cataloging-in-Publication Data

Coleman, Earle Jerome.
    Creativity and spirituality : bonds between art and religion /
Earle J. Coleman.
        p. cm.
    Includes bibliographical references and index.
    ISBN 0-7914-3699-3 (hc : alk. paper). — ISBN 0-7914-3700-0 (pb :
alk. paper)
    1. Art and religion. I. Title.
BL65.A4C65   1998
291.1'75—dc21   97-19143
                                                                CIP

10   9   8   7   6   5   4   3   2   1

For Karen

Contents

Preface   ix

Introduction   xiii

1. Art, Religion, and Relations   1

2. The Perceptible, the Imperceptible, and a Total Response   29

3. Receptivity, Omnipresence, and Sui Generis Emotions   49

4. The Self and Union   71

5. Artistic Beauty, Natural Beauty, and Supernatural Beauty   107

6. The Child-State and Revelation   133

7. Creativity   155

8. The Aesthetic versus the Spiritual   183

Notes   199

Bibliography   215

Index   221

Preface

Since writing a dissertation on Chinese aesthetics, which was published as *Philosophy of Painting by Shih T'ao*, I have focused upon religious aesthetics. My subsequent writings have addressed Buddhist, Christian, Hindu, Jewish, and Taoist theories of art and nature. In teaching aesthetics and philosophy of religion courses for some twenty-five years, I particularly lingered over questions about relations between art and religion. The chief purpose of this book is to explore their shared features. While Chapter 8 discusses possible distinctions between the two, above all, I identify similarities, convergencies, parallels, or common denominators between the spheres of art and religion by turning to spiritual figures such as Lao Tzu and Teresa of Avila, artists such as Mozart and Shih-t'ao, and theologians and philosophers such as Martin Buber and Paul Tillich. Recently I have taught courses on relations between art and religion; and I have published some of my findings in articles. The present book, however, affords me the opportunity to refine my thoughts and to present a sustained analysis of the numerous and fundamental affinities between the categories of the artistic and the religious. To understand any phenomenon always requires understanding another, as when one studies French in order to better grasp English. It is my hope that this study of relations between art and religion will not only be intrinsically interesting, but will somewhat illumine art and religion themselves.

Many people have contributed significantly to the writing of this book. I am grateful to the late Dr. Malcolm F. Stewart of Illinois College and the late Dr. C.Y. Chang of the University of Hawaii for expertly guiding me through Western and Eastern philosophies; Virginia Commonwealth University for a grant and a reduced teaching load; my students at Virginia Commonwealth University; Professors Frank Burch Brown of Christian Theological Seminary, Andrew M. Greeley of the University of Chicago, and Patrick J. Sherry of Lancaster University, whose reviews of the manuscript were invaluable; Arnold Berleant, Professor Emeritus of Long Island University, C.W. Post College, Maurice Friedman, Professor Emeritus of San Diego State University, and Professors James Alfred Martin, Jr. University Professor of Wake Forest University, Thomas R. Martland of the State University of New York, and Holmes Rolston III of Colorado State University were all kind enough to read a prospectus and to offer helpful criticism or encouragement; and especially my wife, Karen, whose support has been unwavering. My colleague, Anthony Ellis, generously assisted with the final preparation of the manuscript. For their ready helpfulness I wish to thank the following editors at the State University of New York Press: Ruth Fisher, Anne M. Valentine, Nancy Ellegate, and Alan V. Hewat. I should also like to thank the publishers of the books and the editors of the journals from which I have quoted for granting me permission to reproduce their copyrighted material.

Reprinted with the permission of T & T Clark Ltd. and Scribner, a Division of Simon & Schuster, from I AND THOU by Martin Buber, translated by Walter Kaufmann. Translation copyright ©1970 Charles Scribner's Sons, New York.

Reprinted with the permission of Long Beach Publications, from my chapter, "Creativity and Spirituality: A Cross-Cultural Inquiry into Relations between Art and Religion," which first appeared in EAST-WEST ENCOUNTERS IN PHILOSOPHY AND RELIGION, Edited by Ninian Smart and B. Srinivasa Murthy. Copyright ©1996, Long Beach, California.

Reprinted with the permission of the Crossroad Publishing Company, from ON ART AND ARCHITECTURE, by Paul Tillich. Edited by John Dillenberger and Jane Dillenberger, translated by Robert P. Scharlemann. Copyright ©1987, New York.

Reprinted with the permission of Hackett Publishing Company, Inc., from WHAT IS ART? by Leo Tolstoy. Translated by Almyer Maude. Copyright ©1996. Cambridge, Massachusetts, and Indianapolis, Indiana. Bobbs-Merrill Company, Inc., Copyright © 1960. Indianapolis and New York.

Reprinted with permission, from my article "On the Inseparability of Art and Religion," which first appeared in *Religious Traditions,* Volume 15 16 17, 1992, 1993, 1994, 83–111. Montreal, Quebec, Canada.

Reprinted with permission, from my article "The Beautiful, the Ugly and the Tao," which first appeared in the *Journal of Chinese Philosophy*, Volume 18, issue 2, 1991, 213–226. Honolulu, Hawaii.

Reprinted with permission, from my article "Beauty and the 'I' of Buber's Beholder," which first appeared in *Religious Education*, Volume 84, Number 1, Winter 1989, 131–149. New Haven, Connecticut.

Reprinted with permission, from my article "Religion as Art and Harmony," which first appeared in *Religious Education*, Volume 86, Number 1, Winter 1991, 5–19. New Haven, Connecticut.

Introduction

Art and religion have often been reciprocal powers, religion inspiring art and it, in turn, communicating the numinous. Indeed, the present distinction between the aesthetic and the spiritual was, to a certain extent, foreign to the ancients, e.g., to early Hindus who had no secular art as such. Although it is hardly possible to recapture their vision, I analyze some of the factors that secured it and that continue to promote a similar outlook today. Early societies were not given to marking off art from religion, nor were they given to marking off either from other aspects of culture. Thus, James Alfred Martin Jr. states: "'Classical' cultures do not designate certain things 'artworks,' certain persons 'artists,' and certain values 'aesthetic.' Similarly, in such cultures there is not an area or segment of life that is thought of as the culture's 'religion' . . . "[1] A trace of this reluctance to distinguish persists in the contemporary native of Bali who, when asked about art, declared: "We have no art; we do everything as well as we can."

Discussions of the relations between the aesthetic and the spiritual are still rather uncommon; and when they occur, discussants often conjoin art and religion in a disparaging way: " . . . hallucinatory experience can be labeled pathological, artistic, religious, and so on, according to one's taste . . . "[2] A prominent contemporary theologian criticizes "aestheticizing theologians" for being "on the high altitude flight of mysticism." Of course, Freudians are prone to characterize both art and religion as exercises in wish fulfillment, interpreting the artist as someone who paints his object of desire and the religious individual as someone who worships an ideal father figure in the sky. Society can be equally suspicious of the starving artist, who persists in the face of economic opposition, and the fasting monk who renounces material wealth and shaves his head. To aggravate matters, religion and art have long been associated with drugs. As Karl Marx said that religion is the opiate of the people, William James asserted that drunkenness is the symphony concert and literature of the poor. While critics often attack the ideas of artists and religious pioneers on the grounds that such figures are mentally unstable, James denounces these assaults for committing the genetic fallacy: "In the natural sciences and industrial arts it never occurs to anyone to try and refute opinions by showing up their author's neurotic constitution. Opinions here are invariably tested by logic and experiment, no matter what may be their author's neurological type."[3] More recently, a number of writers have made valuable contributions to mapping out relations between art and religion.[4]

Concerning such relations, the influential theologian and philosopher Friedrich Schleiermacher is not encouraging: "I could wish to leave the question for your own solution, for me the inquiry is too difficult and too strange."[5] Ananda K. Coomaraswamy is less diffident and categorically equates the two: "Art is religion, religion art, not related, but the same."[6] This assertion by the twentieth-century philosopher, Orientalist, linguist, art historian, and pioneering curator of the Indian collection at the Boston Museum of Fine Arts both repels and attracts. Taken literally and without qualification, the claim is patently false, for however much art and religion may overlap, they are nonetheless different enterprises. At least, the expression "irreligious art" does not seem to be a contradiction in terms. Thus, an Alfred North Whitehead could conceive of religion as the art of cultivating the interior person—without holding that all art is religious. Nevertheless, one returns to Coomaraswamy's identity thesis, for it is revealing as well as repelling. While opposed to any identification of art and religion, I will present some of the myriad ways in which the aesthetic and the sacred interpenetrate. Analysis of these diverse ways may instill a fresh appreciation of Coomaraswamy's admittedly hyperbolical assertion. Other theorists, such as Paul Weiss, insist that art and religion are independent projects, altogether different enterprises.[7] Proposing a mean between Coomaraswamy and Weiss, I argue that art and religion, however different, are complementary responses to the quest for self-realization. At least, Coomaraswamy's overstatement encourages one to reflect upon important but neglected similarities or connections between the aesthetic and the spiritual. For example, the mystical current in religions—with its emphasis upon the experiential, i.e., communion or union with the absolute—invites comparison with aesthetic experience in which one may lose herself through an all-consuming absorption in art or nature.

To exhibit ties between art and religion, I follow a threefold, cross-cultural approach. First, I draw ideas and motifs from religious classics in world literature, such as Lao Tzu's *Tao Te Ching* and *The Interior Castle* by Teresa of Avila, and relate them to aesthetic phenomena. For instance, I juxtapose Teresa's spiritual struggle, in which "seasons of dryness" interfere with her ability to pray, with the artistic problem of "writer's block" in which the "dryness" metaphor signifies the "drying up" of the artist's creative powers. Ironically enough, in Lamentations iii, 9, the author describes the obstacles on his path to prayer as blocks, for he calls them "square stones." Second, I turn to the writings of artists, such as Leo Tolstoy, Vincent van Gogh, Paul Gauguin, Shih- t'ao, and Wassily Kandinsky, for themes and practices that have religious significance. For instance, just as religion enjoins one to become like a child, art urges the would-be artist to return to a primordial innocence. Of course, the artist or the saint is not someone who remains a child or never grows up; instead, she carries her childhood along with her throughout life, integrating it with each successive stage of maturity. Since the child can be childish, i.e., self-centered and petulant, the goal of adults is to become childlike, i.e., possessed of only what is admirable in children. Third, I analyze and evaluate the writings of various theoreticians—philosophers, theologians, art critics, sociologists, and psychologists—who posit views on the relations between art and religion. One recurring theme is Martin Buber's distinction between I-Thou and I-It relations, the former kind of relationship capturing much that is central to art, creativity, and aesthetic experience as well as to the religious life.

I begin with a discussion of five parallels between art and religion. For example, history reveals their agreement in different ages and different societies. Thus, Kandinsky, who contributed monumentally to modern painting, held that when art is not flourishing, religion languishes: " . . . periods, during which art has no noble champion . . . are periods of retrogression in the spiritual world."[8] Similarly, the eminent British art critic, Clive Bell, asserted: " . . . the great ages of religion are commonly the great ages of art."[9] In short, the two often wax and wane in tandem. For example, corresponding to the "God is dead" theological movement of the 1960s, there was the cry "Art is dead" in response to movements, such as minimalist art, in the 1960s.

To explore correspondences between art and religion, I analyze various senses in which one may predicate either of the other. From a religious perspective, the omnipresence of the divine ensures that all things have a religious character. As the ultimate, undifferentiated reality that sustains all being, Brahman is as all-pervasive as salt dissolved in water. Hence, artworks, like other kinds of objects, cannot be devoid of spirituality. Of course, great works of art would be those that express spirituality to a greater degree. Omnipresence may further explain why any subject matter is suitable for the religiously disposed artist. Perhaps omnipresence also illumines the fact of human wonder over the simple existence of a thing, no matter how banal it may seem. If so, an infant's fascination with an unfamiliar object may be spiritual as well as aesthetic. But if omnipresence renders everything religious, this does not distinguish art from natural objects. Moreover, not all art, e.g., a contemporary commercial jingle on the radio, is religious. There are, however, grounds for affirming the converse. That all religion is artistic is more plausible, because each world religion exhibits artistic excellence, whether in the poetry of Chuang Tzu, the epic of the *Bhagavadgītā*, the Beatitudes of Christ, the lyrical calligraphy of Islam, the landscape paintings of Zen Buddhism, or the Hebrew Psalter. As Weiss emphasized, all religions have some art: "If a religion forbids the making of images, recourse will be had to music, arabesques, dance; if it forbids the use of song, men will cultivate the graces of speech; if it frowns on the theatre or the use of musical instruments, it will allow room for architecture or poetry."[10] Moreover, the aesthetic value of sacred texts provides one criterion for the assessment of religions. Accordingly, one may assign low marks to a new religious movement if its writings are devoid of artistic merit as expressed in myths, narratives, poetry, anecdotes, parables, allegories, analogies, metaphors, or other literary vehicles.

To emphasize one role of art in the service of religion, I interpret some artworks as intermediaries, "avatars," or "incarnations" that yoke the human and the divine. Bridging the visible and the invisible, the tangible and the intangible, certain art points to what transcends prose. Religions typically enlist the aid of spiritual figures in order to close the gap between finite humans and the infinite absolute. In Hinduism, there is the avatar or descent form of God, as exemplified by Krishna, which many compare to the incarnation of Christ. In Buddhism, there is the Bodhisattva who stands between humans and the invisible *Dharmakāya*. Hasidic Judaism has the *tsadik* (a Bodhisattva-like figure) and the ten *sefirot* (ten divine powers) that emanate from God. Indeed, all cultures have intermediaries in the form of angels. I hold that one should also understand religious artworks as intermediaries. Art, like nature, can serve as a vehicle by which humans reach for the divine. I further contend that humans, who are aesthetic as well as rational beings, cannot fully encounter God without song, however simple, or without poetry, however elementary. It is telling that one may translate *The Bhagavadgītā* as "The Song of God."

My general procedure is to identify and discuss common denominators between art and religion or between the aesthetic and the spiritual. For example, the latter two find positive value to be omnipresent. Thus, Francis of Assisi finds God everywhere, even in the sun and moon, which he dubs "Brother Sun and Sister Moon." Likewise, the British painter John Constable sees beauty everywhere: "I never saw an ugly thing in my life, for let the form of an object be what it may,—light, shade, and perspective will always make it beautiful."[11] In other words, whatever exists has beauty, because whatever has being has form and whatever has form has its own distinctive beauty. To Constable, all things are aesthetic; and to the pure all things are pure (Titus, I: 15). When Genesis declares that all creation is good, it is perhaps partly on the aesthetic grounds that order is more beautiful than chaos. Francis's poem, "The Canticle of Brother Sun," more explicitly celebrates the beauty of the entire creation from "Brother Sun" to the worm at one's feet. For Francis, the beautiful and the holy are present in all times and places, but for others, beauty exists only at scenic vistas or in art galleries, and religion exists exclusively within churches, temples, or mosques.

Undoubtedly, the most fundamental common denominator between art and religion is a quest for union, unity or oneness. Ironically, this theme is complex, for as William James remarked, "The world is one—in more ways than one." Relating art and religion, I distinguish three senses of union, three kinds of oneness or unity. First, there is the unification of the self, i.e., self-integration. Art and religion, like love, excel at effecting this existential wholeness. Whether one desires union with the divine, another person, nature, or an artwork, self-integration is a prerequisite, for the self that is to merge should be the realized, actualized self. The religiously disposed artist, like the mystic, wishes for unity, wishes to bring order out of chaos, integration out of fragmentation. However, one must first attain some degree of self-integration before she can appropriate a theme, concept, or emotion and create an artwork possessed of significant integrity. Moreover, a focused artwork, being a paradigm of unity, can promote psychic integration in beholders. Indeed, one basic purpose of aesthetic experiences is to restore harmony, integration, balance, equanimity, proportion, or wholeness. Of course, the pursuit may be less self-conscious, as when Amish women integrate pieces of colored cloth into the geometric designs of their quilts and thereby bring harmony into their lives and into their community. Similarly, Kandinsky understands good form in art as that which is capable of evoking corresponding vibrations in the soul. While these attuned vibrations in a beholder's soul proceed from the harmony (Kandinsky sometimes uses the expression "form-harmony") of the work, they derive ultimately from the spiritual vibrations that animated the artist.

A second kind of union is found in one's object of attention, be it the simplicity of the absolute or the integrity of a painting. Even a state of being can possess such unity, since one's spiritual consciousness may have an integrity that is just as deserving of preservation as a great painting. When James of Massa asked Brother Giles, who was one of St. Francis's most illustrious disciples, how he should act during a state of rapture, Giles replied: "Don't add. Don't take away." In other words, when one is enjoying religious ecstasy, he should leave the condition of grace intact. Similarly, the art lover insists that any alteration of a masterpiece reduces its aesthetic value. A kind of reciprocity obtains when a creator, who effects coherency in an artwork, simultaneously experiences greater personal integration. Third, many thinkers regard the union of relationship as the ultimate expression of art, religion, and love. Tolstoy, for example, thinks that art is a failure if it does not elicit a unique feeling of joy and of spiritual union with others. Invariably, the artist tries to identify with her subject matter, model, or form, the saint attempts to become one with her spiritual reality, and the lover strives to unite with her beloved. Each desires an intimacy in which subject-object distinctions diminish or disappear. Each aims for communion, fusion or identification with her respective object of attention. Thus, an Islamic saint may assert: "God is closer to me than my own jugular vein," and a da Vinci may declare, "He who cannot become the object cannot draw it." Ideally, the art lover follows suit by empathizing and becoming attuned to the work. When an artist's insight into things breaks down barriers between the self and the other, interpenetration between them flourishes. Hence, the Taoist painter proclaims: "the mountains are in me and I am in them."

Since "harmony" expresses the highest form of union, I submit that great art and religion are allied practices, because they are both efforts after harmony, i.e., attempts to promote harmony within the self, between the self and others, between the self and nature, or between the self and the divine. Because humans long for wholeness, art and religion are most satisfying when they reconcile tensions, calm and dissipate fears, mitigate sorrows, or wring unity out of opposites. Art and religion find their deepest family resemblance in the yearning for harmony. Their common momentum reflects a yearning to return to the condition of the child, i.e., to a state of relative harmony or tranquillity. As a Taoist would put it, even when children are quite active, they can enjoy a "rest amidst motion." Whether creating art or playing, the child can escape from the storms of daily life to a relative repose. A failure to harmonize one's thoughts, feelings, and willings undermines aesthetic as well as spiritual progress, resulting in enfeebled art and debilitated religion. Of course, this is significant because the harmonies in artworks have a way of effecting harmony in the beholder. Such aesthetic equanimity has its counterpart in the "peace that passes all understanding" of Christianity or the bliss (ananda) of Hinduism. No matter how tumultuous the artwork might be, if it is great, it ultimately induces harmony in the beholder—whether through a catharsis that restores one's emotional balance or by communicating the profound solidarity that a Tolstoy championed. Satire, for example, may arouse one's indignation and lead her to action that resolves some tension or disorder. Since the desire to be whole is a basic human craving, the most significant art eventually engenders harmony in the beholder. Art contributes to such wholeness when it unifies such natural opposites as light and dark, loud and soft, or circle and square, and when it simultaneously absorbs such theological opposites as the sacred and the profane.

Finally, I survey and evaluate various proposed differences between the aesthetic and the spiritual, e.g., the aesthetic is a passive mode of being and the spiritual is an active one. Through illustrations, analysis, and clarification I reject some such distinctions and explain how others are compatible with my proposal that the aesthetic and the spiritual are cognate categories. Ensconced in an "ivory tower," art becomes artificial; isolated or abstracted from ordinary life, religion becomes religiosity. Art and religion enjoy greatest vitality only when they interact, suffuse other aspects of life and are, in turn, suffused by them. Therefore, one can attribute both the aesthetic and the spiritual to phenomena as diverse as a rain dance and the martial arts.

Of course, art history, psychology, sociology, anthropology, and religious studies are replete with discussions of art and religion, but much remains to be said about how the two interrelate. There are few philosophical studies that consider how concepts such as "art," "beauty," "creativity," and "aesthetic experience" find their place or their counterparts in religious discourse and experience. By "art," I mean to embrace all the facets that inspire traditional theories: skillful activity—including craft as well as fine art, representation, the communication of emotions, and the creation of significant forms. By "religion," I mean the set of beliefs, values, practices, and experiences by which one interprets the meaning of existence. While one may use "religious" or "spiritual" interchangeably, the latter sometimes carries a non-institutional, experiential, broader sense. Similarly broad, the "aesthetic" encompasses whatever pertains to art, beauty, creativity, and the appreciation of nature.

Even among philosophical writings, there are surprisingly few sustained, book-length discussions of interconnections between the aesthetic and the spiritual. Concerning the broader significance of my project, religious aesthetics is inherently interdisciplinary, for to clarify relations between art and religion is to illumine religious studies, theology, art appreciation, art criticism, and art history as well as aesthetics. This is so because the success of any inquiry in these disciplines is dependent upon the sort of conceptual analysis that is distinctive of philosophy and that I use in order to clarify propositions, assess arguments, and trace theoretical implications. Finally, the study is multicultural, since it draws material from Western philosophy, Buddhism, Christianity, Hinduism, Islam, Judaism, and Taoism in order to pinpoint and clarify key concepts, doctrines, and activities that link art and religion.

1

ART, ReLigion, and ReLations

Five considerations, which show the interplay between art and religion, support the thesis that the two—although not interchangeable or identical—frequently parallel each other or converge. First and most evidently, one may appeal to their long-standing historical association. That religion and art are universally present in societies is obvious from a turn to different cultures in different eras. Agreeing with the view that when religion diminishes art declines, the Islamic scholar, Seyyed Hossein Nasr, remarks: " . . . whenever there has been a decay or eclipse of the spiritual dimension of Islam the quality of Islamic art has diminished."[1] Positively speaking, one might add that art and religion prospered together in the Gupta period of India, the medieval era of the West, or the Sung dynasty. Again, the so-called axial age of Confucius, Lao Tzu, and the Buddha gave rise to such monumental aesthetic achievements as the Great Stupa in Sanchi. Historically, religious motifs, themes, insights, figures, practices, and values have enriched and animated world art; and it, in turn, has facilitated the transmission of sacred scriptures, doctrines, sermons, experiences, and prayers. Cross-culturally, art reflecting religion, energized by religion, or in the service of religion has frequently prevailed.

For a recent illustration of the ties between religion and art, one may turn to the "God is dead" theological movement of the mid-1960s. A *Time Magazine* cover, dated April 8, 1966, arrestingly declared: "God is dead," thereby introducing to popular culture a doctrine that some trace to Nietzsche. In God-is-dead theology, worse than deceased, God was found to be insignificant. Humans were

1

said to be operating in an increasingly "God-free" way, since God no longer seemed to play a vital role in the daily lives of his creatures. It was as if artists had usurped God's creativity and scientists had stolen God's omnipotence. Radical thinkers argued that the church must go on without any concept of God at all; others concluded that the idea of God as "an old man in the sky" was empty and that humans needed a more meaningful conception. Dietrich Bonhoeffer, the Lutheran theologian who became a martyr at the hands of the Nazis, predicted during World War II that: "We are proceeding toward a time of no religion at all." At the same time, God had nearly vanished from the canvas of twentieth-century Western art. For all the images of God depicted in previous centuries by the Master of Flemalle, Hubert and Jan van Eyck, Mathias Grunewald, Michelangelo, William Blake, and Albert Pinkham Ryder, there is only the occasional depiction by a contemporary such as Paul Klee. Of course, this is not to say that paintings that carry no obvious references to God are devoid of spiritual import. No less an exponent of nonrepresentational art than Kandinsky titled his classic monograph: *Concerning the Spiritual in Art*. Because his paintings are not literal depictions of any deity, but suggestive, evocative compositions, the Chinese Taoist as well as the Christian can find them to be spiritually meaningful.

Not surprisingly, also in the 1960s, a correspondingly critical turn appeared in art; the cry "Art is dead" meant that art had run its course; it was empty of creativity, just as religion was empty of spirituality. On Western painting in the 1960s, John W. Dixon, remarks:

> All signs of the artist's personality are effaced. . . . Sculpture becomes pure geometric forms. . . . The work of art is reduced to pure objecthood . . . the artist works hard to cancel out "interest," that is, any sensuous quality or any complex of internal relations that can give pleasure or direct our attention in time. . . . Here is the artistic statement of the death of God. . . . The minimal art of the 1960's; the color painting of Stella, Louis, Olitski, and the art of many others, make this same affirmation.[2]

Also flourishing in the twentieth century, the anti-artist Marcel Duchamp exhibited "Fountain," an ordinary urinal, in an art museum, leading some critics to conclude that art was effete. Discussing anti-art, Nicholas Wolterstorff interprets Duchamp's action, "What counts is the gesture, along with the reasons for the gesture, not the object with which the gesture is made. In such gestures there is a repudiation of the aesthetic."[3] Interestingly enough, in the last third of the century, the eminent theologian Paul Tillich wrote an essay entitled "The Overcoming of the Concept of Religion in the Philosophy of Religion."[4] In one of his last lectures on art, he talks about non-art and non-religion:

> [T]here are fascinating artistic elements, expressive elements in this new art; but at the same time, one finds an element of something that is "non-art." In other realms of culture, similar phenomena are emerging. There is a religion of non-religion, a religion which has nothing to do with the religion of individuals or groups in the traditional sense. There is a theology that makes use of a language "without God."[5]

Continuing, Tillich complains about contemporary music that neglects the muses and is content to merely link noises. On the disappearance of religion, he notes that psychology, which originally meant knowledge of the soul, has lost its spiritual associations.

Martin Buber, perhaps the most distinguished Jewish philosopher-theologian of this century, wrote about the "eclipse of God" and the "obscuring of eternity." The eclipse occurs not in God but between us and God. To grasp Buber's contribution to aesthetics in particular or to religion and philosophy in general, one must understand his fundamental distinction between two different relationships or orientations toward the world: the I-Thou posture and the I-It posture. With the former stance, one regards the other as a Thou, i.e., as a person rather than as a thing, as free rather than as determined. With the latter perspective, one regards the other as an object that is as determined as are all other mere things. If one adopts the I-It posture he cuts himself off from any divine light. Describing the Nazi regime as an age of the eclipse of God, Buber steadfastly maintained that the dawn would break.

To many, God and art were "dead" in the sense that both had reached a dead end, being displaced respectively by science and a retrogressive pseudo-art. In a recent book, *Beauty and Holiness: the Dialogue between Aesthetics and Religion*, J. A. Martin Jr. offers two chapters that analyze contemporary discussions of the termination of the activities, goals, or concepts of art and religion. Perhaps the "death" of art and religion occurred when the isolating concepts of "fine art" and "religion" displaced genuine art and spirituality and all their rich entanglements with every strand of cultural life. Interestingly enough, in Asia, where art and religion are conspicuously interfused, there was no death of, say, Japanese Buddhism any more than there was a death of Japanese art.

In recent times, pluralism, i.e., the view that one's own group does not have a monopoly on the truth, has dramatically affected— some would say infected—art and religion. The dizzying varieties of contemporary art, with no obvious paradigm for cross-cultural choosing, appreciating, or evaluating, are paralleled by the unprecedentedly bewildering plurality of religions today. Leaders in world religions have entered into dialogue with each other; journals such as *Buddhist Christian Studies* are now multiplying, but, as yet, the typical practitioner of a faith remains puzzled and intimidated by the implications of greater contact with religions other than his own. Concerning interfaith dialogue, one may wonder about the purpose of such conversation. After all, neither party is apt to convert the other in such exchanges. Moreover, the dialogue is sometimes between parties who are quite well versed in each other's religions and are not likely to enlarge their theological education. Perhaps the true value of such dialogue lies in the love or fellow-feeling that it may foster, since genuine dialogue involves being open, receptive, or loving toward the Thou. When Tolstoy affirms that the true value of art is to promote solidarity, brotherly love, or spiritual union, one can scarcely imagine a greater value.

At times, the average person is unable to make sense of the myriad kinds of art that abound, and even critics cannot agree upon aesthetic criteria—whether the six canons of traditional Chinese painting, Greco-Roman ideals, or contemporary manifestoes. From an I-Thou perspective, one should enter into dialogue with twentieth-century artists and their works, not view them from afar as "Its." Similarly, a member of one religion can engage those of other faiths in dialogue in order to understand, evaluate, or temper his own feelings and beliefs. Those who bring nothing but doctrines, dogmas, or propositions to the dialogue situation will fail. Success requires an intuitive receptivity and an existential posture—one that engages the total self, i.e., intellect, heart, and will. Unless one presents her whole being, she is not in a position to affirm the integrity of the other.

Religious claims of exclusivity—"We have the one, true way"— appear less compelling today than they did before recent encounters between and among the world religions. For example, the Christian vision of other religions as unfulfilled spiritual expressions that can only find their culmination in Christianity, has not been corroborated through a significant number of conversions from Hinduism, Buddhism, Islam, or Judaism. Nor has Islam's vision of itself as the fulfillment of Judaism and Christianity been realized. In fine, however well the doctrine of "survival of the fittest" serves the biologist, it does not seem to obtain among the major religions. When pluralism prevails, neither the world of religion nor that of art can be monolithic. Rather than one religion, there are many robust religions; rather than one prevailing school of art, there are more than ever. One can fruitfully compare religions to artworks, for both, at their best, are particular expressions of universal truths. Indeed, some would ask if one religion would be any more desirable than one world art. They might also propose that one religion or art would diminish the diversity, creativity, or fecundity of the human spirit. Generic religion is idolatry and generic art is counterfeit art or debased craft. Thus, particularity, individuality, or uniqueness figures as importantly in religion as it does in art. Naturally, if one enters into dialogue with members of other religions and identifies with them, this can threaten allegiance to her own tradition. Likewise, the artist who is in commerce with other artists risks losing his originality or style. The contemporary writer Anne Roiphe poses a related question: "I am wondering if one feels a primary identification with all the boat peoples afloat on all the waters of the globe, can there ever be a return to the particular group again?" Like a painter who genuinely appreciates other styles but retains her own, a devotee of a religion may respect other religions, but remain committed to her own. Vivekananda, one of the most celebrated of modern Hindus, liked to ask: "If God wanted one religion, why are there so many?" Rather than view different religions as contradictory, Vivekananda viewed them as complementary. Of course, one may also apply such an outlook to the varieties of art. Tolstoy saw the parallel and railed against the exclusivism that marked his time: "The artists of various sects, like the theologians of the various sects, mutually exclude and destroy themselves."[6]

As pluralism in art recognizes the aesthetic values in diverse schools, genres, movements, and cultures, pluralism in religion affirms that there are insights in all faiths. But skeptics argue that when religions contradict each other, they cannot all be right; therefore, they may very well all be wrong. Pluralists, of course, concede that all religions may be wrong some of the time, but this does not entail that all religions are wrong all of the time. They may all be right some of the time, as when they embrace an ethical principle such as the golden rule. Just as different countries, with their respective strengths and weaknesses, united to create the United Nations, different religious traditions, with their respective strengths and weaknesses, have united to form a Parliament of the World's Religions. Religions may glean truths from each other and, just as importantly, rediscover the significance of truths within their own tradition. Of course, the skeptic who holds that all religions are wrong invalidates the point of any such dialogue, and the Philistine who repudiates all of contemporary art does likewise.

It is not difficult to marshal reasoning in support of religious pluralism. For example, one may enlist Descartes's proof that there is an external world in order to defend the value of multiple religions. He argued that if reality consists of only minds and ideas, then God would be deceiving us, for there surely appears to be an outside, independent, physical world. But since to be a deceiver is to be imperfect and since God is perfect, he cannot be deceiving us about the existence of the material world. Similarly, one could ask: If there is but one true religion, why would God deceive us with so many tempting or even convincing counterfeits? Each of the world religions attracts with its art, miracle stories, accounts of revelation, moral codes, sacred spaces, saints or gurus, great thinkers, ascetics, and humanitarians. Indeed, students of comparative religion are prone to discover that the more they study different religions the harder it is for them to elevate one over all others. Any religion that purports to be supreme must come to terms with, for example, the fact that Hinduism has its spiritual masterpiece, the *Bhagavadgītā*, Christianity its New Testament, and Taoism its *Tao Te Ching*. Each text is at once a religious and an aesthetic classic that espouses moral principles of the highest order. People repeatedly turn to an artistic masterpiece, because it forever invites new understanding and appreciation. They also repeatedly turn to familiar scriptural passages, because they forever encourage fresh interpretations and analyses. Since every generation discovers fresh meanings, values, and insights in artistic classics and sacred texts, one may attribute their inexhaustibility to the inspiration of an unconditioned source. William James spoke of the absolute as a "more," and some would add that religious and artistic classics testify to the existence of this "more." Ironically enough, every successful articulation of a sacred text produces an awareness that some inexplicable import remains. It is hardly a coincidence that the writings of the world's religions are great artistic achievements, whether the narrative drama of the *Bhagavadgita*, the poetry of the *Tao Te Ching*, the parables of the New Testament, Sufi stories, or the Hassidic tales of Judaism. One wonders exactly why and how all these writings originated if all members of humanity were to adopt one religion. Since, for example, Hinduism contains ethics, monotheism, a descent form of God, monumental art, and a bewildering number of philosophical schools, one wonders on what precise grounds it can be relegated beneath Judaism, Islam, or Christianity.

Of course, exclusivism, i.e., regarding one's own view as supreme, may be understandable on the personal level, as when a parent declares, "My daughter is the best child in the world." Nevertheless, it is controversial on a social level when humans seek to communicate as equals. If one proclaims that her religion is the one true path, she may be making a psychological statement. After all, if any religion has an epistemological justification for its superiority, one wonders what the evidence is and why there has not been a rush to conversion. One tastes the foods of other cultures directly, but she tastes their religions twice, once directly and once more subtly—if sometimes more forcefully—through their arts. Witness how many American university students are drawn to Zen Buddhism precisely because of the evocative power of its arts. After all, if the food of other cultures nourishes one's body, and if their art moves one emotionally, their religions may have the capacity to stir one spiritually. In fact, Tolstoy suggests that it would be as erroneous for a people to think that their art was the only genuine art as it would for religious people to hold that their religion is the only true one.[7]

Taking religious pluralism to its ultimate conclusion, not only are there multiple religions, and multiple sub-sects, but, in a sense, each person has her own religion, for she brings different understandings and experiences to the faith that she embraces. An individual always filters the elements of any religion through his unique consciousness, thereby yielding one's own personal religion. Similarly, the creators and the appreciators of art bring unique backgrounds to their respective projects, thereby encountering a unique work at every turn. If a painting has five successive owners, it is, in a sense, five different artworks. With each member of humanity holding a distinctive perspective, it is no wonder that new religions, like new currents in art, are always appearing.

Pluralism in religion is appealing because the great religions complement each other; thus, a Hindu perspective on animals may enrich Christian ethics. Mahatma Gandhi learned from the New Testament and the Trappist monk Thomas Merton from Chuang Tzu. Likewise, pluralism applied to art holds that no single theory suffices; thus, theories are complementary rather than antagonistic. An expressionist theory, which puts a premium upon human emotions, represents one important aspect of art. However, a representational theory, with its broadly cognitive thrust, represents another important facet. Again, formalist theory, in which form or structure is paramount, identifies a third fundamental element of art.

For another recent, historical tie between religion and art, one may turn to George Dickie's institutional theory of art in *Art and the Aesthetic*,[8] in which he argues that any man-made object can become an artwork through a kind of "baptism." An artist, critic, or mere appreciator need only declare that an artifact is worthy of apprehension. Understandably, critics attack this account as unilateral, because the focus is upon the proclaimer and not upon any inherent properties that may belong to the object. Dickie's theory applies to religion, too. There is a parallel in the proliferation of so-called new religions, for it appears that one need only declare his cause a religion—no objective properties or ever-present attributes need obtain. One group worships Satan, another a mother goddess, a third has meditation instead of worship, and still another may equate spiritual life with the right dietary or scientific practices. As one may fault Dickie for focusing exclusively upon the beholder at the expense of any intrinsic qualities that the object itself might possess, one may criticize any completely open concept of religion.

A second tie between art and religion arises because the latter, with its quest for the real, can lend weight to art. In short, religion may confer the possibility of revelation, not simply decoration or ornamentation, upon the artist's work. Like science, religion, and philosophy, great art pursues truth. Associating the religious with profundity, Tillich speaks of religion as " . . . the dimension of depth in all sections and levels of culture . . . "[9] For him, to remove religion from art is to arrive at a diminished art, what Tolstoy described as counterfeit or insincere art. At its best, such art can only deliver probable truths or the conditioned truths of the sciences. But artists who are religiously motivated seek abiding, unconditioned truths about the self, others, nature, and the divine. Ideally, the artist sets forth a world view that illumines some aspects of the human condition, e.g., birth, maturity, and death. Artists often condemn as superficial any works that yield only pleasure rather than insight into the significance of life, i.e., the meaning of existence. A Schleiermacher commentator, William E. Horden, elaborates on this theme: "All great art and literature has a concept of the totality of the universe, and this is, whether recognized or not, an experience of God."[10] Of course, one need not turn to monumental works or epic literature in order to sense the boundless, cosmic quality of art. She can, for example, intuit it in a line of poetry from Alfred Tennyson: "Flower in the crannied wall . . . If I could understand What you are, root and all . . . I should know what God and man is." To have this unfettered vision is often the dream of the artist and saint alike.

A third illustration of the relations between art and religion lies in the capacity of art to render religion articulate: art confers the power of speech upon religion. Given its elusive nature, religion inevitably turns to art as a chief means of self-expression. Religion, for example, cannot exist without the art form of humor; therefore, a turn to the great religions reveals rich treasuries of wit. Indeed, one might regard a "humorless religion" as a contradiction in terms. Compare the sobriety of certain contemporary cults to the comic spirit in major traditions such as Zen Buddhism with its endless anecdotes, Judaism with its Hasidic tales, or Christianity with the ironic humor of Jesus, e.g., "It is easier for a camel to pass through the eye of a needle than for a rich man to enter into the kingdom of Heaven." Not only is humor of great instructional value for religion, but it can also play a role in the most profound religious encounters themselves. Complaining to God about her problems and sufferings, Teresa received this reply from her Lord: "Teresa, this is how I treat my friends!" To which she responded with the humor of sarcasm, "That is why you have very few." If the abstractions of theology and philosophy represent the outer layers of religion, then spiritual art represents its otherwise ineffable core. Whether to communicate concepts, intuitions, or feelings, religion needs such art. It enlivens the concepts of theology and philosophy and, ideally, art also fosters a direct, transformative encounter with the divine. In his spiritual aesthetics, Kandinsky affirms the capacity of the artwork to convey "emotions subtle beyond words."[11] Religion without art would be like a sublime silence without the sound that complements and dramatizes it. Religion can be as silent as the contemplative monk, but it is through art that one's I-Thou dialogue with the divine becomes a dialogue with other humans. Through hymns, chants, painting, sculpture, architecture, poetry, and other literature, one meets her fellows spiritually as well as aesthetically. Ludwig Wittgenstein's claim that what cannot be talked about must be passed over in silence is refuted by great music that transmits what ordinary language is powerless to communicate. Indeed, if Tolstoy is correct, one can only communicate his emotions through art and his ideas through language.

When questioned about the relations between religion and art, Huston Smith, the eminent American authority on world religions, replied concisely, "Art can help religion." Indeed, religion is speechless without it. Perhaps religion needs art, because, as Cardinal

Paul Poupard once remarked: "The good needs the beautiful to express itself." One need not be articulate to address God, since God knows one's innermost thoughts and intentions, however ineptly one expresses them. Nevertheless, one enhances dialogue with others to the extent that she draws upon the power of art in order to articulate her ideas. Moreover, artistic expression even benefits one's encounter with the eternal Thou, for it is through art that one sometimes finds himself, the I that meets any Thou. Naturally, such self-discovery allows for greater engagement with any other.

A fourth link between art and religion is evident when they commingle in certain profound experiences, thereby helping to explain the ancients' reluctance to distinguish between the aesthetic and the religious. The awe and sublimity felt in beholding a mountain may be equally aesthetic and spiritual. To see the two merge in the most intense experiences of birth, life, and death is to see their ordinary interrelationship writ large. On the everyday plane, hearing sacred music may trigger religious thoughts. More dramatically, the beauty and religious power of a ritual, such as baptism, are of one piece and include: the innocence of the child, the eloquence of the priest, the symbolism of the water, the sequence of motions, and the solidarity of the congregation praying in concert. Through the moving ritual of a Hindu funeral procession to the Ganges, participants aesthetically transmute death and loss. When van Gogh draws an infant who is aesthetically enjoying the sunshine, the artist glimpses something spiritual in this young child: "I think I see something deeper, more infinite, more eternal than the ocean in the expression of the eyes of a little baby when it wakes in the morning, and coos or laughs because it sees the sun shining on its cradle. If there is 'a ray from on high,' perhaps one can find it there."[12] Demonstrating that the sacred and the mundane interfuse in ordinary life, Zen Buddhists speak about finding enlightenment in the midst of such ordinary activities as carrying water and chopping bamboo. Dramatic everyday illustrations of the intersection between the spiritual and the aesthetic include: the Oriental tea ceremony, Native Americans smoking the peace pipe, the Thanksgiving feast, and the Christian sacrament of communion. Ideally," . . . the self . . . becomes a medium whereby the spiritual world is seen in a unique degree operating directly in the world of sense."[13] Given such cases of profound interpenetration between art and religion, it is perhaps not surprising that some, like Coomaraswamy, identify the two.

Not only are the spiritual and the aesthetic joined in various ways, but they are features of life itself. A religious wedding ceremony is not about life; it is life itself; indeed, it is one of the most important parts of it. The aesthetic, in the form of, for example, religious music at a wedding, is not about the wedding so much as it is an aspect of the wedding. In short, some of the most vital art is not confined to museums or theatres, but is connected to life in the larger world. Marc Chagall refuses to disengage his art from life: "There are hundreds of moments in life which are linked together by art, and turn into paintings I dream about quite outside any kind of realism. It's life itself, and it's got nothing to do with realism or naturalism."[14] Asked to describe his ceramics and pottery, he responded, "They're a continuation of life."[15] Of course, that art or religion that is most continuous with life will be the most vital. The Japanese Buddhist Bon dance, which honors the dead, is not just about the deceased; it is a part of life in which all ages participate in a whirling web of motion, color, chanting, and music. Here, as religion and art manifestly coalesce and vivify life itself, one may sympathize with Coomaraswamy's assertion, "Art is religion, religion art, not related, but the same."

Like ethics, art and religion are axiological spheres; and this provides a fifth basis for relations between the two. They supply the values or standards by which one judges everything else. As religion offers spiritual and moral values, art offers aesthetic values, e.g., when the elegance of a theory compels a scientist's assent. Since one can hardly isolate various kinds of values from each other—witness the relations between moral and aesthetic values in the case of a forgery—if humans are to be whole, they must interrelate various values and integrate them within themselves.

Because art and religion are sometimes threats to each other, their coexistence can be intimidating. Nevertheless, even when the two meet, one need not necessarily overwhelm the other. For there is an obvious alternative: art and religion can be complementary. Indeed, it is the coalescence of the two that can produce the poetry and religious fervor of a Teresa. Of course, if art and religion are sometimes interdependent, this does not entail that they are indistinguishable.

Is All Art Religious?

The various relations between art and religion may lead one to think that every artwork has a religious dimension—however concealed it may be. In other words, one might conclude that all art is religious. I will now critically analyze three considerations that dispose one toward this thesis. First, the doctrine of the omnipresence of the divine apparently entails that non-religious art is impossible. In short, divine omnipresence entails that all things, including artworks, can evoke wonder. A capacity for wonder is especially evident in the child who reaches out in fascination to any new object, perhaps not just because it charms with its unfamiliarity, but because it speaks of being and of potential answers. Celebrating the child, who beholds ordinary things as wonders, religious leaders—from Christ and Lao Tzu to Ramakrishna—enjoin their disciples to become child-like. Of course, to be a wonder is also to have aesthetic import, because the aesthetic is always "trans-mundane," i. e., a departure from the prosaic. Even something as functional and "frill free" as a pencil can be thematic in an aesthetic experience. One can perceive it as a vividly colored band or a streamlined form—whether or not its lead is of the right kind for the purpose at hand. Here, many adults could learn from children, who express delight on receiving a first pencil. Part of their satisfaction is undoubtedly aesthetic, since they have not yet become preoccupied with the practical concerns that can extinguish aesthetic enjoyment. As is illustrated by Mu ch'i's celebrated painting of six persimmons, the great religious artwork frequently hallows the plain and simple.

While Albert Schweitzer held that anything that is alive is sacred, some would add that even inorganic objects have a spiritual essence. Taoists, for example, locate *ch'i*, i.e., vital force or the vibrations of Tao, in stones as well as the blades of grass that grow up between them. In Federico Fellini's film *La Strada*, the actor Anthony Quinn, picks up a rock and declares: "If this stone is useless, then everything else is useless!" The thirteenth-century Dominican priest, philosopher, mystic and poet, Meister Eckhart, whom some compare to Samkara in India, once stated: "The being of a stone speaks and manifests the same as does my mouth about God . . . "[16] And again, "with such an attitude [spiritual outlook] you could tread upon a stone, and that would be a more godly thing to do than for you to receive the Body of our Lord."[17] Indeed, in his sculpture of David, Michelangelo extracted the "Thou" that was latent in the stone. The Nobel Prize-winning novelist, Isaac Bashevis Singer, also considers the lowly stone in his *Love and Exile: An Autobiographical Trilogy*, when he comments on the Kabbalah books, "I realized that their particulars weren't as important as was their concept that everything is God and God is everything; that the stone in the street, the mouse in its hole, the fly on the wall, and the shoes on my feet were all fashioned from the Divinity."

An anecdote from Zen Buddhism suggests that the sacred is present in every artifact. A visitor asked a Zen priest: "If one can discern the Buddha-nature everywhere—in unraked stones as well as raked ones—why do you so meticulously fashion your rock garden?" The priest replied tellingly: "Yes, the Buddha-nature can be discovered everywhere, but we try to make it a little easier to see." As a theist might put the point, God's omnipresence ensures that all things merit appreciation, but not that they are all equally expressive of the divine. In one sense, all persons are not equally admirable spiritually, since some, for example, have achieved greater moral cultivation. From the perspective of the Infinite, every thing may be on the same aesthetic footing, but humans find that some objects more greatly reward their aesthetic attention. Great religious figures are those whose lives embody or "incarnate" the divine to an optimum degree and great religious artists are those who communicate the divine to an optimum degree.

If God is everywhere, it follows that all art is religious, but it also follows that everything else is religious as well. Thus, it would remain to characterize the distinct being of art objects in order to mark them off from other kinds of entities. If everything is religious, it conveys little to assert that all art is religious. Moreover, the list of possible counterexamples is formidable, for few would say that every contemporary novel, all popular music, each piece of modern sculpture—no matter how trite—and every presidential portrait are religious in character.

Of course, to be spiritual, art need not partake of explicitly religious content or symbols. For example, van Gogh's painting of a peasant's shoes transmits something of the sincerity of honest labor. Tolstoy saw such art as religious, because it conveys the nobility of the artist's soul, raises questions about the meaning and value of life, and unites viewers in a feeling of brotherhood or love, as in the *agape*, i.e., spiritual love, of Christianity or the fellow feeling (*jen*) of Confucianism. From this perspective, content is rendered rather accidental. "It is indeed possible to see in a still-life of Cezanne, an animal painting of Marc, a landscape of Schmidt-Rotluff, or an erotic painting of Nolde the immediate revelation of an absolute reality in the relative things . . . they have become 'sacred' objects."[18] Perhaps it would be more accurate to say that their sacred dimension is now transparent, for religions hold that all things are already sacred, the profane appearing only in the eye of the beholder. Because much traditional religious art adheres closely to entrenched conventions, so-called secular art—such as Paul Klee's abstract painting—with its freedom and spontaneity, may strike one with greater religious force. One can also regard the artist as religious when he, like a monk, commits himself to a certain life style, dedicates himself to his "calling," and works to discover and disclose something of ultimate reality.

Tillich posits a second reason to regard all art as religious: art expresses being and a confrontation with being is always spiritually significant. After all, spiritual reality is the source of being and permeates all being. Reflection on the different qualities of being and their hierarchy—from good to better to best, from unattractive to pretty to beautiful—led Aquinas to posit God as the axiological absolute or summit. God's all-pervasiveness ensures the inherent goodness of being; thus, the medievals affirmed that being or existence is better than non-existence. Art is not only a kind of being but it is expressive of being. This is just to say that things can often remain unnoticed until art expresses their being. Ideally, religious art has a threefold significance; it imitates divine creation, communicates human being, and expresses something of the supreme being.

That a thing exists, i.e., has being, rather than does not exist, has religious significance, since it can inspire awe. To ask why things exist at all is ultimately a religious inquiry, for—if there is an answer—it can only be in terms of a metaphysical absolute. Other answers invariably address a how, not a why. It is the ultimate inexplicability of existence that renders it religiously awesome. Hence, painters seek to hint at it in their works and poetry begins after prose fails. As the stark existence of a thing can be evocative of the numinous, it is not surprising that a contemporary Chinese philosopher finds that such existence is also aesthetic, "Existence itself is poetical."[19] It is the brute existence of a thing that strikes, for example, existentialist philosophers with awe, a state that straddles the categories of the aesthetic and the religious as do the concepts of the sublime and the numinous. Existentialists ask: Why is there what there is rather than nothing?—a question so fundamental as to guarantee its religious import. In a discussion of Martin Buber, Maurice Friedman remarks:

Again and again, natural objects "blaze up into presentness.". . . Before we grasp what is over and against us as an object, compare it with other objects, classify and analyze it, and register it in the structure of knowledge, we see it with the force of presence and thereby grasp it in its incomparable uniqueness. . . . Along with the perception of the senses and the categories of the mind, we feel the impact of real otherness.[20]

If natural things have such "presentness," would not artworks have a "redoubled" presence? Outstanding artworks reveal the consciousness of the artist as well as the thusness, i.e., concrete reality or givenness, of media like paint, sounds, and stone. To the disclosures of nature, art adds the revelations of human nature. Even the worst art manifests something of the human spirit and, if humans are sparks of the divine, such art manifests some degree of spirituality as well. Failed artworks are religious in spite of themselves, i.e., religious as things rather than as aesthetic things. Zen Buddhism affirms the presence or suchness of things, each with its peculiar ontological identity. Of course, only someone with the proper mental set can detect the individuating "this-here-nowness" of a thing. Unlike the artist or religious person, most individuals do not grasp a thing in all its concreteness and vivacity. Thus, the enemy of the aesthetic is not ugliness but lackluster observation. For the poet, as well as the religiously disposed, nothing is ever categorically trivial. Hence Chuang Tzu, the lyrical sage of Taoism, observed that a seemingly inconsequential mustard seed, floating in water, can become a boat. Grasping the immediacy of the moment involves seeing things in their "thusness" or "suchness." They are plain and simple; yet, nothing could be more profound, for all things pose the existential question: Why do things exist rather than not exist at all? Clearly, the fact that a thing exists, rather than does not exist, also carries aesthetic significance, for the mysterious is as much an aesthetic category as it is a religious one. Rose Slivka, a prominent crafts critic, holds that the search for "presentness" occurs in crafts as well as arts, because dedicated craftspeople are on a "quest for a deeper feeling of presence."[21]

Commenting on the vitality of a peasant painting by the Dutch artist Jan Steen, Tillich declares, " . . . everything which expresses the power of being is indirectly religious."[22] To express something of the power of being is to express something of ultimate reality; and Tillich believes that Toulouse-Lautrec accomplished this even in his supposedly perverse art. For Tillich, artworks lose their secular status by virtue of their power to manifest ultimate reality. The test of this power lies in the beholder's experience of the work, not in claims about a creator's intentions. Whether an artist's intentions can render a work religious is highly controversial. Biographers of Johann Sebastian Bach report that he wrote "Soli Deo Gloria" (to God only be the Glory) on his evolving manuscripts, including the scores many now classify as secular.

For Tillich, art that lacks any explicitly religious subject matter can still be religious: "Everything in human culture has a

religious dimension if it points to the holy, that is, to that which is
the ground and aim of everything that is."[23] An artwork is religious
if it illumines the meaning of life: " . . . every cultural creation has
a religious dimension insofar as it contributes to the answer of the
question of the meaning of our existence and existence universally."[24] Tillich often identifies Picasso's *Guernica*, a painting that
expresses the violence and horror of war, as a piece that poses
fundamental questions. When Tillich says that "Ultimately no irreligious art is possible,"[25] he means that divine omnipresence entails
that even the most "secular" artwork points, however obliquely, to
the holy. Like other religious thinkers, he turns to the stone for a
model of something that, at first, seems to be spiritually insignificant.
He also recognizes the artist's style as pointing " . . . to the answer he
consciously or unconsciously gives to the question of the meaning of
life."[26] Not surprisingly, contemporary philosophers, who reject religion, are also prone to deny that there is any "meaning of life."
Rather, they believe that there are only particular meanings in life,
but no overarching, general meaning. To the contrary, Tolstoy says
that in every era and culture, there is a grasp of the meaning of life
that reflects the best thought of a people, a comprehension of the
highest good to which the best thinkers of society aspire. He equates
such understanding with what he terms the religious perception and
adds: " . . . it is by the standard of this religious perception that the
feelings transmitted by art have always been estimated."[27] That Paul
Gauguin was also concerned with fundamental questions about the
human condition is evident in the title of a painting that he completed in 1897 and thought that he could never surpass: *Where do
we come from? What are we? Where are we going?*

    There are, of course, serious problems in Tillich's aesthetic
speculations, e.g., in his idea that art expresses being or manifests
ultimate reality. Since he believes that one's direct experience, rather
than reason, verifies whether a work of art succeeds in conveying
being, the revelatory capacity of art remains an experiential rather
than a demonstrable truth. Often, Tillich's assertions are simply
too broad, as when he says of the artist, "He cannot escape religion
even if he rejects religion, for religion is the state of being ultimately concerned. And in every style the ultimate concern of a
human group or period is manifest."[28] Such generalizations proceed
from a singular view of art, but artists sometimes preoccupy themselves with light, color, and sensuous surfaces instead of with hint-
ing at a deeper underlying reality. In addition, art as propaganda
demonstrates that the intense concern that motivates a group may
be political rather than spiritual. When Tillich submits that

"Everything in human culture has a religious dimension if it points to the holy," one wonders what does not point to the holy. A Hindu anecdote relates that someone once criticized a woman, who was resting, because her feet were pointing toward a temple that contained the image of a divinity. Asked to reposition her feet, she said: "Gladly, if you will tell me in which direction God is not to be found." Relating the artist's style " . . . to the answer he consciously or unconsciously gives to the question of the meaning of life," Tillich offers another generalization instead of any one artist's specific answer to questions about the human condition.

Nonrepresentational art provides a third kind of support for the claim that all art is religious. Of course, many laymen today fail to find any sense in non-figurative art, much less religious sense. Still, both Easterners and Westerners have contended that even abstract art is religious. Of course, one can ask if there is any truly abstract art. Discussing Plato's imperceptible forms, Coomaraswamy insists that

> [A]ll the arts, without exception, are representations or like-nesses of a model; which does not mean that they are such as to tell us what the model looks like, which would be impossible seeing that the forms of traditional art are typically imitative of invisible things, which have no looks, but that they are such adequate análogies as to be able to remind us, i.e., put us in mind again, of their archetypes.[29]

In short, nonrepresentational art can be a vivid, poetic reminder of that which transcends direct representation. Moreover, as Nicholas Wolterstorff says, "If he [Gerardus van der Leeuw] means . . . that works of art—even works of abstract art—can be more or less closely fitting to the holy, then I think he is right. . . . Perhaps this is how we are to understand Mark Rothko's and Barnett Newman's abstract works for the chapel in Houston."[30] Newman's nonrepresentational *Stations of the Cross* (1958–1966: Robert and Jane Meyerhoff Collection, National Gallery of Art, Washington, D.C.) seeks to communicate Christ's suffering. If there is a sense in which there is no abstract art—it always communicates specific feelings or moods and conveys particular ideas or intuitions—there is also a sense in which there is no abstract religion, for concrete experiences, rather than the abstractions of theology and philosophy, energize the religious life.

Kandinsky, a father of nonrepresentational painting, asserts, regrettably without any elucidation: "A triangle . . . has a spiritual value of its own."[31] Perhaps he agrees with Plato, for whom the absolute beauty of the immaterial forms of the circle and triangle contrasts with the relative beauty of changing, physical things. Possibly the distinction between Nirguna Brahman (ultimate reality as supra-personal) and Saguna Brahman (ultimate reality as personal) corresponds to that between nonrepresentational and representational art. The abstract expressionism of painters such as Kandinsky was "wholly other" in a way that greatly challenged many viewers. While such art seemed to be quite removed from secular as well as religious life, some viewers saw in it the lyrical, mystical quality of paintings by a Taoist master. Such appreciators experience Kandinsky's paintings not as retreats from the objective world into pure subjectivity, but as insights into a deeper, spiritual realm that grounds and interpenetrates the mundane world. Some found the spirituality of Zen Buddhism in paintings by, for example, Mark Rothko. Such discoveries should not be surprising, since artists universally turn to nonrepresentational art, no less than representational, in order to convey the numinous. Amish quilts, with their simple geometric patterns, have long served as workaday *mandalas*, i.e., designs that are thematic for meditation in Hinduism and Buddhism. Sue Bender noted how art triggered her spiritual pilgrimage:

> Twenty years ago I walked into Latham's Men's Store in Sag Harbor, New York, and saw old quilts used as a background for men's tweeds. I had never seen quilts like that. Odd color combinations. Deep saturated solid colors: purple, mauve, green, brown, magenta, electric blue, red. Simple geometric forms: Squares, diamonds, rectangles. A patina of use emanated from them. They spoke directly to me. They knew something. They went straight to my heart. That was the beginning.[32]

As Tillich stated, "Of course, one cannot show ultimate reality directly, but one can use basic structural elements of reality like line, cubes, planes, colors, as symbols for that which transcends all reality—and this is what non-objective artists have done."[33] Of course, some non-objective artists have used "cubes, planes, colors" non-symbolically and, hence, non-religiously. On a more grandiose scale, one may consider the simplicity of the pyramids and their profound impact upon the beholder. Asians never embraced the realistic, representational art which Westerners can trace to Greece, Rome, and Egypt. This may explain why Chinese art, as Rudolph Otto says, expresses the numinous, the mysterious, the supra-personal rather than the personal. The Tao, after all, is neither male nor female, but beyond all such personal categories. Weiss also champions the spiritual potential of nonrepresentational art:

> [T]he religious painting is articulated by what is comparatively dark, divisible, and stable. From this it would appear that modern abstract painting should prove to be singularly appropriate for religious art, provided that the painter, no less than the spectator, makes the work reveal and point to God as omnipresent.[34]

Of course, there is some force to Weiss's point; still, one might ask if representational painting—which has prevailed in many world religions—is any less appropriate a vehicle. Formalists, such as Clive Bell and Roger Fry, have argued that the misdirecting life associations connected with representational art pose problems for one who wishes to savor the unique aesthetic emotion. Tillich comments on the stained-glass windows of Chartres Cathedral: " . . . to the degree in which these windows are not figurative—the figures are so small that you cannot distinguish them as figures—they have the power to mediate the feeling of transcendent blessedness."[35] Here, Tillich regards non-figurative art as an asset, but one should not forget that much of the world's art is representational and that this variety of art has evoked a rich gamut of religious sentiments, including "transcendent blessedness." Moreover, non-figurative art has produced a vexing problem for certain contemporary artists. One who wishes to transmit her ethnic, religious, cultural, or national heritage, and who elects to do nonrepresentational work, faces a curious challenge, a kind of "identity paradox." One twentieth-century Chinese painter is illustrative. Growing up in China, she came to love Chinese calligraphy, poetry, painting, music, philosophy, religion, and cuisine. For years, what she cherished influenced her paintings. Eventually, however, she wanted the freedom to depart from traditional artists, schools, and canons. When she began to paint abstractly, the paradox arose: Even if one has appropriated a rich tradition, the yearning for freedom can drive her to create art that is not obviously Chinese. Few, if any, can distinguish abstract paintings as "Chinese," "German," "French," "British," or "American." At first, a beholder may conclude that none of the abstract artist's entire tradition is manifest in her art. On reconsideration, however, the beholder may decide that it is dubious that an artist could completely suppress all of her rich heritage, even when she paints abstract works. Perhaps aspects of her culture are more subtly present. An abstract painting by a Chinese artist may contain yellow bands that are traces of bamboo as rendered by traditional masters. Whether one's art is representational or nonrepresentational, she may communicate her own spirit as well as the ideas, intuitions, and experiences that sustain her tradition.

Not only is art often religious, but it sometimes serves as religion. It is no wonder that social philosophers, such as Andre Malraux and John Dewey, have characterized art as a surrogate religion. Some beholders approach artworks, which cost millions of dollars, with the reverence and whispers that befit sacred objects. It is as if moving from one painting to another on museum walls has replaced walking the stations of the cross, a devotion in which Anglicans and Catholics meditate and pray before fourteen representations of Christ on his final journey from praetorium to tomb. In 1934, Dewey had two salient observations about art museums as shrines. First, he said that these buildings, which displaced cathedrals, were erected as status symbols, signs of "cultural good taste," or as "a kind of counterpart of a holier-than-thou attitude." While there are exceptions, as in the case of the recently completed National Cathedral of Washington D.C., contemporary museum architecture generally overshadows that of churches, cathedrals, temples, or mosques. The museum has become the place to pause, contemplate, search for meaning, and discover something about one's self. As untouchable as the holiest of holies, the artwork is beyond our reach. Second, Dewey states that the isolation of museums, opera houses and galleries from ordinary life shows: " . . . that they are not part of a native and spontaneous culture."[36] Lamenting the compartmentalization of art and religion, he points to the ironic possibility that the grandeur of imposing edifices, be they art museums or cathedrals, may be inversely proportionate to the actual state of aesthetic or religious sensitivity in the societies that erect them.

It is, of course, possible that art is not replacing religion at all. Indeed, art may just be a disguised form of spirituality. Rather than speak of art as usurping the role of religion, it may be more accurate to assert that religion appears under the guise of art. There are "saints" in both domains—ascetic monks and starving artists; alongside faith healing, there is artistic healing through catharsis; and, for the religious pilgrimage, there is, say, a journey to the Louvre. Occasionally the museum and the temple intersect. In 1992, the art show "Mystic Visions" drew substantial crowds to the Virginia Museum of Fine Art, a state institution in Richmond. When the Tibetan Buddhist monks, who were creating a sand *mandala*, engaged in prayer, there were no vocal complaints to the effect that such activity violated the separation of church and state. Apparently, the exotic appearance of the monks, coupled with their artistic activity, rendered them harmless in the eyes of those who are normally eager to preserve the separation. It was as if the aesthetic could somehow neutralize the religious.

All Religion Is Artistic

Even if not all art is religious, it remains to consider the corollary: all religion is artistic. Every religion has its artistic expressions—however understated or subtle they may be. Devoid of art, religion would be a kind of blind plodding—lacking in the vision of the artist—and, therefore, correspondingly inexpressive. Historically, the religious life invariably issues in art, whether in the luminous poetry of a Francis of Assisi, the sublime landscape paintings of the Ch'an Buddhist Mu ch'i, or the lyrical calligraphy of Islam. Since all religions have some art, even the austerity of the Amish and Shakers does not prevent them from creating respectively the strong, simple beauty of their quilts and the lean elegance of their furniture.

In the lives of the saints, deeply felt religious experience often crystallizes in the form of an aesthetic prayer. More to the point, one wonders if there can even be a genuine prayer that is not aesthetic. Every authentic prayer meets Tolstoy's requirements for art: however plain and simple, it must be a sincere communication and it must be a transmission of emotion. Like the actor who wishes to feel something of the emotions that he intends to convey, one who prays must participate emotionally in order to avoid routine recitations with their stillborn emotions. Perhaps if prayer is to be a "fine art," rather than a mere means to some end, like the boat one uses to reach the other shore and then discards, prayer must be an end in itself, as when one is completely content to rest in God.

It is no accident that, for example, the *Bhagavadgītā*, like many other religious classics, is an artistic masterpiece, for aesthetic expression, not ordinary discourse, is the language of religion. Witness the poetry of the *Tao Te Ching*, the Jataka tales of Buddhism, the epic of the *Ramayana*, the narratives of the Sufi, the parables of Jesus, the allegories of Chuang Tzu, the dialogues of the *Upanishads*, the *Bhagavadgita* or "The Song of God," and the colorful mythologies of every tradition. And what would Hinduism be without the magnificent hymns that are the Vedas or Catholicism without the drama that is the Mass? For that matter, no religion could exist without poetry, calligraphy, architecture, painting, music, sculpture, or dance. To illustrate the relevance of drama, for example, according to Ignatius Loyola, one cannot read scripture as a detached observer; one must become a participant and plunge into the "drama," as a method actor identifies with his character. Specifically, Ignatius directs the reader of scripture to exercise his imagination in order to envision, and thereby create, a detailed, living, diorama of persons, places, and events.

Nicholas Wolterstorff wonders: "must a good hymn be aesthetically good?" In other words, if a hymn effectively praises God, must it also be aesthetically significant? He replies affirmatively, reasoning that although art is not the ultimate value in a religious setting, artistic merit is nonetheless a value that enriches the gestalt of worship.[37] As Wolterstorff points out, not all artworks are equally appropriate for a particular religious occasion. Depending upon the circumstances, some works may disturb, misdirect, or distract one significantly during a religious moment. Voluminous music, no matter how evocative of religious awe it might be in the setting of a Christian cathedral, would be out of place in a Chinese tea ceremony.

All religions need art, for it is the art of world religions that first draws individuals to them and then sustains their religious life. Consider the aesthetic simplicity of the Chinese landscape painting, the entrancing complexity of a gothic cathedral, an elegantly sensuous sculpture of the gyrating Shiva, or the hypnotic quality of the Bon dance in Japanese Buddhism. Again, it is the austere beauty of Zen Buddhist flower arrangements that leads one to inquire into the spiritual tradition itself. In *The Catholic Myth: The Behavior and Beliefs of American Catholics*, the priest and sociologist Andrew M. Greeley contends that the appeal of Catholicism lies in its poetry. By poetry, he means art in the broad sense: music, stories, architecture, folklore, rituals, customs, paintings, sculptures, and poems, together with such sub-categories as parables, metaphors, and symbols. In effect, Greeley argues that Catholics like Catholicism because of its aesthetic components, the poetic appeal being so great that they are willing to remain Catholics in spite of doctrines, rules, and officials that they dislike.

That art is essential to religion, rather than simply a helper, is apparent in the need for intermediaries. Every religion affirms the existence of angels, bodhisattvas, avatars, incarnations, saints, or *sefirot* who mediate between humans and the absolute. Because humans usually perceive a great gap between themselves and the divine, they posit transitional figures. The extent of the gap is evident in that God is all-powerful, but humans struggle, for instance, to open modern, plastic packaging. God is all-knowing, but even Socrates declares that his wisdom lies in recognizing his own ignorance. God is all good, but humans do not even wish to be good; so, Augustine, feeling guilty over his entanglement with a mistress, prays: "Lord, Give me chastity—but not just yet!" Considering the chasm between humans and God, the need for a bridge is obvious. Accordingly, religions recognize spiritual intermediaries who serve to tie humans to the divine. In India, the avatar links the human and the divine. In Ethiopia, an orthodox hymn to the Blessed Virgin Mary declares, "And it was through thee that created human nature was united in indivisible union with the divine Being of the Creator." Interestingly enough, this hymn continues by contrasting the mundane artist with the supreme artist: "What an unheard of thing for a potter to clothe himself in a clay vessel. . . . What humility beyond words for the Creator to clothe himself in the body of a human creature." In Japan, there are the *Nirmānakāya* (earthly body of the Buddha), the Bodhisattva (one who turns back from the brink of nirvana in order to aid others), and the *Sambhoghakāya* (visionary body of the Buddha), all of which stand between humans and the invisible *Dharmakāya*. To these, Judaism adds the *tsadik* (a figure whose exemplary righteousness renders him a conduit between God and ordinary men) and the *sefirot* (ten divine powers, "beings," or "personal aspects") that radiate from God.

Religious artworks are also intermediaries, "avatars," or "incarnations," as it were. It is dubious that humans can, for example, really know God without a song or poem—however basic it might be. Art may partake of the divine in two senses. First, one may expect a trace of the divine inspiration that infected the artist to be evident in the work. If great art involves a divine transmission, i.e., if afflation is true, then the work would necessarily be spiritual. Second, the artist herself is, in a sense, divine, since she possesses a soul, *atman*, Buddha-nature, or transcendental self that is of the same substance as the absolute. As the incarnation or avatar is the coincidence of the human and the divine, the ideal artwork embodies a union of the mundane and the transcendental. A striking candidate for this synthesis exists in the icons of Byzantium, i.e., devotional images that, in the Orthodox Church, serve as channels between the devotee and the sacred personage who is represented. To fully confront one of these arresting portraits is to have an I-Thou meeting in which the presence of the painted figure engages one head on, face to face; and one "meets" the being whose spirit animates the painted image. Whether one confronts a human, the divine, or an artwork, the I-Thou relation involves encountering a particular presence rather than a generalization or an abstraction. This may help explain the aversion that many art lovers feel toward the sale of artistic masterpieces and the disdain that some have toward art criticism. Does not Kandinsky insist that a painting express the inner spirit of the artist? Because no one should own or possess a person and because an artwork carries the Thou of its artist, one may wish to safeguard even this sort of personhood against the wrong sort of private ownership or hoarding. That masterpieces sell for great amounts and that their creators often lived under austere conditions only exacerbates the situation. Again, those like Tolstoy, who view art as an irreducibly social phenomenon, naturally resent art collectors who refuse to show their masterpieces.

Coomaraswamy speaks eloquently to why religion needs art when he addresses beauty, one of the most central concepts in aesthetics. In its highest expressions, art yields a beauty that is inseparable from the spiritual vocabulary of illumination or enlightenment. In short, beauty is tantamount to lucidity, intelligibility, illumination, and revelation, concepts that apply equally to a religious awakening. Since beauty pertains to clarity or enlightening radiance, ugliness belongs to vagueness, failure to communicate, or the inarticulate.[38] In the end, religion can no more dispense with art than it can with truth. Ugliness corresponds to the uninformed or shapeless, to that which does not convey its essence or form. For Coomaraswamy, everything, from a sea shell to a painting, is beautiful to the degree " . . . that it really is what it purports to be, and independently of all comparisons; or ugly to the extent that its own form is not expressed and realized in tangible reality."[39] The fulfillment of a thing's being is religiously significant, for the greater the actualization of an individual being the more it approximates the fully actualized absolute. Given the above considerations, when a religion suffers from a paucity of great art, one has grounds for suspecting a commensurate lack of spirituality; and, when art does not point beyond itself to that which occupies religion, e.g., ultimate truths, universals, insights into human nature, unchanging realities and verities, one has grounds for judging such art to be penultimate.

Religion and Art as Essential Aspects of the Human Condition

Because religion and art are universal, pervasive, interacting forces, one can neither understand nor appreciate a culture without some understanding of its spiritual and artistic expressions. Although an individual might repudiate religion or art—and even this is dubious—there is no civilization that is quite bereft of them. Just as human beings are sexual and cognitive animals, humans possess aesthetic and religious sensitivities and impulses. As Epicureans realized, if some members of society refrain from sexual activity, society can survive, but if all members refrain, society ends. Although an individual may not participate in the aesthetic or the spiritual, if all people were to avoid participation, such creatures could not satisfy the present concept "human." When cave dwellers started painting pictures and engaging in spiritual practices, they took two of the major steps to becoming human beings.

One can also argue that the inexhaustible richness of art and religion renders them immune to rejection by the individual. Were someone to state, "I reject all art," he would be making a manifestly uninformed and wholly unwarranted statement, for he could not renounce that with which he was unacquainted. Obviously, no one can be familiar with the entire gamut of world art from antiquity to the present. One could hardly rule out the classical Spanish guitar, jazz piano, opera, haiku poetry, ballet, Fellini films, Mark Twain's wit, Sung dynasty landscape paintings, a still life by Cezanne, all cottages, huts, skyscrapers, residences, mosques, temples, and cathedrals, Picasso's classical, blue, rose, surreal, and cubistic periods, all literary masterpieces from all cultures, and all sculpture from primitive to postmodern. Such a list is endless, for it would also include what some consider non-art, as when the Balinese people resist distinctions between art and non-art. Clearly, no one knows enough to assert, "I renounce all art."

One can develop a parallel argument for religion. Suppose a person disavows Christianity in the form of conservative Protestantism. To totally repudiate Christianity, one would also need to know all other forms, such as: the pietistic Amish, the liberation theologians of Catholicism, Christian feminists, the mystical gospel of a Teresa of Avila, the Christianity of a more recondite and scholarly mystic like Meister Eckhart, the abstract theology of Paul Tillich, Augustine's extensive writings, and Thomas Aquinas's voluminous, architectonic exposition of theology and philosophy. As if rejecting Christianity, with its two to three hundred, variegated denominations, not to mention their sub-groups, were not problematic enough, rejecting other world religions and their sub-divisions poses insuperable problems. For example, one should master Sanskrit, Chinese, and Japanese in order to study Buddhism. Given the inexhaustibly diverse expressions of art and religion, no one can know, much less thoroughly evaluate, the varieties of either. After all, even the atheist may find merit in such non-theistic religions as Confucianism and Therevada Buddhism. While the wholesale rejection of all varieties of religion and art is impossible, one need not remain neutral. Affirmation is possible, because everyone has some religious stirrings—evoked by, for example, the starry heavens above—that allow her to feel a rapport with the most spiritually accomplished souls; and everyone has some aesthetic sensitivities that allow her to appreciate and feel oneness with some of the most gifted artists of her culture.

After condemning aristocratic art, Tolstoy wonders: "How could it occur that humanity lived for a certain period without real art, replacing it by art which served enjoyment only?"[40] Tolstoy answers that only a small portion of humanity—the upper classes of European Christian society—appreciated it. Meanwhile, according to Tolstoy, most human beings depended upon what he considers to be genuine art: the epic of Genesis, the Gospel parables, folk songs, and fairy tales. For him, " . . . to say that a work of art is good but incomprehensible to the majority of men is the same as saying of some kind of food that it is very good, but that most people can't eat it."[41] He reasons that if art is a truly important matter, rather than an idle pastime or superfluous ornament on life, it must be essential for all mankind. In other words, whatever is fundamental should be available to all. Moreover, he finds art to be " . . . one of the indispensable means of communication, without which mankind could not exist."[42] Therefore, he reasons that so-called art, which is not understandable to all, is not art at all. In addition, if true art is intelligible to all humans and if humans are also religious creatures, then to speak about a religion that can only address a select number is to speak about an impostor. Accordingly, a classic in mystical literature, *The Cloud of Unknowing*, describes contemplation as: " . . . a practice so simple that even the most uneducated peasant may easily find in it a way to real union with God in the sweet simplicity of perfect love."[43] Tolstoy praises straightforward artistic expressions, because they are sincere, unaffected but affecting transmissions of feeling that elevate the human spirit, inspire wonder toward the grandeur of life, and foster rapport with one's brothers and sisters. Criticizing hedonistic art, he claims that our human nature puts limits upon what we can enjoy, but our spiritual mission, i.e., the advancement of humanity, is unlimited.[44]

Parallel to the religious dictum "Seek and you shall find," there is the aesthetic invitation: "Practice art and you shall achieve." Tolstoy, who believes that art and religion are basic to human nature, inspires the thesis: "All can have a modicum of success in either art or religion." Both religion and art are integral to the human condition and if nothing in nature is in vain, steadfast responses to their respective impulses will be rewarded. Just as one may believe that every soul who searches for religion has some capacity to receive it, Gauguin affirms the aesthetic capacity of humans, "Perhaps I have no talent, but—all vanity aside—I do not believe that anyone makes an artistic attempt, no matter how small, without having a little—or there are many fools."[45] In fine, there is no one who cannot sketch, paint, write, sculpt, dance, sing, play a musical instrument, compose, or frame a simple poetic line; nor is there anyone who is unable to recite a traditional prayer, meditate, sing, chant, lose herself through absorption in nature, or be spiritually moved by liturgy.

2

The Perceptible, the Imperceptible, and a Total Response

Having seen various interconnections and interdependencies between art and religion, we may consider some of the manifold common denominators between the two, e.g., their audio-visual emphasis. Inner states, in which auditory and visual phenomena prevail, are an obvious link between the artist and the saint. Both are more prone than others to hear voices and have visions. Discussing the interior life of artists, Evelyn Underhill makes the similarity explicit:

> [T]he painter really sees his unpainted picture, the novelist hears the conversation of his characters, the poet receives his cadences ready-made. . . . In the mystic the same type of activity constantly appears. Profound meditation takes a pictorial or dramatic form . . . "interior voices" and "imaginary visions" which are sometimes . . . indistinguishable from the ordinary accompaniments of intense artistic activity.[1]

Because vision and hearing dominate in the fine arts, art museums, libraries, and schools have audio-visual departments, but not gustatory-olfactory-tactile departments. Symphonies present sounds, not aromas, tastes, or tactile data. Of course, there are exceptions, e.g., a sculpture show at which visitors wear blindfolds and experience the artworks through touch rather than vision. Naturally, a painting can pique one's sense of smell; describing five versions of Marc Chagall's *Le Cantique des Cantiques*, his friend Verdet says: "The surface of each picture seems scented . . . "[2] Since the tactile and visual features of a painting are not mutually exclusive, one can admire the tactile aspects of a still life painting while appreciating its visual qualities. More often, one elevates hearing and sight over the other three senses. Just as hearing and vision are primary in aesthetic experiences, they prevail in religious experiences; thus, Evelyn Underhill's classic text, *Mysticism: A Study in the Nature and Development of Man's Spiritual Consciousness*, includes a chapter on "Voices and Visions," but lacks corresponding chapters for taste, touch, and smell. Audio-visual experiences far outnumber tactile, gustatory, or olfactory experiences in religion as well as art. Why is this so? Answers run the gamut from the Aristotelian view that vision is the most cognitive sense to the idea that organizing aromas, rather than sounds or colors, poses an insuperable problem. Perhaps touch, taste, and smell are less prominent in religion and art, because they focus attention upon the states of our own bodies; and religion and art seek more than bodily satisfactions.

Of course, mystics do sometimes have tactile, gustatory, and olfactory experiences of the divine, but these cases represent a minority report. Tactile sensations figured importantly in the visions of the mystic Beatrice of Nazareth, who testified that she felt the Lord penetrate her body and pierce her soul.[3] Also, Teresa reports tasting a sweetness after she received the sacrament of communion on Palm Sunday.[4] And the 34th Psalm enjoins one to taste and see for herself how good the Lord is! (34:8). While some sense the numinous in the pungent aroma of incense or the smoke of the peace pipe, others find the divine in the earthy smells of a farm. Some accounts of olfactory experiences are negative, as when Teresa describes an encounter with the demonic in which two nuns detected the offensive smell of brimstone. Whether the experience is positive or negative, it is the auditory and visual data that are preeminent in religious reports.

Those who favor the abstract, conceptual, or intuitive over the sensory or perceptual call into question even vision and hearing. As William James asserts: ". . . the absence of definite sensible images is positively insisted on by the mystical authorities in all religions as the sine qua non of a successful orison, or contemplation of the higher divine truths."[5] From Plato, through Descartes, Spinoza, and Leibniz, to Hegel and contemporary idealists, philosophers have been suspicious of so-called sense knowledge. Spinoza associated it with human bondage. Schopenhauer recognized a hierarchy of the arts in which one rises from the concreteness of architecture, past painting and sculpture, to the more abstract arts of poetry and music, ones that the artist creates and appreciates entirely within his own consciousness. Others have favored literature, on the grounds that it is more abstract than painting or music, because the reader, rather than actually perceiving vivid images or hearing harmonies, imaginatively conjures up sights and sounds from the text. Moreover, literature is not proprietary to any one sense—as is painting or music; thus, a Braille book allows one to "read" a novel through touch and records or tapes ("talking books") enable one to receive the novel by listening. Of course, a defender of visual art could hold that when literary art—devoid as it is of images as seen and sounds as heard—yields to such physical expression, it produces some of the greatest moments in the history of art, for the stage drama is words "made flesh."

As James's remark illustrates, there is a rather widespread and uncritical tendency to belittle the significance of visions and voices in religious experiences. Concerning "divine visions and voices," Underhill claims: "The best mystics have always recognized the doubtful nature of these so-called divine revelations and favors . . ."[6] Teresa, for example, claimed to hear through her soul, not her bodily ears. By contrast, Francis of Assisi, a paradigm medieval mystic, insisted that he actually heard the voice of God. Some have urged that prayers be spoken aloud, chanted, or sung rather than be relegated to internal expressions. A rabbi once said that if one speaks out loud, then she affirms that she is really talking to someone. In short, one goes from introspective thought to dialogue. A poet might add that poems do not fully exist until one reads them aloud, for only then do literary works also become dramatic transmissions. Francis's stigmata were a microcosmic expression of the macrocosmic vision in which he saw Christ on the cross. Like the artist who experiences the world in terms of concrete data, Francis shies away from abstractions and reports that the voice, which he heard emanating from the cross at St. Damiano, was heard by his physical ears. Again, among North Americans such as Black Elk, warrior and medicine man of the Oglala Sioux, the incandescent vision is the centerpiece of spiritual experience. Under the spell of visions and voices, artists such as Standing Bear have painted visionary scenes depicting, for example, the center of the world.

There are two basic kinds of religious or mystical experiences; in one, images and voices—together with data from the other senses—abound, as in the case of Francis of Assisi or Black Elk. In the other, one intuits what is imperceptible, a distinctionless unity, an undifferentiated oneness, as in the case of Plotinus, Samkara in Hinduism, or the Taoist who experiences *p'o*, i.e., the uncarved block or single reality from which all multiplicities arise. Moreover, one can find both emphases in one tradition; thus, Christianity celebrates St. Bonaventure with his Neo-Platonic leanings as well as Francis with his visionary perspective. Rather than speak of visionary versus non-visionary experiences, Teresa identifies two kinds of visions; the higher, intellectual vision represents God "without any likeness of Him."[7] Through it one learns of God's omnipotence and of his omnipresent love. The lower sort of vision is aesthetic or "perceptual" in that the eyes of the soul behold God's beauty and glory. While penultimate in nature, the aesthetic variety of vision is important enough to help establish the veridical character of religious experiences. To the idea that they might arise from our own imagination, she replies, "There is no ground whatever for the supposition; for the very beauty and whiteness of one of our Lord's hands are beyond the imagination altogether." (Earlier in her autobiography she reports an experience in which the Lord showed her the great beauty of his hands.) Teresa asserts that after seeing "the great beauty of our Lord . . . everything I see is loathsome."[8] She elaborates,

> As to fine and beautiful things, such as water, fields, perfume, music, etc., I think I would rather not have them, so great is the difference between them and what I am in the habit of seeing, and so all pleasure in them is gone from me. Hence it is that I care not for them, unless it be at the first sight: they never make any further impression; to me they seem like dirt.[9]

That Christian mystics can vary considerably is evident by a turn to a Francis who ennobles even dirt to the status of "Brother Earth." In any case, Christians from the earliest times have practiced both the kataphatic way of praying with images and the apophatic way that is devoid of images; moreover, the two ways of devotion sometimes alternate within an individual.

On praying, Teresa insisted that vocal prayer and mental prayer are inseparable; we must say the physical word to hear the word within.[10] In a dramatic expression of this sentiment, the Tibetan

Buddhist monk chants his prayers or meditations, making his inner states resonate in audible, physical vibrations that he and his fellows then receive. In this way, "the word becomes flesh." One appreciates chants, whether Gregorian or Tibetan, for their intrinsic, auditory qualities, attending to them for their aesthetic significance as well as for their power to deepen one's contemplative states. Poets argue that one does not grasp a poem until it is "made flesh," i.e., spoken aloud, for to read a poem is not just to silently scan the words; one must read it aloud in order to participate in it completely and to engage others fully.

Coincidence of the Universal and the Particular

Another common denominator of art and religion is that they are both vehicles in which the universal and the particular coalesce. Nevertheless, particularity is more apparent than universality. Religion exists only in the form of a particular religion, not as an abstract entity. There is Islam, Christianity, or Judaism, but there is no religion in general. Similarly, art exits only in the form of an actual, particular creation, not as a mere intellectual abstraction. In this sense, there is no abstract art, for every work is a unique, concrete particular. Of course, religion and art often attempt to transcend provincialism by capturing universal truths. Being from this town or that city, this era or that dynasty, this ethnic group or that nation, the artist nevertheless wants her work to be universal in import. Similarly, the spiritually inclined always seek something beyond the particulars of the here-and-now world in order to arrive at what is general, what can account for the individuals, and that without which they are not fully intelligible. While there can be no art without particulars—"this serpentine line," "that unexpected color combination," or "this idiosyncratic brush stroke"—these elements are empty unless they are informed by the suffusing illumination of universals. These generalizations, timeless truths, or abiding motifs elevate the work beyond sheer technical accomplishment, e.g., van Gogh's painting of a particular peasant's shoes captures something that is universal to laborers, the dignity of honest work.

In the Chinese tradition, many art lovers turn to Mu-ch'i's celebrated painting of six persimmons for a taste of the universal. Hisamatsu comments on its serenity: "This sort of calm or composure seems also to be excellently expressed in the phrase 'rest amid motion.'"[11] From the premise that to have form necessarily entails disquiet, he concludes that only the Formless completely avoids disquiet. Of course, 'rest' belongs to the enduring, formless universal and 'motion' to the changing, formed particular. Individual brush strokes are responsible for various forms, but the unity of brush strokes evokes a sense of the formless One. In short, the One expresses itself in the many and the many express the One. The One, without the many, would be detached from human significance; the many, without the One, would be without abiding significance.

Spiritual thinkers affirm the existence of Platonic universals, i.e., eternal truths or realities, and understand both religion and art as syntheses of the universal and particular. When Clive Bell addresses the significant form of an artwork, he equates the divine and the universal: " . . . we become aware of its essential reality, of the God in everything, of the universal in the particular . . . "[12] Indeed, this interpenetration of the universal and the particular may account for the cross-cultural appreciation of art. Perhaps one can appreciate the art of every culture, because each, in its own distinctive way, is expressive of the universal. Attracted by the universality of a foreign art, one lingers over its particularities; and this allows him to transcend his own culture and to appreciate the distinctive creativity of another tradition—no matter how exotic or unfamiliar. Rudolph Otto testifies to such aesthetic participation when he says of the art of China, Japan, and Tibet that it "surpasses all others in the unusual richness and depth of such impressions of the 'magical,' and even an inexpert observer responds to them readily."[13]

Although religion and art are culturally determined expressions, at their noblest they seek what is not exclusive to any society, i.e., what is universal. Against the naturalist or nominalist, who holds that only particulars—which one experiences through the senses—exist, one can argue that humans need universals, not only to account for one particular or another, but in order to set all of them into perspective and consider the meaning of life. While one can identify particular reasons for particular events, one must go beyond all particulars and postulate the existence of a general principle if he wishes to have a sufficient reason for why there are any particulars at all rather than nonbeing. This move toward the general or universal culminates in positing God, the Tao, or the Dharmakaya.

Time belongs to particulars, eternity to universals. An artist, who captures the universal, grasps what is unchanging, unconditioned, e.g., a truth about human nature or a recurring feature of existence. Working in the temporal but yearning to express what is timeless, the artist pursues the enduring truths and values that sustain humankind. As the contingent points to the necessary and the unfinished points to the finished, the temporal points to the eternal. Thus, many artists and spiritual figures search beneath all temporality and change for whatever might abide. Indeed, if all things are constantly changing, if there is nothing that is constant, one wonders how there can be any meaning in life. After all, meaning presupposes persistence, unity, coherency. In the end, art—as much as religion—can be a quest for the invisible. Accordingly, Paul asserts that visible things are temporal, but invisible things are eternal (2 Corinthians 4:18). Hence, the artist faces the seemingly impossible task of trying to render the invisible visible.

This is not to say that one may ignore particularity. Despite any artist's struggle to transcend what is particular or provincial, abiding artworks—like enduring religions—are always particular, i.e., unique, expressions of universal truths. Generic religion is idolatry and generic art is counterfeit art or debased craft. Particularity, individuality, or identity is as important to religion as it is to art. Of course, pluralism, which affirms the validity of different religions and which may greatly emphasize their shared traits, runs the risk of, at best, obscuring the peculiar historical identities of religions and, at worst, reducing religions to colorless, generic phenomena. Clearly, it is the distinctive arts—including rituals— of a faith that help stamp it as unique. Anonymous art reaches us, for example, in vague elevator music or mass-produced reproductions of paintings by which the unique becomes the commonplace; and anonymous religion arrives in the sermon of the television clergyman that reproduces those of other television preachers.

Transcendence of Time and Space

Whatever is universal transcends time and space; and such transcendence is another common denominator of aesthetic and spiritual states. In order to realize what is true eternally and everywhere, various artists and mystics wish to transcend time and space—the very two forms that Immanuel Kant took to be the most fundamental and insurmountable modes by which humans apprehend the world. Nonetheless, numerous artists and mystics have contended that time and space "disappear" in their respective experiences. Both live in the eternal present; fully participating in the moment, they talk about a kind of living immortality in which what is immediately present has displaced all concern for the past or future. Like the artist, whose work may cause her to forget time and place and whose art may also allow appreciators to escape such fetters, Francis of Assisi enjoyed more than the spatial-temporal world. In *The Little Flowers of St. Francis*, we learn that he lost awareness of time and space while contemplating God: "For his mind had been concentrating on and rapt in the splendors of Heaven and he had actually not perceived the changes of time and place or the people who met him."[14] Such seemingly irrational states of mind encouraged strangers and relatives alike to mock, insult, and even stone Francis. Thus, he fared worse than the artist whom society, at turns, neglects, ridicules, or condemns. According to *The Cloud of Unknowing*, " . . . you must forget all about time, place and matter in this spiritual work."[15] Just as the mystic advocates living fully in the "eternal now," an artist may try to capture the "present moment." Criticism is later, in the future, or after the fact of creativity; and unless criticism is itself creative, it lacks the vitality of the artwork. Moreover, the artist cannot worry about what the critics will say, for such a preoccupation compromises her freedom. It is a natural corollary that the art lover dwells in the present, savors the qualities of the work, and avoids misdirecting thoughts about the past or future. As the theologian Langdon B. Gilkey has observed:

> When an event that we label art thus stops the heedless flow of time in an enhanced moment, a moment of new awareness or understanding, a moment of intense seeing and participation in what is seen, then (as the Zen tradition has taught us) the transcendent appears through art, and art and religion approach one another.[16]

Spiritual moments, like aesthetic ones, are different from those of conventional time; thus, the mystic's taste of "eternity" may endure for only an hour. And one may complete the aesthetic, whirlwind experience of reading *Around the World in Eighty Days* in a matter of hours, even as the story unfolds in its own internal time. Dwelling upon the past or the future is an obstacle to aesthetic immersion as well as to the religious life. With the suspension of time and space, determinism yields to freedom and spontaneity, thereby giving rise to creativity in art and enlightenment in religion. Bell remarks on the sublime in art: " . . . he who can feel the profound significance of form, is raised above the accidents of time and place."[17]

Invariably, the artist leaves ordinary space behind, transforms it, or augments it. After praising Cezanne for not covering his entire canvas and saying "That's where his genius was,"[18] Chagall adds, "Kafka didn't fill everything up either, but with him it was words. The gaps are invisible, but they exist."[19] At times, space takes on an elusive, spiritual significance for the artist. "On the threshold of the unknowable, Cezanne prefers leaving a space to producing something arbitrary."[20] Like the characters in a play who transcend any single performance, God and human spirits are in the world, but not trapped by it. When actors move through ordinary space, they change it into aesthetic space, compressing or expanding it, making it inviting or intimidating as they will. In the religious drama that is the Mass, when the priest elevates the communion host, he consecrates ordinary space and represents the sacrifice of Christ for all humankind. In both the stage drama and the ecclesiastical drama a kind of boundlessness obtains. When Belden C. Lane mentions: "the incapacity of any fixed place or institution fully to contain the holy,"[21] his point applies equally to the aesthetic, for the beautiful may be no less place-bound than the sacred.

Discussions of space, whether in art or religion, invariably lead to such notions as "emptiness," "nothingness," or the "void." Artists and saints may purge themselves of all attachments, defenses, and artifices in order to stand nakedly before the void, i.e., that which is undifferentiated, without limits, or boundless. For the artist, it is the gnawing nothingness of infinite potential that precedes creation; for the saint, it is the unspeakable absolute that is utterly simple and without qualifications. Zen would add that the "gnawing nothingness" and "unspeakable absolute" are identical. Since the absolute is a kind of nothing, one may describe ultimate reality in the negative terminology of "emptiness" or "nothingness." What is formless is the source of all forms but itself is devoid of form. It is nothing in the sense of being no particular thing but the thingless source of all things. It is the formlessness of Oriental paintings, especially in the case of serene landscapes with their wisps of mist suggesting *ch'i* or Tao energy, which renders them so enchanting for even an uninformed viewer. Examples abound to show the *via negativa*, i.e., way of negation, in the world's religions. The Spanish Kabbalist Joseph Gikatila spoke of God as nothing, meaning that no human can comprehend any aspect of the divine. In a like vein, Meister Eckhart talked about the ultimate, transpersonal One or Godhead—that is more primordial than the Father, Son, and Holy Ghost of the Trinity—as nothing and about passing into this divine abyss of so-called nothingness. For Hindus, Brahman is "neti, neti" ("not this, not this"), since the absolute reality lies beyond all predicates. In a different sense, the artist says "not this, not this," as she discards and edits in her quest for the ideal. The great artist is a great "denier," as is the spiritual person who exercises self-denial. For more than two millennia, the Chinese have spoken of Tao as *wu* (nothing") or *p'o* (the uncarved block or undifferentiated source), since this cosmic power is no thing among things, but the primordial ground of all things. Buddhists have sometimes favored the Sanskrit term *sunyatta*, which literally means emptiness, as a label for their ultimate reality. While *śūnyattā* denotes swelling in the sense of what is hollow or empty, it further denotes what is pregnant with unknown potential. Buddhists also recognize the undifferentiated *Dharmakāya*, i.e., that which is nothing in particular but is the root for everything else. Rabbi Dov Baer explains a cross-cultural sense of nothing: the righteous produce not something from nothing, but nothing from something, because their physical acts generate non-physical, holy sparks. From physical acts that are something, they generate immaterial goods that are nothing, i.e., not material things at all.

Emptiness for the artist may also mean returning to consciousness that is devoid of rules, a primordial consciousness in which intuition and speculation preside over logic and theories. Concerning the emptiness needed to receive God, Thomas à Kempis says, "Where our Lord finds the vessel empty and void, there He gives His blessing . . . "[22] One must rid himself of all wrongful attachment to earthly things. Chapter forty-three of *The Cloud of Unknowing* urges one to empty his mind of everything but God; all creatures—even one's own self—must recede. Of course, artists relegate even their own well-being to a place beneath art. That they sometimes sacrifice themselves for their art is no less true because it is a cliché. While religious martyrs are typically more common and sensational, artistic martyrs are scarcely unknown.

Regarding the sacred void by which architecture can symbolize the transcendent divine, Tillich says that the architect must shape space so as to reveal the numinous character of the building.[23] Such emptiness is not mere vacancy; by being devoid of finite things, empty space has "room" to receive and suggest an infinite presence. The *Tao Te Ching* celebrates the value of space by observing that it is upon its emptiness that the utility of a room depends. Of course, the space of architecture is a reconstituted, aesthetic space. But even this space itself is penultimate, for it points to the ultimate nothingness: the Tao which is the non-being that gives rise to all spaces and solids. Architecture, which provides one of our three most basic needs, has profoundly different expressions of nothingness. For example, it expresses the transcendence of the divine in the cavernous space of a soaring gothic cathedral and the immanence of the spiritual in the elegant plainness that pervades the intimate space of a tea house. In a sense, architecture presents the divine as unmanifest, since invisible space is its primary medium and, by contrast, painting and sculpture present the divine as manifest in paint and stone.

The contemporary architect I.M. Pei credits the *Tao Te Ching* with influencing the prominence of space in his east wing of the National Gallery of Art in Washington, D.C. Perhaps like thinking was at work in Frank Lloyd Wright who once declared: "The trouble with architecture is the architects. They don't understand that it isn't the roof or the four walls that make a house, but the spaces between them—the living spaces."[24] Again, the emptiness or void (wu) in a Chinese landscape painting at once invites the viewer's participation in the scene and points beyond to the invisible Tao. Sue Bender reports a similar phenomenon, "The Amish often leave a space, a seeming mistake in the midst of their well-thought-out plans, to serve as an opening to let the spirit come in."[25] Painting, which embraces *hsu* (the formless) or *k'ung* (emptiness), conveys what Taoism calls the image of the imageless, the form of the formless. In the emptiness of the painting, all subject-object categories fade as the void suggests the invisible, inaudible, intangible Tao. Since the Tao underlies all else, the unifying ideal of Chinese painting has long been to somehow express this invisible reality.

While the Taoist emphasizes the continuity between humans and the Tao, Otto conceives the spiritual as wholly other. Accordingly, creature consciousness is the feeling of one's nothingness before the *numen* or "wholly other." Otto refers to the numinous as "that which is nothing." "By this 'nothing' is meant not only that of which nothing can be predicated, but that which is absolutely and intrinsically other than and opposite of everything that is and can be thought."[26] Otto comments upon its aesthetic significance: "Besides silence and darkness, oriental art knows a third direct means for producing a strongly numinous impression, to wit, emptiness and empty distances . . . vacancy is, as it were, the sublime in the horizontal."[27] To him the void becomes the main subject in a Chinese painting. Indeed, he says that the void is " . . . a negation that does away with every 'this' and 'here,' in order that the 'wholly other' may become actual."[28] In a strikingly similar way, Kandinsky speaks about the color white:

[A] symbol of a world from which all colour as a definite attribute has disappeared. This world is too far above us for its harmony to touch our souls. A great silence, like an impenetrable wall, shrouds its life from our understanding. White, therefore, has this harmony of silence, which works upon us negatively, like many pauses in music that break temporarily the melody. It is not a dead silence, but one pregnant with possibilities. White has the appeal of the nothingness that is before birth, of the world in the ice age.[29]

Like the character *p'o*, which is a synonym for Tao and which represents a tree before humans divide it up, white is without differentiations. Both represent consummate harmonies that resolve all discords. One may describe either in terms of non-being or nothingness, but their emptiness is rich rather than vacuous.

Total Response

Like love, great art and religion both require a complete commitment, a total personal response of the whole individual, an unstinting investment of one's heart, mind, and will. With his characteristic flair for exaggeration, Picasso once remarked, "The artist goes through states of fullness and emptiness, and that is all there is to the mystery of art." Still, there is a truth in such hyperbole if we think of emptying as not holding back, letting all of one's powers, faculties, or resources pour forth into the work. The artist can empty herself when she summons all her physical, emotional, and spiritual energies and releases them without reserve. As L. Frank Baum so unforgettably illustrated in *The Wonderful Wizard of Oz*, since humans have a threefold nature, full immersion in a task requires the engagement of one's cognitive, affective, and volitional aspects. Not surprisingly, Buber insists that the involvement of one's undivided being stamps the I-Thou relation: "The basic word I-You can only be spoken with one's whole being."[30] So-called "wholehearted" participation is not just affective but cognitive and volitional as well. There is no holding back of any aspect of one's self, for the I-Thou relation engages the integrated person, not the partial or pseudo-self of the ego. A supposedly religious person who proclaims his creed but does not act accordingly is a hypocrite; and a so-called artist who gives only a part of himself is a craftsperson in the worst sense, i.e., a mere mechanic. Correspondingly, art appreciation calls for the engagement of all of the beholder's powers—spiritual, intellectual, and affective. Of course, this sort of commitment renders one quite vulnerable, but no more than an artist who devotes her whole being to a project.

The I-It orientation, which science exemplifies, does not want and cannot accommodate one's whole self; witness the scientist who distances herself from her emotions during the course of research and experiments; the last thing she needs to be is "passionate," i.e., completely involved in her work. Indeed, if the scientist becomes as ecstatic as a Teresa, he runs the risk of being deemed mad. Participation with one's entire being means engaging in a situation of dialogue, reciprocity, or mutuality, rather than holding the aloof posture of a detached spectator. The I is swept up in the synthetic nature of the relationship, rendering critical analysis difficult if not impossible. Without such participation, i.e., genuine encounter or engagement with the other, there is religious talk, but not the spiritual dialogue of which Martin Buber writes. Similarly, in a flawed painting, the would-be artist breaks Tolstoy's commandment that the artist must communicate. Instead, the pseudo artist's only goal is to manipulate an It, not to address a fellow Thou.

Buber insists that "The more perfect the participation is, the more actual the I becomes."[31] Indeed, Francis of Assisi carries the I-Thou perspective to the universe at large, adopting this stance toward all the objects, beings, elements, and states that make up creation. He is perhaps unsurpassed in his capacity for affirming the personal dimension in life. While personification was as old as religion, Francis broke ground by extending the domain of the personal to all creatures, objects, natural forces, and states of being. By addressing the Thou of everything, he discovered that the divine, i.e., eternal Thou, had imparted personhood to all things as an author leaves a signature on all of her writings. The total involvement of one's person does, however, produce an ironic effect: "For an action of the whole being does away with all partial actions and thus also with all sensations of action (which depend entirely on the limited nature of actions)—and hence it comes to resemble passivity."[32] It is because all the artist's energies—affective, cognitive, and volitional—work together that her activity may strike the beholder, and often the artist herself, as effortless. Again, it is because all of his powers—spiritual, intellectual, and emotional—hold sway together that a Confucius can do what is right effortlessly. In other words, he can do whatever he wants to do without overstepping the boundaries of what is right.

Sometimes, full participation may come by doing "nothing." The Chinese principle of *wu-wei*, which literally means "non-action," is not a prescription for stagnation or vegetation. Instead, it means that one should do nothing strained, artificial, or contrived; in positive terms, one should act spontaneously or naturally, i.e., as fire burns upward and water runs downward. Speaking about how to obtain spiritual delights from the Lord, Teresa states: " . . . there is no better way than the one I mentioned, of not striving for them."[33] By not straining to do anything one contributes greatly to a task. The *Tao Te Ching* teaches that although nothing is done, everything is accomplished. Clearly, the text is not prescribing total inactivity, but advocating natural action as the proper course. Acting without calculation is the ideal, as illustrated in a famous Taoist story about two artists who were in a contest to paint the best snake. The artist who finished first then proceeded to paint feet on his snake. Of course, this artist lost, because it was unnatural to add feet and *wu-wei* was violated. Stoicism, a perennial and cross-cultural religion-philosophy, enjoins more than acceptance of the inevitable; its dynamic side enjoins one to gracefully harmonize with the flow of the universe. One who follows *wu-wei* leaves no traces, i.e., he apparently does nothing, no assertiveness is evident in his actions; yet, he achieves all things. Consider the great painter who appears to be doing nothing—a stroke here a dash there—but who thereby achieves a masterpiece, seemingly without effort. Shih-t'ao, the premier Chinese painter of the Ching Dynasty, describes the ideal artist: "When he grasps the brush it is as if he were doing nothing."[34] With *wu-wei* there is action, but one acts intuitively rather than rationally. Similarly, the Amish, " . . . worked relaxed, 'unconsciously conscious.' 'We grew up learning to sew, cook, quilt, can and garden,' Emma said, 'hardly realizing when it happened.'"[35] Again, for Buber, the activity of the whole human being " . . . has been called not-doing, for nothing particular, nothing partial is at work in man . . . "[36] In fine, one achieves wholeness or integration of the psyche. It is also because all her faculties are at work that the artist seems to work so effortlessly.

Ernest Hemingway once lamented the partial, insincere commitment to art of certain young men:

> [T]hose boys who used to be sent to Paris with two years in which to make good as writers or painters after which, if they had not made good, they could go home and into their fathers'

business . . . the way to paint is as long as there is you and colors and canvas, and to write as long as you can live and there is pencil and paper or ink or any machine to do it with, or anything you care to write about, and you feel a fool, and you are a fool, to do it any other way.[37]

Here, one remembers the simple fact that art and religion both refer to ways of life rather than to individual acts. A would-be photographer, who accidentally manages to take one splendid photograph, is not thereby an artist. Nor is the so-called religious figure "religious" because he has performed one isolated good deed. Because art and religion are ways of living, it follows that there are phases, stages, or periods through which one goes, as with Picasso's blue period or Augustine's Manicheanism. Besides declaring that one swallow does not a summer make, Aristotle taught that one ethical deed does not a moral agent make. Thus, one may condemn the use of a drug on the grounds that it lends undue weight to the isolated experience; and one does not approach perfection, whether artistic or spiritual, hastily.

Buber extended his I-Thou orientation beyond the human sphere to the realm of nature. Indeed, one of Buber's most dramatic passages applies his philosophy of dialogue to an encounter with a tree. The thesis is that if we allow the tree to engage us, it becomes a Thou that may serve as a conduit to communion with the eternal Thou. Buber acknowledges that speaking about mutuality or reciprocity between a man and a tree is problematic, for the tree " . . . has to deal with me as I must deal with it—only differently."[38]

It is part of our concept of the plant that it cannot react to our actions upon it, that it cannot "reply." Yet this does not mean that we meet with no reciprocity at all in this sphere. We find here not the deed of posture of an individual being but a reciprocity of being itself—a reciprocity that has nothing except being. The living wholeness and unity of a tree that denies itself to the eye, no matter how keen, of anyone who merely investigates, while it is manifest to those who say You, is present when they are present: they grant the tree the opportunity to manifest it, and now the tree that has being manifests it. Our habits of thought make it difficult for us to see that in such cases something is awakened by our attitude and flashes toward us from that which has being. What matters in this sphere is that we should do justice with an open mind to the actuality that opens up before us.[39]

In this passage, Buber, for whom the tree becomes a gateway to the absolute, uses language ("reciprocity of being," "wholeness," "unity," "manifest," "awakened by our attitude," and "open mind") which is as applicable to aesthetic experiences as it is to spiritual ones. He emphasizes that I can enter into a relation in which the tree stops being an It; to address the tree as a You is to address the eternal You, for " . . . in every You we address the eternal You, in every sphere according to its manner."[40] In this relationship, one encounters what Buber calls "the tree itself,"[41] an expression that invites comparison with the phrase "the artwork itself." To appreciate and relate to the tree is to taste an innocent, aesthetic delight; it is to enjoy a state that ignores exclusively practical demands. In the I-Thou relation, one must be receptive to the tree, i.e., let it disclose its innermost nature. Only then will the tree stop being an "It" and become a "Thou." The wholeness of the tree is just as important as the wholeness of the I that meets it. Those who seem to enter most readily into such dialogue include the Native American Black Elk who reports: "I made a prayer to the herb,"[42] the child who addresses the trees and stars, and a poet like Francis who meets with "Brother Sun." Of course, if God underlies all things, then to address them is also to approach the infinite Thou that pervades them. When the Oglala Sioux hear low thunder, they acknowledge it as coming from thunder beings, personal emissaries, subordinates of God. In any case, the Sioux recognize no unadulterated category of the impersonal. For the spiritually inclined, the more one approaches natural phenomena the closer he gets to God. There is a corresponding Arabic saying: "The further you go into the desert, the closer you come to God."

Buber does not limit the I-Thou outlook to human relations and the contemplation of trees. As with an aesthetic perspective, the I-Thou stance is an attitude by which one humanizes and sanctifies anything to which he attends. Hence, Buber's concern for animals is not surprising. As an eleven-year-old, calmly petting a horse, he suddenly became aware of the sensation on his hand. This awareness upset him, because he interpreted it as a shift of attention from the Thou to Buber's own ego. His esthetic rapport with the animal gave way to self-centeredness alone. He also extended the I-Thou orientation to works of art, for every work expresses the Thou of a creator.

In the act of creation, there is "dialogue" or reciprocity; the form acts on the artist as she acts upon it.[43] When, for example, the sculptor chips away at some substance, the emerging matter speaks back; sounds, shapes, aspects of surface influence the sculptor as she guides further emergents from their substrate. She articulates a form and the evolving form makes recommendations that steer its further shaping. In short, the material dictates to the sculptor as she dictates to it. The materials with which the artist works constitute an incipient Thou and contribute to the Thou of the completed piece of art. Therefore, true artists respect their materials; and treated respectfully, materials yield their possibilities to artists. C.Y. Chang comments on this reciprocity in creativity: "When the poet has achieved the mind of no-mind, his subjectivity interfuses with the objective reality of things. 'Things are grasped in the Self and the Self is grasped in Things.'"[44] Jacques Maritain has spoken with elegant circuitousness on the reciprocity, mutuality, or twofold nature of the creative process:

> In order for a novel to be poetry, a particularly powerful creative intuition is required, capable of carrying its influx up to the inner recesses of other human selves living in the work. This is possible only because the creative intuition of a great novelist involves—starting with some primordial emotive awakening of his own self—that poetic knowledge of other subjectivities in and through his own, that knowledge through affective connaturality which makes him penetrate his characters and foresee their actions through the medium of his own inclinations, and which extends and develops all along the development of the characters and the production of the work, in such a way that the novel is made both by the poet and by his creatures.[45]

The I-It orientation frustrates reciprocity because it involves a subject-object stance in which one holds back something of himself. One views matters, as does the scientist in the lab, at some remove and with some reserve. While such psychical distance is obviously appropriate at times, Buber has warned that if it is one's constant posture, he will not be fully human. For Picasso, painting wasn't an activity of one faculty, but a passionate pursuit, a way of life that called for the immersion of his total being. To be an artist or saint is to go beyond isolated acts to a pattern of living, i.e., a way of life. Meister Eckhart speaks similarly of prayer as an act that should engage all our faculties: "We ought to pray so powerfully that we should like to put our every member and strength, our two eyes and ears, mouth, heart and all our senses to work; and we should not give up until we find that we wish to be one with him who is present to us and whom we entreat, namely God."[46] In a like vein, when a critic asked a modern painter how he painted, the artist replied that he painted with his genitals. His point was that he painted with everything, i.e., with all of his powers and resources—including his body as well as his heart, mind, and soul. The spiritually inclined artist would agree with Buber: "'Inner' actuality, too, is only where there is reciprocal activity. The strongest and deepest actuality is to be found where everything enters into activity—the whole human being, without reserve, and the all-embracing god; the unified I and the boundless You."[47]

If one invests her life in a project, be it art or religion, her economic well-being is not necessarily a part of this total engagement. The artist's zeal for his work—a passion that economic sacrifices need not diminish—furnishes one obvious analogue for the priest's vow of poverty. The great Chinese painter Ni Tsan gave away his belongings and spent the rest of his life painting, writing poetry, and travelling. Picasso could not always even keep his own creations, because he sometimes burned original paintings to keep warm during winters in Paris. Since ownership disposes one toward an I-It stance and since Francis of Assisi owned virtually nothing, his poverty enabled him to have an I-Thou relation with anything. He lived by the maxim: "To appreciate everything, possess nothing." In *Walden*, Thoreau recounts the story of a poet (Thoreau himself) who walked through a farmer's landscape and believed that the farmer suspected him of having stolen some apples. Thoreau was amused because he did take something with him, an aesthetic enjoyment of the land—something that one can neither steal nor own. Contemporary artists, such as Christo, sometimes taunt art collectors by creating artworks that are so mammoth as to preclude their being housed or stored.

Since I-Thou relations require the investment of one's total being, the participants assume enormous risks. One may wonder if it is not absurd to devote all to religion, since, for example, God may not exist. Or, one may wonder if it is not absurd to devote all to art, since the capricious, critical art world may reject his creations. While a commitment to art and religion can be exclusive of other values and interests, the I-Thou perspective begins in exclusivism, but ends in a boundless inclusiveness. At first, the Thou may be one's sole center of attention, but rather than phase everything else out of his consideration, one may allow all other things to live in the Thou. A book, a sight, a person that one meets, and even a favorite food can all be moored in the Thou, for the I no longer encounters them in isolation; instead, whatever their former significance, one can now interpret them in relation to his

Thou. For the I, the Thou is the only "context" in which anything else can enjoy vital existence. Indeed, everything is enriched by its setting in the Thou, as a painting is set off and accented by its frame. The richness of Buber's I-Thou relation is that everything else can live in it. Exclusivity gives rise to potentially boundless inclusiveness. Naturally a work of art may also serve as the host for an unlimited series of interpretations, associations, and connections. Beatrice of Nazareth discovers a like phenomenon in the soul's relation to the Lord, " . . . she desires Him so strongly that she can consider neither saint, nor man, nor angel, nor creature, unless it is in that common love in which she loves everything with Him."[48] One test of love is that loving the object of one's attention promotes loving all things. In addition, Soren Kierkegaard thinks that an important attribute of a saint is the ability "to will one thing." Obviously, this singlemindedness is also evident in the committed artist. With complete involvement in a project comes a way of life rather than a series of disconnected acts. In *The Cloud of Unknowing* we find: "Why do you suppose that this little prayer of one syllable is powerful enough to pierce the heavens? Well, it is because it is the prayer of a man's whole being."[49] Not surprisingly, some Zen Buddhist paintings consist of a single, energetic stroke.

3

Receptivity, Omnipresence, and Sui Generis Emotions

An attitude of receptivity or openness is another shared feature of the aesthetic and the spiritual. Usually, this state of readiness or acceptance precedes the mystic's illumination and the artist's inspiration or afflation. After the New England Transcendentalist Margaret Fuller exclaimed, "I accept the universe," Thomas Carlyle replied, "Gad! She'd better!" While Carlyle apparently saw no alternative, William James observes that one can either adopt a posture of "dull submission" or take up a religious stance, i.e., "a mood of welcome."[1] In the preface to his novel, *The Spoils of Poynton*, Henry James discusses the genesis of the work and emphasizes that the creative artist must be receptive to the germ of a story. Similarly, in the spiritual classic *The Cloud of Unknowing*, we read: "Let it [grace] be the active doer and you the passive receiver. Do not meddle with it (as if you could possibly improve upon grace), but let it be for fear you spoil it entirely. . . . Be as wood to a carpenter or a home to a dweller . . . for knowledge is a hindrance here."[2] St. Teresa explains receptivity to the will of God through an archetypal metaphor: "For indeed the soul does no more in this union than does the wax when another impresses a seal on it."[3] Artists, such as Samuel Taylor Coleridge, asserted that they sometimes wrote with no sensation or awareness of effort. The novelist Thackeray reported that it felt as though an occult power were guiding his pen. Again, van Gogh writes of his lucidity in moments when: " . . . I am not conscious of myself any more, and the picture

49

comes to me as in a dream. (Letter 543)."[4] It is important to realize that such "passivity" does not dispose one toward a feckless quietism; rather, to be passive is to do something, namely, to prepare oneself for fresh vision and action. Receiving need be no less active than presenting, for to cease one activity does not preclude engaging in another. William James observes that "Receptivity... often comes about, not by doing, but by simply relaxing and throwing the burden down. This abandonment of self-responsibility seems to be the fundamental act in specifically religious as distinct from moral practice."[5] One must, to some degree or other, succumb. Artists "surrender" to a medium, a literary or musical theme, an emotion, an emergent form, the divine, or to an idea that has arrived for development. For example, in the preface to *The Spoils of Poynton*, Henry James reports that while writing he was "beguiled and led on." The artist not only controls a medium but she is controlled by the medium, i.e., learns from it, is steered by it, or falls under its sway.

One finds a classic account of a person submitting himself to the will of God in Jean-Pierre de Caussade's eighteenth-century spiritual work, *Abandonment to Divine Providence*. It is important to note that such total surrender, far from being a loss of freedom, is an expression of it, for abandonment begins with an exercise of free will and culminates in a newfound freedom. Teresa speaks about the soul consenting to become a prisoner of God[6] and eventually declares, "I seem to be in every way free from myself; and though I thought that my obedience would be a burden, I have attained to the greatest freedom."[7] Similarly, the artist who allows herself to be "beguiled and led on"—whether by the germ of a story, an artistic medium, an abstract motif or rhythm—enjoys liberation from the routine and the opportunity to attain new aesthetic heights. Augustine adds that through submission one avoids a kind of enslavement: "Surrendering ourselves affectionately to His Mercy we do not let ourselves be overcome by the delights of bad habits drawing us into sin."[8] By conforming to the will of God or entering into accord with the Tao, one capitulates to her own true nature and thereby achieves the deepest fulfillment that is possible. One has left unreason behind and with it all disturbances; hence, one naturally enjoys great inward peace. In prayer, acting with the simplicity and trust of a child, one may place herself entirely into the hands of God.

Receptivity is integral to the I-Thou relation, because the I is acted upon as well as an actor. To love another without any reciprocity constitutes adulation rather than relation. Again, if an

artwork does not change its creator, there is no real mutuality
between the two. To enter into the I-Thou relation is not to assume
power or control; the emphasis is upon receiving rather than using
or manipulating, upon relinquishing rather than grasping. According to Buber, with the I-It posture of science and magic, control is
fundamental. He states that when the person who says I-It turns
toward particulars, " . . . he uses the objectifying telescope of distant vision to arrange them as mere scenery."[9] One controls rather
than beholds. Perhaps the tendency to reach for a camera—which
one can control through buttons, lenses, filters, and the like—and
photograph a landscape is sometimes a subterfuge by which one
avoids any actual encounter with nature as fully present. The artistic photographer, by contrast, allows the landscape to affect him
as he affects it. Such a relational posture is non-magical, non-
exploitative. The I-It perspective is preoccupied with magic, i.e.,
gaining power over persons or things, not in entering into relationships with them.[10] Bad art is as mechanical as adherence to the
formulas of the magician. Such art manipulates rather than engages. One produces it under conditions of restraint—one's whole
self is unable to participate—and seeks to engender conditions of
restraint. Liberation or release is as important in art as it is in
religion.

As science and magic are inherently impersonal, art and religion are unavoidably personal. One who wishes to have an I-Thou
relation with a tree must suspend the detached, causal, means-end
perspective of science or magic and adopt the personal, relational
posture that coalesces with aesthetic appreciation. One can affect
the tree by leaving it undisturbed and by giving it her whole self,
as she would invest her total being in the creation or appreciation
of an artwork. The tree can affect a beholder by addressing her,
since the being of the tree invites her into relationship; and she can
further affect it by accepting its invitation to relation, by taking up
the I-Thou stance toward the tree. Naturally, there is no freedom
in the domain of science, for this is the I-It realm of inexorable
cause and effect. That science has a branch that is called "mechan-
ics" is telling. In the world of relations, however, the I and the
Thou transcend the mechanical and meet each other in a free reciprocity that is undiminished by any causality. In fine, creativity,
vitality, spontaneity, and unpredictability prevail. As magic and
science rotate around causal chains, religion and art seek to transcend those chains; thus, religion pursues freedom. In Hinduism,
for example, *moksha* is the term that expresses ultimate liberation.
Of course, artists, like Shih-t'ao, struggle to break from bondage to

any school, style, or genre. Ideally, the artist's project begins and ends in freedom. First she freely chooses a method, and ideally, what she creates is the very embodiment of the free human spirit.

Unlike the scientific perspective that keeps a certain distance between the observer and the natural phenomena under investigation, the aesthetic orientation encourages one to relate to a thing, to feel rapport with it, to sympathize with it, to empathize with it, to identify with it; in a word, to become engaged with it, rather than detached from it. Only such engagement can transform the It into a Thou. The It-world of science is the world of non-aesthetic quantities in which one can see and record the velocity, dimensions, and varying positions of a red globe, but still miss the beauty of that very sunset. This It-world is one of sheer quantity and objectivity, but the I-Thou world contains aesthetic qualities and personal insights. As Louis Z. Hammer has observed, "The artistic imagination leads the person to the world that has been set at a distance and enables him to retrieve that world."[11] Stated differently, art can re-unite the I with the Thou. According to Buber, artistic creation requires encounter or confrontation with an incipient Thou:

> This is the eternal origin of art that a human being confronts a form that wants to become a work through him. Not a figment of his soul but something that appears to the soul and demands the soul's creative power. What is required is a deed that a man does with his whole being; if he commits it and speaks with his being the basic word to the form that appears, then the creative power is released and the work comes into being.[12]

The I-Thou posture, elucidated so powerfully by Buber and lived so gracefully by Francis, applies to an aesthetic attitude as well as to a spiritual one. For the classifying, analyzing, non-personal, I-It outlook of science, with its dualism of spectator and object, Francis substitutes the empathizing approach of the I-Thou outlook by which he enters into rapport with others. A child, who is so absorbed, rescues her blanket from thingness by naming it and thereby endowing it with personhood. While science speaks in the impersonal language of "the temperature is sixty-five degrees," Francis communicates in the personal language of "Brother Sun" and "Sister Poverty." He is no more interested in nature in general than an art lover is interested in art in general. Indeed, G.K. Chesterton uses the distinction between the general, in the sense of "abstract," and the particular in order to separate Francis from the pantheist:

" . . . he is the very opposite of a pantheist; he did not call nature his mother; he called a particular donkey his brother or a particular sparrow his sister."[13] In fine, Francis loved individual creatures and creations, not nature as a diffuse, general whole or amorphous abstraction. Clearly, Francis is no more a polytheist than he is a pantheist, but his prayers that refer to the sun, moon, water, and fire render him vulnerable to such a misinterpretation. Interestingly enough, some have accused the Native Americans—who also bestowed similar praise upon the sun, wind, and other elements—of worshipping idols. This in spite of the fact that Indians, such as Walking Buffalo, have spoken to the contrary: "We saw the Great Spirit's work in almost everything: sun, moon, trees, wind, and mountains. Sometimes we approached him through these things. Was that so bad?"[14]

When T.S. Eliot wrote about a person who left a place only to return to it and see it for the first time, the poet could have been writing about the aesthetic perspective or the spiritual perspective, since either enables one to see matters afresh. Since both pertain not merely to features of experience but to ways of apprehending things, i.e., attitudes or outlooks, it makes sense to speak of perceiving things aesthetically: "She studied the clouds, not for meteorological purposes, but for the sheer joy of tracing their formations." It also makes sense to speak of seeing things from a spiritual perspective: "The poorest of the poor, the weakest of the sick, and the worst of the depraved should all be seen as one's brothers and sisters." Both interests animate one line of a daily prayer of Mother Teresa of Calcutta: "Lord, give me this seeing faith, then my work will never be monotonous." Just as we need faith for religion, we need a "seeing faith" if aesthetic experience is to supplant the humdrum.

Rudolph Otto explicitly links the aesthetic and the religious through the idea of receptivity. According to him, a disposition to know the holy is universal, but this receptive capacity remains uncultivated in most; hence there are many adherents of a religion but only a few prophets. Likewise, in art, what appears as mere receptivity in the majority of humankind reappears at a higher level in artists' creativity, invention, or works of genius. "The prophet corresponds in the religious sphere to the creative artist in that of art . . . "[15] The aesthetic attitude doctrine holds that a proper mental set is the prerequisite for having aesthetic experiences. To illustrate, one can hardly relish the humor in a comic play if he is in a depressed state. In short, this doctrine identifies a positive frame of mind, an optimal openness to any aesthetic qualities that objects possess. Offering a spiritual counterpart for the aesthetic attitude, Otto refers to " . . . the mental predisposition necessary for the experience of holiness . . . "[16] Praying, fasting, meditating, and chanting may all be used as instruments for effecting this outlook. This ideal state is thematic in Martin Buber's Hasidic novel, *For the Sake of Heaven*, which treats the life of perpetual prayer; and there is a parallel in Joyce Carey's novel, *The Horse's Mouth*, which relates the life of an artist whose every moment is an aesthetic one. Typically, the saint seeks continual union with God; and the aesthete does not want the aesthetic experience to end.

Some philosophers describe the aesthetic attitude in terms of mental distance. They argue that such psychical distance is essential for having an aesthetic experience, because unless one puts her narrow, personal self-interests at some remove, she will be unable to behold an object aesthetically. One should, for example, be able to appreciate a masterpiece irrespective of whether she or her enemy owns it. The Catholic priest Henri Nouwen talks about the temporal variety of psychical distance:

> What is most close, most intimate, most present, often cannot be experienced directly but only with a certain distance. . . . Only in retrospect do I realize that something important has taken place. Isn't this true of all the really important events in life? When I am together with someone I love very much, we seldom talk about our relationship. . . . But later . . . we realize how much it all meant to us . . . [17]

B.C. Lane, developing an essay on spiritual geography, states, "We know all the most meaningful places only in retrospect."[18] He explains this by observing that the places that are most sacred to us are always those which we have had time to internalize, reconstitute, and conjure up afresh as memories. Perhaps memories are precious, not because they are all that one has left of experiences, but because, in a sense, collected in the chemistry of imaginative reflection, memories include more than was present in the original experiences. In a classic article, Edward Bullough discusses aesthetic distance in terms of degrees, arguing there can be too little or too much.[19] The unsophisticated countryman who rushes onto the stage in order to help the heroine of a play illustrates underdistancing; the twelve-year-old who cannot relate to Hamlet illustrates overdistancing. While fewer theoreticians write about the aesthetic appreciation of nature than about the aesthetic appreciation of art, the desert dweller Edward Abbey notes a case of

overdistancing in the desert: " ... like many other mechanical gad-
gets it [the flashlight] tends to separate a man from the world
around him. ... If I switch it on I can see ... only the small pool of
light which it makes in front of me; I am isolated."[20]

The ideal aesthetic appreciator is disinterested enough to suspend any preoccupation with her own desires. She relinquishes her
ordinary practical attitude in order that self-centered concerns and
prejudices do not dictate how she apprehends art and nature. To
reduce one's idiosyncratic interests is to open one's larger self to
what is universal. Of course, one who is disinterested is not unin-
terested, but, like an ideal judge, impartial. Therefore, disinterestedness is the ideal in art criticism in which one's prejudices
are not to determine how she interprets or evaluates works. A
critic's need to abstract strictly personal considerations becomes
especially acute if, for example, she is the one being satirized in a
comic play. One's ego recedes if he is a theatre goer who identifies
with an actor or an actor who identifies with the role he plays.
Disinterestedness can flourish, because such identifications entail
a temporary bracketing—however partial—of one's everyday interests and problems. To enjoy art for art's sake, one must, to some
degree, go beyond narrow self-interest.

One can relate a disinterested attitude to love. The purity of
Francis's love for animals is expressed in reports that he bought
and released them before they could be sold at market. What
Underhill attributes to the artist applies equally to the religious
person: "We perceive things not as they are, but as they affect
ourselves. The artist, on the contrary, sees them for their own
sakes, with the eyes of disinterested love."[21] Accordingly, the Catholic priest Anthony De Mello contradicts the bromide that love is
blind:

> Love springs from awareness. It is only inasmuch as you see
> someone as he or she really is here and now and not as they
> are in your memory or your desire or in your imagination or
> projection that you can truly love them, otherwise it is not the
> person that you love but the idea that you have formed of this
> person ... [22]

When he states, "You cannot love what you are not constantly
discovering anew,"[23] the object of affection may be an artwork or
natural beauty as well as a human or the divine.

Church fathers, such as Clement, identified disinterested love
as detachment, the supreme state of the believer. Indeed, Meister

Eckhart elevates "detachment" to the status of the ultimate virtue: "All other virtues have some regard for created things, but detachment is free from all created things."[24] Eckhart reasons that, as great as love is—it compels us to love God—detachment is even greater for it compels God to love us. "To be empty of all created things is to be full of God."[25] Eckhart speaks of detachment as "naked nothingness," but such a nothingness is a great potentiality, for in this nothingness is the greatest receptivity.[26] Here, he compares the heart to a wax tablet, as does Teresa, arguing that the tablet is never so good for writing upon as when it has no writing at all. Likewise, it is only after the artist has abstracted his ego from all things that he can return to them and see them fully for the first time. Of course, one's appreciation of art should be disinterested, i.e., not self-seeking. Disinterestedness, detachment, or distance does not entail an attitude of disdain toward created things; on the contrary, possessed of detachment, one greatly appreciates them, but without clinging to them.

Detachment is a prerequisite for contemplative activity; and something like the contemplation that transfixes saints is valuable for artists. Thus, there have always been artists, as well as religious figures, who felt the need to go beyond ratiocination to contemplation or meditation. Certainly, conceptual analysis has a place among artists, saints, and art appreciators, but in the most profound experiences, reason yields to the immediacy of a mystical intuition. Accordingly, even the most intelligent art theory, theology, or art criticism is penultimate. Clearly, soul-searching contemplation is at the heart of artistic as well as religious lives. It is noteworthy that F.C. Happold's description of mystical contemplation sounds strikingly like an account of the aesthetic attitude: "In the state of contemplation there is found a self-forgetting attention, a humble receptiveness, a still and steady gazing, an intense concentration, so that emotion, will, and thought are all fused and then lost in something which is none of them but which embraces them all."[27] To a degree, many artists employ the same medium as do all mystics: contemplation. Humility is an essential ingredient in the awakening of either the aesthetic or the religious life. Taoism, which regards humility as a supreme virtue, uses the metaphor of the valley to capture the yielding receptivity of the Tao. That the motif is cross-cultural, if not archetypal, is evident from the fact that thinkers such as Augustine also recognized the valley as a symbol of humility. Unless a cup is empty, it cannot receive anything. To empty oneself of ego is fill oneself with humility.

An exclusively practical orientation has always been the bane of art and religion alike. The twentieth-century artist Man Ray was attacking the dragon of "usefulness" when he attached nails—that would shred and ruin any cloth—to the bottom of an iron. By so destroying the iron's function, the artist released its formal, sculptural qualities. Exhibited in an art museum, the iron invited viewers to appreciate it on non-utilitarian grounds. To take an example from nature, many would describe the desert as worthless or useless, but it is because it is devoid of mundane utility or profit that the desert yields untold aesthetic delights. If deserts are only good for disclosing beauty and for manifesting God, this will hardly diminish their value to artists and religious searchers. The desert fathers, Christ, and Mohammed were all undoubtedly moved by the aesthetic power of the desert, a beautifully skeletal landscape for those who can take their beauty and spirituality straight. Roger Fry explains how the practical can inhibit aesthetic appreciation:

> The needs of our actual life are so imperative, that the sense of vision becomes highly specialised in their service. With an admirable economy we learn to see only so much as is needful for our purposes . . . the normal person really only reads the labels as it were on the objects around him and troubles no further. Almost all the things which are useful in any way put on more or less this cap of invisibility. It is only when an object exists in our lives for no other purpose than to be seen that we really look at it, as for instance at a China ornament or a precious stone, and towards such even the most normal person adopts to some extent the artistic attitude of pure vision abstracted from necessity.[28]

Thomas R. Martland credits both art and religion with giving us new eyeglasses that yield a fresh, however temporary, vision of the world.[29] Calling to mind the aesthetic attitude doctrine, the Trappist monk Thomas Merton identifies the transformative power of prayer: "Prayer does not blind us to the world, but it transforms our vision of the world, and makes us see it, all men, and all the history of mankind, in the light of God."[30] One may compare Fry's above remarks with this passage from Evelyn Underhill's landmark work on mysticism:

> This new method of perception will reveal unsuspected qualities in the external world. First, you will perceive about you

a strange and deepening quietness; a slowing down of our feverish mental time. Next, you will become aware of a heightened significance, an intensified existence in the thing at which you look. As you, with all your consciousness lean out towards it, an answering current will meet yours. It seems as though the barrier between its life and your own, between subject and object, had melted away.[31]

Similarly, from the perspective of artistic creation, one is to identify with her object. In short, the boundary between the self and nonself fades or disappears. If, as Fry says, it is our practical perspective that renders the aesthetic invisible, surely this outlook can obfuscate the spiritual, no matter how close at hand it may be.

While obviously important, the practical is never entirely decisive for either the mystic or the artist. Even the architect, who tends to be the most pragmatically determined of all artists, is not willing to let practical considerations alone dictate the form of a building. As the soul enlivens the human body, the aesthetic dimension brings vitality to any work of architecture. Therefore, the utilitarian banner cry, "form follows function," can scarcely serve as the basis for architectural aesthetics. Again, when one preoccupies himself with utilitarian considerations about the afterlife, he has left religion behind. Asked about the life to come, Confucius replied: "Worry about leading a good life here and now; the afterlife will take care of itself." With art and religion, one appreciates things, partly at least, for their inherent features, rather than exclusively for their utilitarian value. I-Thou relations are similarly trans-practical, for they are never wholly utilitarian. To view the other exclusively in terms of his usefulness is to adopt the I-It stance. By contrast, to take up the relational, I-Thou attitude is to resist an unduly practical perspective. Interestingly enough, the saint and the artist, by assigning the practical its proper status, do not render themselves effete; rather, they go on to transform the world.

Intrinsic value is at the heart of religion, art, and love. Ideally one values a religious ideal, an artwork, or a human relationship, for its own sake alone, quite apart from any external benefits that accrue. If one values an artwork for its own sake ("art for art's sake"), he can speak of it as "purposeless." As Buber puts it, "The purpose of the relation is the relation itself—touching the You."[32] For Immanuel Kant, judgments of pure beauty are those that pronounce something to be beautiful apart from any conception of its usefulness or comparative merits. Kant's illustrations of such "free" or unconditioned beauty include flowers: "Hardly anyone but a botanist knows what sort of thing a flower ought to be; and even he, though recognizing in the flower the reproductive organ of the plant, pays no regard to this natural purpose if he is passing judgment on the flower by taste."[33] Further examples offered by Kant include exotic birds, seashells, and wallpaper designs, for one need not base judgments of such beauties on intellectualizing, conceptualizing, categorization, or classification. Only the person who suspends his analytic processes can exercise taste. Buber agrees that the wrong way to contemplate a tree is to categorize it under a species and regard it as an instance.[34]

Having an aesthetic or a spiritual orientation, one appreciates intrinsic as opposed to merely extrinsic value. To "art for art's sake" and "spirituality for spirituality's sake," St. Bernard of Clairvaux adds "Love for Love's sake": "Love is sufficient of itself; it is pleasant of itself and for its own sake. Love itself is a merit, and itself its own reward."[35] When the practical rules over art, the result is the aesthetically dispiriting, slack, or humdrum, for propaganda or advertising flourishes. When the practical dominates in spiritual matters, religion becomes magic, i.e., a quest for mechanical techniques to engender desired effects. When the practical prevails in human relations, each treats the other merely as a means rather than as an end, as an It rather than as a Thou. Whenever the practical rules over human relations with nature, exploitation follows. Of course, great Christian thinkers elevate the divine above nature. In chapter twenty-four of *The Cloud of Unknowing*, one reads that humans should love God over all creatures and strictly for his own sake. In *The Imitation of Christ*, Thomas à Kempis declares, " . . . those who love Jesus purely for himself, and not for their own profit or convenience, bless Him as heartily in temptation and tribulation and in all other adversities as they do in time of consolation."[36] Christian thinkers, such as the anonymous author of *The Cloud of Unknowing*, tend to hold that art is a penultimate end, one that gains its deepest meaning from being moored in the ultimate significance and value of religion.

As Clive Bell states, to view objects as ends in themselves is uncommon: "Mr. Roger Fry has pointed out that few can hope ever to see a charging bull as an end in itself and yield themselves to the emotional significance of its forms, because no sooner is the label 'Charging Bull' recognised than we begin to dispose ourselves for flight rather than contemplation."[37] For Bell, it is only when artists perceive things as ends that such things can serve as a means to ecstasy.[38] He soon explicitly compares the spiritual and the aesthetic:

For the mystic, as for the artist, the physical universe is a means to ecstasy. The mystic feels things as "ends" instead of seeing them as "means." He seeks within all things that ultimate reality which provokes emotional exaltation; and, if he does not come at it through pure form, there are, as I have said, more roads than one to that country. Religion, as I understand it, is an expression of the individual's sense of the emotional significance of the universe; I should not be surprised to find that art was an expression of the same thing. Anyway, both seem to express emotions that are different from and transcending the emotions of life.[39]

When considered as an end in itself, art may be a threat to religion. Aestheticism, for example, elevates artistic values over all others. Of course, the theist insists that there is a hierarchy of ends in themselves, with God at the summit. Therefore, art need not be idolatry, i.e., something that usurps God's place and stands between humans and the divine. After all, a lower end is a step toward the end of ends. As with a stained glass window, one can first appreciate its design and then treasure the light that gives the window its luminous beauty and which is the necessary condition for any and all beauties. Sue Bender provides a religious example of the intrinsic value of labor: "The Amish find meaning in work itself. Work is never viewed as a stepping stone to personal success or advancement but a challenge to do whatever your are doing to the best of your ability."[40] As the monastic life shows, dedicated work can be as worshipful as hymns and prayers. For the saint and the artist, everything is or is potentially an end in itself. To the baker who makes a loaf of bread and allows the process to engage his heart, mind, and will, the activity will have intrinsic as well as extrinsic value.

One may call an artwork "good for nothing" if its only value is to sustain aesthetic contemplation. Similarly, a religious act can be strikingly impractical and, in this sense, "good for nothing." Loving one's enemies or imitating Christ may be of no personal benefit to the agent. Of course, God is "good for nothing," in the sense that there is no power sufficient to reward him. The tales of the Taoist sage Chuang Tzu discuss the usefulness of uselessness, i.e., the value of the useless. Specifically, he tells of a tree that escaped destruction only because it was misshapen and did not lend itself to human purposes. The tree preserved its life owing to its useless nature. Artworks too can preserve their intrinsic value only if they retain something of their uselessness, only if their practical aspects do not exhaust their worth. Likewise, acts are religious only if one does not perform them exclusively for their usefulness.

Omnipresence

An early Hassidic song declares, "Wherever I Go—only Thou! Wherever I stand—only Thou! Just Thou; again Thou! Always Thou! Thou, Thou, Thou! When things are good, Thou! when things are bad, Thou! Thou, Thou, Thou!" A prayer attributed to St. Patrick (389–461) celebrates the omnipresence of Christ:

> Christ, be with me, Christ before me, Christ behind me,
> Christ in me, Christ beneath me, Christ above me,
> Christ on my right, Christ on my left,
> Christ where I lie, Christ where I sit, Christ where I arise,
> Christ in the heart of every one who thinks of me,
> Christ in the mouth of every one who speaks of me,
> Christ in every eye that sees me,
> Christ in every ear that hears me.

A Navajo daily prayer finds beauty to be ubiquitous:

> With beauty before me, I walk
> With beauty behind me, I walk
> With beauty above me, I walk
> With beauty below me, I walk
> From the East beauty has been restored
> From the South beauty has been restored
> From the West beauty has been restored
> From the zenith in the sky beauty has been restored
> From the nadir of the earth beauty has been restored
> From all around me beauty has been restored.

In similar language, Mohammed yearns for the omnipresence of light: "Oh God, give me light in my heart and light in my tongue and light in my hearing and light in my sight and light in my feeling and light in all my body and light before me and light behind me . . . light on my right hand and light on my left hand and light above me and light beneath me . . . " As the divine is often associated with light, light is often linked with beauty. In the early Kabbalah we find: "Let there be light: This means Beauty, for the Torah came forth from Wisdom."[41] Therefore, whatever illumines, whatever enlightens, is profoundly beautiful and profoundly spiritual.

As already noted, the omnipresence of positive value is a feature of both the aesthetic and spiritual perspectives. This is simply to say that one can detect the beautiful and the holy in all places. That the aesthetic and the spiritual are omnipresent is thematic in Henri Nouwen's focus upon the here and now: "Just as a whole world of beauty can be discovered in one flower, so the great grace of God can be tasted in one small moment."[42] Of course, only heightened receptivity allows the artist or saint to recognize the omnipresence of positive value. Artists excel at finding beauty in all quarters; thus, a photographer from Chicago, Charles Swedlund, captures the stark beauty of "found objects" in his photographs of a garbage-strewn alley. Similarly, St. Teresa finds the sacred in everything: "I believe that in each little thing created by God, there is more than what is understood, even if it is a little ant."[43] The illustration is cross cultural, for the Taoist Chuang Tzu also locates the Tao in an ant. To underline the omnipresence of the spiritual, Taoism teaches that the Tao is in even urine and dung. Affirming the inseparability of the sordid and the sacred, St. Teresa prays that God will use her in order to praise him, " . . . men shall see that on a dunghill so foul and rank He has made a garden of flowers so sweet."[44] No object is too homely to be devoid of aesthetic import; witness van Gogh's painting of a peasant's shoes. No action or agent is too vile to lack spiritual value; therefore, Meister Eckhart declares: "In every work, even in evil, I repeat in one evil both according to punishment and guilt, God's glory is revealed and shines forth in equal fashion."[45] Clearly, if the supreme reality is everywhere, it cannot be absent from even the lowliest of things. Therefore, the religious person unflinchingly traces one implication of omnipresence and concedes that "even in idolatry there are holy sparks." Underlining the omnipresence of the divine, Buber explains that there is no God-hunting, because there is no place where one cannot find him.[46] Similarly, the artist need not search for beauty, because no thing is devoid of it.

Saints dignify and sanctify ordinary objects and activities by, say, offering them up to God; and artists transfigure pedestrian things in the creative process. However prosaic an act or entity might be, it is transformed and rendered extraordinary in the chemistry of spiritual and aesthetic experiences. Otto is struck by the fact that the catalyst that evokes a numinous state of mind can be quite routine, the resultant emotion being far out of proportion with that which occasioned it.[47] This is also true of aesthetic experiences, since something as seemingly inconsequential as a housefly may elicit one. Of course, from the belief that God is present in all beings, it does not follow that God is present to all beings. Such is the irony of omnipresence: although God is everywhere, he is not easy to find. Typically, the searcher expends great energy in order to know the presence of the divine. Since art is a key aid to this discernment, no religion is utterly devoid of artistic expressions. Lane quotes from Augustine to show that it is possible for everything to have sacramental significance: "Taking the broadest definition of a sacrament as a 'sign of a sacred reality'—as Augustine did—anything in the world could be seen as a sacramental, since all of creation is a sign of God."[48] The aesthetic and the religious coalesce in the poetry of Walt Whitman for whom every blade of grass and "every cubic inch of space is a miracle." In the poem "Miracles," from *Leaves of Grass*, Whitman revels in the miraculous:

Why, who makes much of a miracle?
As to me I know of nothing else but miracles,
Whether I walk the streets of Manhattan,
Or dart my sight over roofs of houses toward the sky,
Or wade with naked feet along the beach just in the edge of
    the water,
Or stand under trees in the woods,
Or talk by day with any one I love, or sleep in bed at night
    with any one I love,
Or sit at table at dinner with the rest,
Or look at strangers opposite me riding in the car,
Or watch honey-bees busy around the hive of a summer
    forenoon,
Or animals feeding in the fields,
Or birds, or the wonderfulness of insects, in the air,
Or the wonderfulness of the sundown, or of stars shining so
    quiet and brave,
Or the exquisite delicate thin curve of the new moon in
    spring;
These with the rest, one and all, are to me miracles,
The whole referring, yet each distinct and in its place.

To me every hour of the dark and light is a miracle,
Every cubic inch of space is a miracle,
Every square yard of the surface of the earth is spread with
    the same,

Every foot of the interior swarms with the same.
To me the sea is a continual miracle,
The fishes that swim—the rocks—the motion of the waves—
    the ships with men in them,
What stranger miracles are there?

Just as the I-Thou sanctifies the other—whether a person, tree or
painting—Whitman's poetry elevates all entities. Because believers
can always appreciate the formal qualities of God's creation, they
know a priori that it's possible to experience any object aesthetically. In Kantian terms, "One can appreciate every object aesthetically" is a synthetic a priori truth. It means that every particular
can give aesthetic satisfaction. While a claim about matters of fact,
it purports to be universally and necessarily true. Naturally, non-
spiritual thinkers need a different justification for such a claim.
The question is: How can they know in advance that every particular will reward aesthetic appreciation? If the answer is that the
appreciator brings the aesthetic attitude with him to an object, this
may undermine the objectivity that some assign to beauty, reducing it to wishful thinking or mere human projection. Ironically
enough, notwithstanding the omnipresence of aesthetic and spiritual values, there is a common and persistent tendency to think
that art exists only in museums and that religion exists only in
mosques, churches, and temples. Obviously, art flourishes beyond
museums; and religion often begins with a rejection of the established church or temple. One can compartmentalize neither art nor
religion, for creativity and spirituality, like water, resist confinement
and spill out of any and all institutional settings to nourish all
other aspects of life. Only after immersion in life can these two
currents return to their respective institutions with a replenished
vitality.
    The I-Thou relation, like the omnipresent God who is the Thou
of our most exalted relation, is latent everywhere. Philip Wheelwright has identified Buber's basic metaphysical postulate as "the
potential availability of relationship in any and all situations, however seemingly unpromising."[49] This, of course, places the respon-
sibility of establishing relationships upon every individual. To take
up an I-Thou relationship is a religious act, because one must meet
a human Thou before he can meet the eternal Thou. For Buber, to
hallow the mundane is to worship the divine. Meister Eckhart
addresses the consecration of the ordinary, "It is not what we do
which makes us holy, but we ought to make holy what we do."[50]
One can also transform everything into art; in which case, the

concept loses its meaning as a category that marks off selected items from all others. In Judaism, the Baal Shem Tov recognized everything corporeal, including the coupling of husband and wife, as subject to being hallowed through the proper intention. The hallowing of the mundane occurs when a person leaves the sanctity of an I-Thou relation in order "to bring the spark of the spirit into everyday living in the world of things."[51] That van Gogh had an I-Thou relationship with nature and its transcendent source is evident in the intense sparks that he carried to his landscape paintings.

"One cannot live in the pure present: it would consume us . . . "[52] With this observation, Buber responds to the paradox of omnipresence: If God is everywhere, then why do not humans discover him in all places? Perhaps it would overwhelm a person to encounter the divine everywhere, for such meetings call upon one to invest his whole being. Teresa points out that if one continually felt God's presence with great clarity, she could not do anything else, not even dwell among people.[53] Even in the case of meetings between finite humans, the "Thou" usually returns to its status of being a mere object among objects. Accordingly, William James spoke of mystical states as transitory. Presumably, it is only for God that finite Thous never slip to the status of Its and that "a thing of beauty is a joy forever." Like states of artistic inspiration, I-Thou encounters are fragile respites from the mundane. But, from a religious perspective, neither exists merely for ephemeral pleasure; both afford a glimpse—however momentary—of that which is not time-bound. Buber elaborates: " . . . every thing in the world can—either before or after it becomes a thing—appear to some I as its You. . . . The It is the chrysalis, the You the butterfly."[54] Of course, the omnipresence of the Thou may be unrealized, but the unappreciated person or painting merely awaits re-animation by a sensitive I who approaches.

Constant prayer would seem to be the logical human response to God's omnipresence. After all, if God is constantly presenting himself, it would seem that humans should constantly acknowledge him; and scripture does enjoin one to pray without ceasing (I Thessalonians 5:17). One may question if such a practice is possible and, if so, what form(s) it takes. At times the call for constant prayer may just refer to sustained prayer, as when St. John of the Cross speaks of a soul delighting in prayer for one or more nights. Other times, "unending prayer" means having an abiding vision or image. Just as the aesthete reports that an aesthetic experience lingers and shapes future experiences, Teresa reported that, in addition to transitory visions of Christ, one of her visions of Jesus did not disappear, but persisted and informed her everyday life.[55] On and following the Feast of our Lady's Nativity, Teresa reported seeing the Virgin Mary: "I had this vision constantly for some days . . . "[56] In one vision, Christ appeared and resembled his depictions in paintings: "The vision made me very much afraid, for it was so clear, and so close to me, that it made me think whether it was an illusion or not. He said to me: 'Be not afraid of it, for the union of My Father with thy soul is incomparably closer than this.' The vision has remained with me until now."[57] This may be another case of the indebtedness of religion to art, for Teresa compares her vision of the Lord to him "as He is painted in the pictures of our Lady of Anguish." One wonders if her intellectual vision of Christ could possess such vivacity were she unacquainted with paintings of him.

The anonymous author of *The Cloud of Unknowing* urges one to focus continually on contemplative love and to take up a definite orientation: " . . . with your attention centered upon the blind awareness of your naked being united to God's, you will go about your daily rounds, eating and drinking, sleeping and waking, going and coming . . . you will be offering to God continually each day the most precious gift you can make."[58] In the *Dark Night of the Soul*, which details the tribulations of the soul's progress, St. John of the Cross talks about the soul seeking God without stopping, whether eating, speaking, thinking, or sleeping. Here, to engage in constant prayer is to adopt an ever-present attitude. In the union of "spiritual marriage," the soul remains centered in God, just as one might center himself in the beautiful, as in the case of the composer who, on hearing a kitchen plate shatter, exclaimed: "Ah, C-Sharp."

Sui Generis Emotions

To posit that the aesthetic and the spiritual are everywhere and embedded in every thing is not to say that they lack any characteristic traits. Those who immerse themselves in art or religion report that they experience distinctive affective states. In other words, the emotions of art and religion are different from those of ordinary life (though sometimes like each other); thus, distinctive emotions constitute another common denominator between the aesthetic and the religious. That watching a tragic drama elicits "aesthetic" sadness, rather than normal sadness, is evident, because we wish to repeat the former experience but not the latter.

Again, if a spectator responds to a drama by feeling unmitigated rage, she cannot sustain the aesthetic attitude. An actress transmits stylized emotions, which are under her control, and her own person—mind and body—is the medium. Of course, with natural self-expression, there is no control of a medium. Witness the person in a temper tantrum. Therefore, philosophers of art sometimes speak of esthetic emotions as distanced, detached, or filtered. Religious emotions are also distinctive. Clearly, "the peace that passes all understanding" differs from ordinary states of repose—however serene they may be. Teresa speaks of a joyful suffering or pain in which the awakening soul: " . . . feels that it is wounded in the most delightful way. . . . It knows clearly that the wound is something precious, and it would never want to be cured."[59] She also says, "It is impossible to describe or explain the way in which God wounds the soul or the very grievous pain inflicted, which deprives it of self-consciousness; yet this pain is so sweet, that there is no joy in the world which gives greater delight."[60] Both a saint and the reader of a tragic novel welcome repetition of their "painful" experiences, because, for example, they provide distinctive pleasures, effect a catharsis, or deliver illumination.

Surely there is a felt quality of aesthetic or spiritual emotions that marks them off from routine feelings. Through art or religion, one experiences emotions that are apart from the mundane, even if the most commonplace ingredients are thematic. According to Clive Bell, who was hardly reluctant to generalize about art, the transcendence of the material world is the essence of art. "All artists are religious," and when it comes to saints and artists, "the materialistic conception of the universe does not seem to explain those emotions which they feel with supreme certainty and absolute disinterestedness."[61] Lane, in a discussion of Baroque spirituality, eloquently describes the artistic expression of Teresa's experiences that is evident in El Greco's paintings: "His ethereal, elongated figures seem caught up in an ecstatic suffering as they yearn to ascend heavenward. In their austere beauty, they agonize with unconcealed joy—engrossed as they are in the process of turning pain into eternity."[62] Teresa also reports a vision in which a cherub repeatedly plunged a gold spear into her heart, penetrated to her entrails and drew them out as the spear was removed.[63] However grotesque the picture presented, like aesthetic sadness, this wounding experience is decidedly positive, for she tells us that "the pain is not bodily, but spiritual; although the body has a share in it, even a large one."[64] Discussing Gianlorenzo Bernini's sculpture *The Ecstasy of St. Theresa*, one art historian describes Teresa's elation as "palpably physical." According to Andrew M. Greeley, " . . . both the saint and the sculptor used erotic images to describe what it is like to be caught up in God's love."[65] Teresa's ecstatic experience was not simply one of mundane joy or pain, since in the final pages of her autobiography, she reports that her suffering is not sensory and that her "wound" is not physical, for it has its locus in her soul.

The Cloud of Unknowing is careful to observe that when contemplatives empathize with Christ's agony, their pain is different from his, "A person deeply committed to contemplation shares in Christ's redemptive suffering, not exactly as Christ did himself, but in a manner similar to Christ's."[66] Presumably only those who possess the stigmata would undergo Christ's exact feelings. For all others, participation in Christ's ordeal is strictly imaginative or aesthetic, as when the actor identifies with the emotions of his character. P. Pourrat speaks of Francis's "veritable participation" in Jesus's pain.[67] As his stigmata testify, surely no actor ever identified more with the character he was playing than Francis did with the suffering figure of Christ. Obviously, to speak of Francis as "sympathizing with," "empathizing with," "vicariously experiencing," "identifying with," or "imaginatively projecting himself into" the suffering Christ is also to engage in aesthetic discourse. In short, Francis's experience was an admixture of aesthetic and spiritual elements.

After abstracting moral and rational aspects from the holy, Otto finds that what remains is: " . . . a unique 'numinous' category of value and of a definitely 'numinous' state of mind. . . . This mental state is perfectly sui generis and irreducible to any other."[68] Nonetheless, he later makes an explicit comparison between the aesthetic and the spiritual: "Musical feeling is rather (like numinous feeling) something 'wholly other,' which, while it affords analogies here and there will run parallel to the ordinary emotions of life, cannot be made to coincide with them by a detailed point-to-point correspondence."[69] Ultimately, Bell wishes to reduce the categories of the aesthetic and the spiritual to something more fundamental: " . . . both art and religion are manifestations of man's religious sense . . . his sense of ultimate reality."[70] On Bell's side is the fact that art and religion can conjure up the same sort of awesome, sublime emotions and especially a sense that one has encountered the ineffable, whether one interprets it as the numinous or the beautiful. Just as the holy evades conceptual expression and one must directly experience it, beauty is indefinable; and one must behold it in an immediate experience. Although Bell's "significant form" and Otto's "wholly other" are both unique notions, they converge on the metaphysical. At the conclusion of his chapter, "The Metaphysical Hypothesis," Bell speaks of "the God in everything," or the ultimate reality that underlies the appearance of all things. He posits that artists, perhaps unconsciously, apprehend this thing in itself and that it inspires them to communicate the altogether distinctive emotion that marks aesthetic encounters. For Bell, the form of an artwork, appreciated as form alone, gives one a taste of ultimate reality. For Otto, the "wholly other" is the actual presence of ultimate reality. Since the self and self-cultivation are basic to both art and religion, analyzing this notion may help to clarify relations between the two.

4

The Self and Union

Socrates' maxim "know thyself" captivates the mystic and the artist alike, since both seek to realize their own true character, self, soul, *atman*, or Buddha nature. Hence, the quest for self-realization is a major common denominator between religion and art. Chapter thirty-three of the *Tao Te Ching* begins: "One who knows other men is intelligent, but one who knows his own self is enlightened." Self-realization requires that the artist allow his own unique state of mind to issue forth in his work. Of course, the priest is no less occupied with self-discovery and cultivation of the self. Both art and religion struggle to deny and root out a lesser self, because taming this ego is an essential task for aesthetic and spiritual advancement. Religions and philosophies frequently distinguish between the ego and the transcendental self. One must go beyond the narrow self in order to develop the true self. When Augustine asserted that "He who pleases himself pleases a fool," he was thinking of the baser self, for the satisfaction that attends cultivation of one's higher self is inseparable from wisdom. As Carl Jung stated, "However one may define self, it is always something other than the ego . . . "[1] Moreover, one's higher self is always continuous with the other, be it a finite Thou or the eternal Thou. It is in this nobler self that Frederick Buechner locates the root of creativity: "I think that among other things all real art comes from that deepest self—painting, writing music, and dance, all of it that in some way nourishes the spirit and enriches the understanding."[2] Obviously, the self to which Socrates refers is not the ego, for one is normally and effortlessly under its spell. Religiously speaking, one's true self

71

should supersede the limited, empirical self, because the higher self is either of the same substance as, made in the image of, or identical with the divine. "Thomas à Kempis distinguishes between two wills rather than two selves, "For that little will which you forsake here, you will always have your will in heaven where you will have all that you desire."[3] In the dark night of the soul, instead of two selves or wills, John recognizes two parts of the soul, one that is sensual and lower and one that is spiritual and higher. In any case, one distinguishes between the authentic self and its counterfeit. Only when the superficial, self-centered ego does not interfere is it possible for an individual's deeper self to merge with her object of attention—whether a person, an artwork, nature, or the divine. Paradoxical as it sounds, it follows that one's greatest moments occur when he or she is "absent," i.e., when one's ordinary, lesser self or ego recedes. For many beholders, art is an escape from reality or from one's personal problems. However, like religion, art can also effect an escape from the ego. If one curtails his ego, his higher self can participate in the feelings of others. Tolstoy identifies a problem among artists, art critics, and members of the public who he asserts

> have never (except in childhood and earliest youth before hearing any discussions on art) experienced that simple feeling familiar to the plainest man and even to a child, that sense of infection with another's feeling, compelling us to joy in another's gladness, to sorrow at another's grief, and to mingle souls with another—which is the very essence of art.[4]

Of course, it is just such a union or mingling of souls that also constitutes the essence of religion. If artists are sometimes devoid of such fellow feeling, art critics can fare even worse. What the anonymous author of *The Cloud of Unknowing* says about critics of meditative souls, one might equally apply to art critics:

> [W]orldly-minded critics who find fault with contemplatives should also be excused on account of their ignorance . . . these people understand little or nothing about the contemplative life. The ardor of young God-seekers baffles them. They cannot understand how these young people can cast aside careers and opportunity . . .[5]

Buddhists sometimes describe the true self as nothingness or emptiness, not because it is literally vacuous, but because it is unlike anything that one has previously encountered and is ineffably rich in creativity. When an imaginative person takes up a pencil and blank sheet of paper, she has yet to express anything, but there is infinite potential. In addition to the sense of emptiness as inchoate potentiality, there is the emptiness of purgation. When Christ emptied himself (Philippians 2:5–11), he also fulfilled himself, for he became fully humble. To receive, be it artistic inspiration or divine grace, one must attain emptiness, i.e., one must become a receptacle, a vessel that is empty of ego. Such emptiness is a boundless openness, like the wide open spaces of a vast landscape, which seem to be nothing at all, yet continue without apparent limits. C.Y. Chang notes that Wang Pi identifies the Tao with "emptiness and selflessness."[6] This is not an ontological denial of the self as in the *anatta* doctrine of Therevada Buddhism, but a rejection of all self-centeredness or selfishness.

Ideally, aesthetic experience is, at once, a revelation of that which is (objective reality), of who one is (subjective reality), and of their unity. One may attribute any opposition between the subjective and the objective to the divisive ego. With the emergence of the true self, one's continuity with the other—whether another person, the divine, nature, or an artwork—becomes apparent. Concerning creativity, even Freud—a thoroughly non-mystical thinker—believed that one must suppress the ego and allow free association if inspiration is to occur. Greatness in art or religion requires a non-egoistic answer to the question: Who am I? One must probe below the superficial self for one's own true nature. Consider the numerous self-portraits by Chagall, Rembrandt, van Gogh, or Gauguin. These painters were not content to portray the transitory, empirical self; instead, they sought to capture the enduring self or soul. Therefore, each rendered his own likeness again and again. Unless one renounces her petty self, she lacks the unfettered vision by which to behold spiritual reality, much less to artistically express it. One may compare an obsession with the self in religion or art to solipsism in metaphysics, for all such preoccupations are barren. The distinction between the ego and the higher self can also explain Barnett Newman's remark: "I don't express my self in my painting. I express my not-self." In art, spirituality, and love, one loses his baser self. Something of this spirit appears in St. Matthew's point that anyone who wishes to save his life will lose it (16:25). Discussing contemporary artists, Nicholas Wolterstorff asks: Will not he who loses himself find himself? And: Will not an artist's narcissistic preoccupation with finding his self result in his self being hopelessly lost?[7] The task of life is to cultivate the self and let the ego atrophy; thus, the "creation" of the genuine self parallels the creation of art. As Thomas Merton remarked, "In art we find ourselves and lose ourselves at the same time."[8] What one finds is her spiritual nature; what one loses is her self-indulgent ego. To uncover the higher self, some individuals turn to prayer, some to moral reform, some to meditation, and others to art. In any case, by glorifying the divine, one actualizes her higher self. A Shinto morning prayer recognizes the two sides of every person: "I pray that this day, the whole day, as a child of God, I may not be taken hold of by my own desire, but show forth the divine glory by living a life of creativeness, which shows forth the true individual."

The solitude of the monk's cell and of the artist's studio is evidence that withdrawal from the world sometimes facilitates finding one's self. Cistercian monks, for example, teach that when one has left everything else behind, only the self remains. Of course, social relations precede and follow times of solitude, because some social flourishing is a prerequisite for successful coping with one's solitariness. Therefore, any characterization of religion and art as solitary pursuits should also acknowledge their social dimensions. It is telling that Zen Buddhists, for instance, like to practice silent meditation in the company of their fellow monks. Tolstoy's transmission theory of art reminds one that art requires a receiver as well as a sender. Not only do artists need a general community with which to communicate, but their distinctive interests and problems lead them to artistic communities from New York to Taiwan. The artist and the saint join the scientist in pursuing unity, in working to bring order out of chaos, integration from fragmentation. The first two, however, seek to effect a unification of the inner self as well as to find unity within the external cosmos. After all, one who is searching for herself does not want to find a fragmented psyche.

When it comes to finding one's self, harmony is the alpha and omega. Unless one's mind enjoys some degree of harmony, self-discovery is impossible. It is when one is unruffled from within and undisturbed from without that she finds her real self. This found self, in turn, bears the promise of achieving an even more profound harmony. A taste of enlightenment brings serenity and serenity brings further enlightenment. A related spiral of exchange occurs in the dialectic between the artist, her subjects, and her artworks. Capturing the inner harmony of things, she achieves inner harmony herself and, with this enhanced harmony, she produces artworks that are even more harmonious. In other words, self-realization is inseparable from the institution of a profound harmony.

As if knowing the self were not difficult enough, some thinkers believe that one must first try to know God in order to fully know the self. Teresa asserts: "We shall never completely know ourselves if we don't strive to know God."[9] If humans are made in the image of the divine and are, as it were, God writ small, then they can scarcely comprehend their true character apart from some awareness of its cosmic prototype. However, Teresa later observes that what we can know of God amounts to virtually nothing, " . . . for even in our selves there are great secrets that we don't understand."[10] A profound humility led Teresa to greatly doubt her prospects for knowing the divine. Somewhat more optimistic about such possibilities, Augustine adds that knowledge of God is necessary for self-actualization; without such awareness of the divine, the self does not come to be and develop: "He [man] is when he sees Him Who Is, and in seeing Him Who Is, he is also himself, as far as his capacity allows, beginning to be."[11] Religion must have existential import; it is a way of being, not only a way of knowing. Similarly, we turn to art not only to gain insight into life, but in order to become fully human. In addressing faith, Thomas Merton emphasizes being over knowing: "We believe, not because we want to know, but because we want to be."[12]

Contrary to Teresa, Thomas à Kempis, states that knowledge of the self precedes knowledge of God, "If you cannot understand or grasp such things as are within you, how can you then comprehend those things that are above you?"[13] John of the Cross agrees with the focus upon oneself as the starting point, "Let me know myself Lord, and I shall know Thee."[14] John reasons that one extreme can well know another. Addressing God, Thomas à Kempis allows that the discoveries of self and the divine may be simultaneous: " . . . in seeking You again, I have found both You and myself."[15] If humans are sparks from the divine, to know God is to know something of one's true self and to know one's true self is to know something of God. An enlightened soul sees her self as well as God, for the light that proceeds from the divine reaches and illumines her true nature. It is the prospect that an artist might simultaneously discover her own self and God that lends great profundity to the creative act.

Religious experiences are transformative; they change the self in abiding ways, as when they effect moral reform. Similarly, one's aesthetic experiences would hardly be profound if they did not reconstitute the self, e.g., by expanding one's world view; it is only frivolous, superficial, aesthetic enjoyments that leave one unaffected.

In book ten of his *Nichomachean Ethics*, Aristotle argues that the latter kind of pleasure is mere amusement, but only genuine aesthetic experiences can give rise to happiness. Some thinkers use the dramatic language of death to express the transformation of the self: "The death of the ego yields the birth of the true self." To uncover her genuine self, the mystic must "kill" or root out her ego. Dramatically declaring that self-effacement is a prerequisite for self-realization, the Persian mystic Shaykh Ahmad-e Jam states:

> "All those by the knife of submission killed
> Each moment from God with new life are filled."[16]

Using the metaphor of the butterfly as the emerging soul, Teresa emphasizes that prayer, i.e., union with God, greatly transforms the soul. Indeed, it is the touchstone of one's spiritual experiences that they change the person. Among artists, the impostors are those who produce without undergoing changes in themselves, e.g., the art forger who counterfeits any number of styles but never develops one of his own. That artists go through periods or phases is one sign of their transformations. Therefore, at their best, both art and religion accomplish a metamorphosis of the self. Of course, the transformed self transforms what it meets. Therefore, just as the religious individual sanctifies the commonplace—whether by saying grace before dinner, or by consecrating the communion host—the artist turns the ordinary into the extraordinary. Witness Chih Pai-shih's painting of a housefly on a plate, which transforms these homely objects into vehicles for the most profound meditation. In the Taoist tradition, transformation occurs through non-differentiation: " . . . our nature reaches its highest development only when we cultivate ourselves spiritually to the point that we achieve union with all things."[17] For Buber, self-realization can only occur in a social, dialogical context—as is also true in the case of the artist. Here the immediate Thou being addressed is the artist's model, theme, or medium; and the artist creates in order to be. The painter's self-portraits and the religious person's introspections, meditations, and prayers begin to disclose something of their true selves just when they start to affirm the reality of others. It is only after self-interest recedes that one's deeper self can advance in aesthetic or religious communion. Buber believes that humans are born with a kind of innate "Thou," a congenital yearning to meet and establish relations with the other; therefore, encountering a Thou is the very means to one's own self-cultivation. If one is to discover her true self in all its fullness, the I must meet a Thou. Because the other is latent within the I, as an incipient or innate Thou, to meet the other is a twofold self-realization, a discovery of the active I and an awakening of that dormant aspect of my self that beckons always—however faintly—for encounter. Therefore,". . . the innate You is realized in the You we encounter . . ."[18] Aesthetic interest colors Buber's description of the infant's yearning for a You:

> The innateness of the longing for relation is apparent even in the earliest and dimmest stage . . . at times when there is obviously no desire for nourishment, soft projections of the hands reach, aimlessly to all appearances, into the empty air toward the indefinite. Let anyone call this animalic: that does not help our comprehension. For precisely these glances will eventually, after many trials, come to rest upon a red wallpaper arabesque and not leave it until the soul of red has opened up to them. Precisely this motion will gain its sensuous form and definiteness in contact with a shaggy toy bear and eventually apprehend lovingly and unforgettably a complete body: in both cases not experience of an object but coming to grips with a living, active being that confronts us, if only in our "imagination." (But this "imagination" is by no means a form of "panpsychism"; it is the drive to turn everything into a You . . .).[19]

The "red wallpaper arabesque" reminds one that Immanuel Kant turned to abstract wallpaper designs in order to illustrate the nature of aesthetic appreciation. In this passage, Buber replaces Nietzsche's will to power and Thomas Hobbes's will to live with the will to relate. When Buber speaks of "the drive to turn everything into a You," he addresses a fundamental tendency in human nature. By animating the apples and oranges in the event of his still life, the painter creates a "Thou," for they participate in the being of the eternal Thou. Van Gogh stands before cypress trees and imparts something of himself in painting them, allowing beholders to see the trees from a fresh perspective, as made in the image of van Gogh. Still, the painting cannot be all van Gogh; he must meet the tree as a Thou if he is to paint the being of the tree. Painting and all other art forms demand the expression of an I-Thou relationship. A great painting is not an act of self-expression in any narrow sense. Only in the dialectic between the I and Thou, only in the enlivening of the Thou, can one rise above egoism and shallow art. In life and in art, self-discovery entails affirmation of and dialogue with the other, i.e., the flowering of the innate Thou. For relational beings like humans, there is no self apart from the I standing in relation to a Thou. Therefore, artists transcribe nature in terms of themselves, but also in terms of the other, the Thou whose spark is within us, the Thou that begins inside us, but can only be met in mature form apart from us.

Richard Cartwright Austin argues that without nature we cannot fully be ourselves: "If we lose contact with nature, we lose touch with much of the joy of life and an important part of our human calling . . . the human personality is incomplete, and human life is impoverished."[20] Representative of landscape painters East and West, Claude Monet thought that by expanding our vision of the world, we enlarge our knowledge of the self. Meeting one's self in nature can be just as disturbing as meeting oneself in art. An interviewer asked a Catholic priest, who had spent time praying in the desert: "Aren't you afraid to be out there all alone?" He answered: "Two things terrify me when I am praying: I might meet God and I might meet my self." Otto, having described the supreme, spiritual being as a harmony of the personal and supra personal, adds that within us also there is not just the personal but the "wholly other."[21] Perhaps it is the radically distinct, intimidating "wholly other" dimension of one's self that accounts for his reluctance to pursue self-discovery.

One stereotype has it that the artist possesses an enlarged ego. Even when this is the case, the artist may be seeking his true self or soul, for a large ego is compatible with seeking, even if finding one's true nature requires subjugation of the ego. Interestingly enough, in his classic study of Cezanne, the gifted art critic Roger Fry remarks on the indispensability of humility:

> A Veronese or a Frans Hals may dispense with humility. Their virtuosity is sufficient for their spiritual needs. But every artist who is destined to arrive at the profounder truths, a Rembrandt, a Velasquez, or a Daumier, requires an exceptional humility.[22]

According to Tillich, "An artist who expresses only himself is like an adolescent who writes sentimental verses, without artistic validity."[23] He adds: "If a work of art expresses only the subjectivity of the artist, it remains arbitrary and does not penetrate into reality itself."[24] Like the devotee of religion, an artist must leave behind the ego so that her larger self, which is continuous with others, can achieve insights by moving from the provincial to the universal. Obviously, it is not as if the ego can generate no art whatever; instead, the claim is that art that flows from the nobler self far surpasses any egoistically motivated work. Of course, artists and saints sometimes struggle with and succumb to their egos, but their greatest contributions come only after they have overcome their egos, thereby opening the door to communication and rapport with others. On this view, an artist who exhibits a considerable ego, will do his best when he restrains it, even if the ego reasserts itself as soon as he completes the creative act. After all, aesthetic inspiration is as transitory as mystical illumination.

A charming story about Picasso illustrates the aesthetic need to subdue one's ego. After producing a forgery of a child's drawing, Picasso became frustrated, because his friend Matisse looked at the sketch and immediately identified it as a counterfeit. A short time later, playing with his son on the floor and sharing the exuberance of a child inspired Picasso to again try his hand at creating "children's art." Since he had become a "child" again, Picasso now produced an artwork that fooled Matisse, who unhesitatingly pronounced it to be a genuine piece of children's art. Of course, Picasso's ego may have been in ascendancy just before he started playing with his son and may have reasserted itself just after he completed the drawing. Following Tolstoy, one can argue that the ego cannot drive great art, since such art must communicate; it must address the other—ideally to the point of being universal. And, one wonders how the self-absorbed artist could grasp, much less transmit, universal truths. Just as no artist can strike a universal chord until she transcends her limited self, religion teaches that one cannot reach God—the ultimate universal—until she lets go of her provincial ego.

A year before her death, Teresa spoke of her soul as being "so forgetful of its own interests as to seem, in some measure, to have lost itself. . . . Everything is directed to the honour of God, to the doing of His will more and more, and the advancement of His glory."[25] For Teresa, the further one goes into herself, the more she loses her self, i.e., ego. Similarly, the fourteenth century painter Wu Chen maintained that when he began to paint, he did not know that he was painting; he completely forgot that it was himself who held the brush. Another expression of "egoless" art appears in the faceless dolls fashioned by the Amish.

According to Taoism, "When a man is in this creative process he is truly egoless: as egoless as the Moon and the stars."[26] As Keats remarks: "A poet is the most un-poetical of anything in existence; because he has no Identity—he is continually in for—and filling some other Body—the Sun, the Moon, the Sea."[27] Jacques

Maritain agrees: "The creative Self of the artist is his person as person, in the act of spiritual communication, not his person as material individual or as self-centered ego."[28] Albert Einstein identifies a lack of self-centeredness in religious leaders: "A person who is religiously enlightened appears to me to be one who has, to the best of his ability, liberated himself from the fetters of his selfish desires and is preoccupied with the thoughts, feelings, and aspirations to which he clings because of their super-personal value."[29]

The humility that religions espouse, e.g., "the Tao is like water which seeks out the lowest places," is evident in the artist who considers himself a vehicle. Paul Klee describes such an artist: "His position is humble. And the beauty at the crown is not his own. He is merely a channel."[30] Klee submits that the artist is one who transmits, just as Confucius insisted that he was a transmitter, not an originator. Attracted by an expression of humility, Picasso gestured toward a sheet of tin hanging upon a door and exclaimed: "I have never in any museum seen a picture as beautiful as this one. The man who painted this picture was not thinking of his glory."[31] Here, Picasso reminds one of the extraordinary appeal that humility generates. All religions recoil from self-centeredness and this flight is equally basic to creation and art appreciation. The artist who is self-centered leans toward the provincial and can scarcely communicate what is of universal human significance. Moreover, if self-interest preoccupies the appreciator, he will apprehend the artwork as a mere means rather than as an end in itself.

It is the task of the religious person and the artist alike to transcend both subjectivity and objectivity. Of course, "subjectivity" pertains to one's narrow self, but what does it mean to go beyond "objectivity"? If one totally objectifies the divine, spiritual reality, the absolute becomes remote, abstract, and wholly distinct from oneself. There are two religious paths to circumvent such abstraction. First, one may identify with the divine, as in the Hindu declaration "Tat tvam asi." Here, the believer proclaims that Atman is Brahman, i.e., the individual soul is identical with the divine. Second, and more commonly, one may engage the divine in an I-Thou relation. To avoid objectifying the divine, the individual must learn to either identify with or worship this absolute. In a sense, the artist also denies the objectivity or total otherness of objects, for she identifies with them in order to capture them aesthetically. Such an identification is not the product of ratiocination, but of an unconscious, intuitive realization.

Rekha Jhanji observes that transcendence of the ego and desirelessness allow both the art lover and the mystic to enjoy a sense of liberation; this freedom, in turn, yields a joy that relates to play: "It is this purity of joy which led Abhinavagupta to see a parallel between mystical ecstasy and aesthetic enjoyment, for the mystic, too, sees the world as a play (*līlā*) of the divine creator."[32] This reference to play invites a further comparison between the artist and the mystic as fellow seekers of a childlike, primordial innocence. Sacred texts, from the *Tao Te Ching* to the New Testament, urge one to become like a child; and artists yearn to recover a childlike spontaneity. Accordingly, Tolstoy denounced art schools, because he thought that they invariably pervert the sincerity of the child artist.

Since self-realization involves one's inner reality, the spiritually disposed painter, such as Kandinsky, may concern himself with expressing inner feelings rather than with manifesting external reality. The artist transmits "to those observers capable of feeling them lofty emotions beyond the reach of words."[33] Similarly, religions are sometimes wary of perception; thus, the *Upanishads* discourage dwelling upon sense impressions, for such an interest interferes with the inward turn by which one discovers her true self: " . . . man looks toward what is without and sees not what is within. Rare is he who, longing for immortality, shuts his eyes to what is without and beholds the Self."[34] Christianity reminds one that she cannot see the beam in her own eye if she only fixes upon the sliver in someone else's eye. Of course, this found self is a wonder to behold and is, therefore, aesthetic. One describes his inner nature in terms of such paradigmatic aesthetic ideas as: "tranquillity," "harmony," "balance," "unity," and "radiance." When religion and art address what is ineffable, they find the perceivable world to be penultimate or incomplete. Thus, a Kandinsky turns to his own interior spirituality or a Taoist paints forms in order to convey the "form of the formless." Appreciating nature, rather than art, is sometimes the key to self-actualization. A spirited defender of the American wilderness, John Muir, stated: "When a man plants a tree he plants himself,"[35] an assertion that one might paraphrase as, "By planting a tree a man finds or establishes himself." For if humans are to find themselves, surely it must be through meaningful action; and few actions can be any more significant than cooperating with nature in order to produce new life. That one chooses to perform this act at once says something about the person and helps make that person who he is.

Like a self-centered individual, the disciplines of art and religion can be unduly self-referential. A recurrent criticism holds that art is too often about art itself, i.e., art is "incestuously" preoccupied with earlier styles, movements, gestures, and statements. One may accuse the artist of ignoring her own nature and drawing exclusively from art history. A parallel critique of religion would hold that it is often about past religion, for it occupies itself with upholding the established doctrines, creeds, and rituals rather than with spiritually confronting present needs and evolving accordingly. Bad art and bad religion try to dwell in the past and are naturally inhospitable to the present.

Kant was not sanguine about the prospects for discovering the higher self that he calls the transcendental unity of apperception and which he credits with the organization and unification of all mental states. Identifying this self as that which underlies and organizes our experiences, Kant concluded that it could not be thematic in them. Of course, mystics agree that one cannot intellectually grasp the transcendent self, but they add that one can realize it in a profound intuitive experience. Typically, meditation is the prescribed route for this achievement. Here, an artwork can be a medium in two senses, for it may serve not only as a means of communication but also as a vehicle to promote meditation. When the ego reigns there is always some measure of discord, since the ego stands over and against the other, but with the cultivation of a distinctionless harmony, the true self is born. The creation of genuine artworks parallels the creation of the genuine self, just as leading a religious life promotes the cultivation of one's spiritual self. The Sanskrit term *karma* literally refers to a carving out, for the individual's actions serve to carve out his nature. Similarly, as the sculptor works upon the marble, she is at once sculpting this material and forging her own character.

To say that self-discovery is communal is to say that it can only occur in a social, dialogical context. The great religious or artistic leaders always stand in some sort of communion with their fellows—whether though writings, teachings, preaching, artworks, personal encounters, or the establishment of a community. For relational beings like humans, no complete self exists apart from all other souls. Religious self-discovery entails affirmation of and dialogue with the other—even if, as in the Vedanta school of Hinduism, one ultimately interprets the "other" to be identical with one's own *atman*. That the union afforded by community is of paramount importance follows from the fact that the vast majority of artists—of every quality, era, and culture—create in order to reach an audience. Being social creatures, artists do not wish to keep their works to themselves. Not surprisingly, when some Catholic priests elect to celebrate a private Mass, i.e., one without a congregation, fellow priests sometimes criticize the practice. The Mass is a drama and what is a drama without an audience? In short, a private Mass is like an unappreciated artwork.

Union

There are three varieties of union that unite art and religion: self-integration, the unity of the other—whether an artwork or the divine—and union between the self and the other, whether as communion or identification. Moreover, the three kinds of union are themselves united by interrelations, e.g., one who is self-integrated is in the best position to appreciate an artwork; and a work that possesses integrity can enhance the appreciator's self-integration.

The early Kabbalah interprets the expression "The Lord is One" (Deuteronomy 6:4), not merely as a statement of numerical identity, but as a declaration of God's unity. Because God is one and humans are made in his image, they are morally bound to achieve their own optimal self-integration. Using an aesthetic analogy, Buber insists that one should regard the Thou as a whole:

> Even as a melody is not composed of tones, nor a verse of words, nor a statue of lines—one must pull and tear to turn a unity into a multiplicity—so it is with the human being to whom I say You. I can abstract from him the color of his hair or the color of his speech or the color of his graciousness; I have to do this again and again; but immediately he is no longer You.[36]

"Unity" refers to the wholeness of a being who is participating in a lived relationship.[37] Like artworks, humans are wholes; and to analyze a human into various parts is to lose the vital, breathing Thou. While psychology and art criticism are analytic and discursive, I-Thou relations and aesthetic experiences tend to be synthetic and intuitive. Further, the objectification and quantification that are inherent in the former can be inimical to the latter, as when the physician's detached, measured evaluation of a patient prevents the doctor from entering into an I-Thou relation with her. Likewise, an art critic's analytic evaluation of a painting may divert her from meeting the Thou of the work. In short, both an I-Thou encounter and art appreciation are holistic experiences.

Perhaps the Oriental art form of the *mandala* best illustrates the import of self-integration in art and religion. Manifesting a consummate integrity, the *mandala* effects wholeness in the beholder. A long-standing vehicle for meditation, this variety of iconography, which one may sketch, paint, sculpt, draw in sand, embroider on a banner, or even dance, depends upon symmetrically arranged circles within larger concentric circles and exists in the rituals and contemplation of Hindu and Buddhist Tantrism. Traditionally, there is a central Buddha figure that subordinate deities or attendants encircle; the latter may be malevolent as well as benevolent. Of course, one may interpret even the most gruesome, weapon-wielding fiend as a metaphorical reminder that only the undaunted warrior is fit for battle against the defiling enemies of passion and ignorance. At a still higher level of interpretation, one apprehends the opposite powers as complementary forces that ensure the wholeness and equilibrium of the cosmos. Indeed, one now discovers that the cosmic deities are within himself; seeing all gods as self-contained, one realizes his own divinity or identity with the absolute *Brahman*, or *Śūnyattā* (void). To speak of ultimate reality as empty, void, or nothing is really to say that there is an ineffable reality that is no thing, for it is the foundation of all things and one should not confuse it with any particular thing, just as one should not confuse an artist with any of her creations.

The quest to reestablish primeval consciousness, that integrity of being which only rapport with the One can fully restore, inspires both Hindu and Buddhist *mandalas*. In *The Archetype and the Collective Unconscious*, Carl Jung applied the fresh perspective of analytical psychology to the *mandala* and theorized that the psyche as microcosm corresponds to the *mandala* as macrocosm. Jung also reported that *mandalas* surfaced spontaneously in the dreams of his schizophrenic patients, even though they were unacquainted with Eastern thought. He speculated that such patterns were instinctual, therapeutic responses to the problem of psychic disintegration. The *mandala* serves as a matrix in terms of which the disoriented patient may detect, relate, and reintegrate the apparently opposed aspects of her self. Tibetans who contemplate the *mandala* hold that its own unified field enables them to reintegrate fragments of their psyche. Defining the emergent as "the archetype of wholeness," Jung affirmed the universality of the *mandala* by recognizing the basic similarities in *mandala* forms irrespective of the culture or age in which they appear. Sacred symbols like the cross, swastika of Hinduism, the rose window of a cathedral, and the sand paintings of the Native American are all variations on the *mandala* theme of a single point from which all things emanate and to which they return.

After condemning log houses because there is no power in the form of a square, the Native American Black Elk celebrates the circle:

> [E]verything an Indian does is in a circle. . . . Everything the Power of the World does is done in a circle. The sky is round, and I have heard that the earth is round like a ball, and so are all the stars. The wind, in its greatest power, whirls. Birds make their nests in circles, for theirs is the same religion as ours. The sun comes forth and goes down again in a circle. The moon does the same, and both are round. Even the seasons form a great circle in their changing . . . the life of a man is a circle from childhood to childhood.[38]

Black Elk makes it seem easy to find the center of the cosmic circle: " . . . anywhere is the center of the world."[39] Apparently, because the divine is everywhere, the center is wherever we turn. Of course, it is no easier to discover the divine center than to discover one's own center, i.e., the center of selfhood, that which is most important and around which all other things rotate. Discussing Chagall's painting *Hommage à Apollinaire*, which features a half-man and half-woman figure as the centerpiece of a circular composition, the art historian Franz Meyer writes,

> The circle is symbolic of the whole and becomes on a new level the symbol of the unity of soul and psyche, of conscious and unconscious, of immobility and activity, as reflecting the link between man and beast. The totality experienced in the circle is found in religious art of all epochs, as a sign of perfection framing representations of the godhead. In Byzantine art, for instance, it occurs in representations of Christ's transfiguration, from which Chagall may have unconsciously drawn his inspiration.[40]

Diego de Yepes, one of Teresa's early biographers, testifies that she had a vision of the soul as a castle, in the form of a beautiful crystal sphere—a three-dimensional *"mandala,"* which contained seven dwelling places, with the King of Glory dwelling in supreme splendor in the central one. From this locus, " . . . He beautified and illumined all those dwelling places . . . "[41] Augustine concludes that self-integration is dependent upon the divine, "I find no secure place for my soul except in you, and in you I pray that what is scattered in me may be brought together so that nothing of me may depart from you."[42]

As self-integration refers to the unity of the I, a second sort of union refers to the unity of the Thou. Whether an artwork or God is the focus, a harmony of elements obtains. When the parts of an artwork culminate in an inevitable whole or when the divine attributes cohere in a commanding oneness, this unity exists. In the context of personal relations, one might call it the unity of the other. Religious examples include the Christian God, who embraces the Father, Son, and Holy Spirit in the unity of a perfect equipoise, and the Tao. A synonym for Tao, *wu* or nonbeing refers to a supreme harmony or higher unity that blends all elements into an undifferentiated state. Other instances of the unitary ultimate include: Plato's Form of the Good, Plotinus's One, and the unicity of the absolute for countless mystics, whether Kabbalist, Christian, or Sufi. Just as the unity of an artwork may promote unification in the beholder, the paradigmatic simplicity of the absolute may foster self-integration in the religiously inclined, a self-integration that, in turn, conduces to deeper communion or identification with the divine.

Traditionally, an artistic masterpiece is a synthesis of elements such that to alter one part is to vitiate the whole. To tamper with the integrity of art is to risk vandalism; to tamper with the integrity of religion is to risk desecration. Aristotle draws an ethical parallel when he defines virtue as a mean between extremes; adding to a virtue results in an excess and subtracting from it yields a deficiency. In book two, chapter six of his *Nicomachean Ethics*, Aristotle pinpoints an aesthetic mean when he says that the good craftsperson attends to what is intermediate as he makes his work. Teresa's visions, like the artistic masterpiece that can suffer no additions or subtractions without undergoing aesthetic impoverishment, have an even more dramatic integrity, "This is true of all visions without exception: we can contribute nothing towards them—we cannot add to them, nor can we take from them; our own efforts can neither make nor unmake them. Our Lord would have us see most clearly that it is no work of ours, but of His divine Majesty . . . "[43] In Ecclesiastes 3:14, one reads that the deeds of God are not subject to human alterations: " . . . whatever God does endures forever; nothing can be added to it, nor anything taken from it (RSV)." While one may not try to add to or subtract from artistic masterpieces or religious visions, he may nevertheless find them to be inexhaustible phenomena. Therefore, Hamlet is subject to unending analyses; and Catherine of Siena once prayed, "You, O, eternal Trinity, are a deep sea, into which the more I enter the more I find, and the more I find the more I seek."

As the first kind of union is that of the I and the second is that of the Thou, the third is that of the I and Thou in relationship. Expressing the union of communion, Tolstoy develops a communication theory of art. In this three-part model, the artist undergoes an emotion, embeds it in a medium, and "infects" spectators who are then able to re-experience the feeling. One's aesthetic relation with nature can yield an interpenetration; in the journal of the naturalist John Muir, one finds: "Now we are fairly into the mountains and they are into us . . . the boundary walls of our heavy flesh tabernacle seem taken down and we flow and diffuse into the very air and trees and streams and rocks . . . we are a part of nature now. . . . How glorious a conversion . . . "[44] While John the Baptist baptized with water, Muir prefers an aesthetic-spiritual immersion in all of nature. The coalescence or interpenetration of subject and object marks peak experiences in religious and aesthetic lives. It is the saint's direct experiences that convince her that God is in her and that she is in him. According to St. Catherine of Siena, the soul is in God and God is in the soul just as the fish is in the sea and the sea is in the fish. Of course, one can also believe in such interpenetration because of inferences from scripture. If God is omnipresent, then he is in each person; and, since humans are dependent creatures, each person must be rooted in God. Of course, there is interpenetration when one speaks of the music being in him, i.e., moving him, but also of himself being in the music, i.e., empathizing with its ebb and flow, projecting oneself into it and moving with it. Similarly, the void in a Sung Dynasty landscape painting moves the beholder and invites him to move within it, i.e., to "step inside" the scene.

While the intellect constantly distinguishes between the subject and the object, intuitive aesthetic and spiritual experiences undermine one's confidence in harsh dichotomies or bifurcations between one's self and the supposed nonself. When William James quotes Malwida von Meysenbug's experience of union, a coincidence of the religious and the aesthetic is apparent:

I felt that I prayed as I had never prayed before, and knew now what prayer really is; to return from the solitude of individuation into the consciousness of unity with all that is, to kneel down as one that passes away, and to rise up as one imperishable. Earth, heaven, and the sea resounded as in one vast world-encircling harmony.[45]

Basic as they are to human existence, sex and reproduction leave their imprint upon religion and art. From nuns who are "Brides of Christ" to monks in Tantrism, the language of sexual union is pervasive in many accounts of peak, spiritual experiences, because the intimacy of sexual intercourse serves as an analog for union with the absolute. Not surprisingly, an analysis of artistic creativity reveals the terminology of reproduction: the artist "conceives," passes through a "gestation" period, undergoes "labor," and eventually "gives birth." This vocabulary of reproduction underlines how natural a creative process should be. Religions also have their own reproductive metaphors, e.g., "being born again."

To unite with the dusty world is to get closer to the Tao; so the *Tao Te Ching* urges the reader to appreciate the everyday world or the "suchness" of ordinary things. One should identify with all things, because she and they have a common root. Accordingly, Taoist painting requires the painter's ontological identification with all things. Instead of trying to escape from the dusty world, the Taoist favors absorption in things without attachment to them. A certain detachment is the very prerequisite for penetration into the ten thousand things.

Since humans are social creatures, it is by participating in a community that they can subdue their egos and begin to cultivate their true selves. In Christianity, for example, expressions like "the communion of saints" point to the essential solidarity to which all should contribute. Thus, Tolstoy holds that art, like religion, exists to effect just such a fellowship or community among all humans. Moreover, the value of solidarity exists prior to its realization through art. Here, Nietzsche was wrong; the artist does not create new values, at least, not ethical-religious values. To do so would be to produce disvalues, since real values are those that abide from generation to generation. Of course, the artist creates concrete expressions of values or general principles. Architecture, for example, can foster the value of solidarity. A building that invites and unites its inhabitants nourishes what is best in the human spirit. A building that alienates its occupants—from each other or from outsiders—is just as much an architectural failure as a building with structural problems. If inhabitants become monads rather than interrelating agents, moral and aesthetic condemnation is appropriate. Perhaps the sterile, dispirited architecture of, for example, many government-supported housing projects is not unrelated to the hopelessness, hostility, fear, and criminal behavior that abound in them.

For Tolstoy, the goal of union among men is what motivates the creative process: "Art begins when one person, with the object of joining another or others to himself in one and the same feeling, expresses that feeling by certain external indications."[46] In short, art fosters the union of communion through the communication of feelings. For theists, it is ultimately impossible to separate communion with one's fellows from communion with God, since, for example, Christ promised that he was present wherever two or more gathered in his name. Again, Buber taught that one meets the eternal Thou by meeting the finite Thou. The union of communion furthers self-integration, because one must subdue his divisive ego if he is to successfully unite with another.

To cultivate rapport with things is extremely important to the artist as well as to the saint. Underhill quotes a relevant passage from Henri Bergson: " . . . could we enter into immediate communion with things and with ourselves—then, we should all be artists."[47] To which Buber, who addressed a tree, or Francis, who sang to the sun and moon, could add that to establish such rapport is also to be a spiritual being. Paul Gauguin's life demonstrates that one sometimes achieves communion through simplification. Reminiscent of the theologian who defines sin as alienation from God, Gauguin praises those who avoid separation from existence, nature, and the absolute: "A Maori hut does not separate man from life, from space, from the infinite."[48] Of course, one may wonder how to effect a rapprochement with nature or the infinite. Following a period during which he lamented man's alienation from nature, Gauguin sanguinely reported:

> Civilization is falling from me little by little. I am beginning to think simply, to feel only very little hatred for my neighbor—rather, to love him. All the joys—animal and human—of a free life are mine. I have escaped everything that is artificial, conventional, customary. I am entering into the truth, into nature. Having the certitude of a succession of days like this present one, equally free and beautiful, peace descends upon me.[49]

Like Thoreau, he found beauty in the simplicity of asceticism. Of course, extreme cases of self-abnegation abound in art as well as in religion. Just as the Buddha walked away from his family and Christ enjoined his disciples to distance themselves from their families, Gauguin left his family to travel to the South Seas. His letters demonstrate that he was always desperate for cash and sometimes could not even afford to buy his precious art supplies. With practically no material goods, his riches included the warmth of his native friends and of Tahiti itself. One may compare his gradual shedding of civilization to the *Tao Te Ching*, which teaches that the ordinary man gains day by day, but the sage loses day by day. While the ordinary man constantly acquires trivial data, dubious, unexamined principles, and popular doctrines of society, the man of Tao works to lose all such obstructions to genuine wisdom. Like the talented photographer, who must know which pictures to discard, the Taoist winnows out all that is unnecessary for spiritual cultivation and enlightenment. As Henri Matisse argued in his terse essay, "Notes of a Painter," "All that is not useful in a picture is detrimental."[50] William James explicates this link between the artist and the religious person:

That law which impels the artist to achieve harmony in his composition by simply dropping out whatever jars, or suggests a discord, rules also in the spiritual life. To omit, says Stevenson, is the one art in literature: "If I knew how to omit, I should ask no other knowledge." And life when full of disorder and slackness and vague superfluity, can no more have what we call character than literature can have it under similar conditions. So monasteries and communities of sympathetic devotees open their doors, and in their changeless order, characterized by omissions quite as much as constituted of actions, the holy-minded person finds that inner smoothness and cleanness which it is torture to him to feel violated at every turn by the discordancy and brutality of secular existence.[51]

Meditation is the classic path to oneness with ultimate reality; so, of the three traditional Hindu routes to liberation, some emphasize *jnana marga* (the way of mind) over *karma marga* (the way of action) and *bhakti marga* (the way of devotion or love). Typically, individuals inflect each of the three paths at some point in their spiritual lives. Thomas à Kempis, for example, urges individuals to become one with the absolute through action and specifically through the imitation of Christ. Of course, Christians have taught that one can best approach God by approximating Christ's life. Union with

God is only possible when one affirms, out of love: "Thy will be done." In short, the union of surrender to God is a prerequisite for the union of ecstasy.

Some have faulted Chinese painters for "copying" the masters, but this activity enables one to master traditional techniques, absorb classic compositions, and acquire a rich vocabulary of brush strokes. In short, the artist develops the repertoire that is essential for innovation. Moreover, reproducing the masters allows one to "meet," i.e., enter into rapport with, great artists. There is no better way to penetrate an artist's consciousness than to reenact his creative process and to reexperience his primordial joy of creation. In Nathaniel Hawthorne's *The Marble Faun*, the author praises Hilda, who reproduces the paintings of masters, because she is no mechanical copyist. Instead, by following the same, step-by-step procedures of the original painter, she encounters him, communes with his soul, and savors the spirit of the painting. Contrasting her with imitators who mechanically produce copies of great paintings, Hawthorne exclaims, "Hilda was no such machine as this; she wrought religiously, and therefore wrought a miracle." It is hardly unexpected that in a recent survey of professional writers of essays, stories, novels, poems, or plays, "Half of the writers, men and women, reported that they had had intense experiences of mystical communion."[52]

In the first variety of union, the self is thematic; in the second, the other is thematic; and, in the third, one's relation to the other is thematic. In the last case, there are two basic religious possibilities: either one places herself in accord with the absolute (the union of rapport) or she discovers that she herself is the absolute reality (the union of identity, i.e., monism). Whether one adopts the union of communion or the union of identity, harmony is the ultimate goal. Having examined the union of rapport or communion, it remains to consider monism.

Religious monism takes two basic forms: First, there is the monism of dissolution or annihilation in which all beings eventually pass into the absolute and thereby lose their identities in its sublime oneness. Each individual, like a drop of water returning to the ocean, merges with the infinite—as in the Upanishadic metaphor of the soul, like salt, dissolving in water. Second, there is the monism of ontological identity, which asserts that the individual is divine. This is the unity of numerical identity, as when one predicates concave and convex of the same line. Here, the wider, Parmenidean claim is that everything always has been, is, and always will be identical with Brahman.

When Teresa speaks about her soul dissolving into Christ, it is actually a case of pseudo-monism, for her theism persists and invariably reasserts itself. Writing about the seventh dwelling place in *The Interior Castle*, Teresa describes her spiritual marriage to Christ in terms of a bright light that enters a room from two windows but becomes one beam. During the experience, she is unable to distinguish between her soul and the God with whom she has united. Similarly, in *The Living Flame of Love* (1.13), John of the Cross speaks metaphorically of the soul as a crystal and of the divine as a penetrating light. Although the two are distinct, distinguishing between them becomes impossible as the intense light pervades the crystal, for to be filled with light is to appear as light itself. In short, Teresa and John agree that monism is psychologically true, but ontologically false. Ultimately, as the form and matter of a vase are aesthetically inseparable yet ontologically distinct, the human and the absolute interpenetrate, while all the time retaining their respective natures. Therefore, despite her moments of "dissolution" into the divine, Teresa concluded that the soul continues to exist in all its separateness and individuality. After all, if one abolishes all distinctions between the self and God, the life of dialogue becomes problematic. Indeed, if there is no dualism of the self and the divine, there can be no human-divine relationship, no advance from separation to union and love. During Teresa's union of the "spiritual marriage," the soul is blind, deaf, and devoid of all understanding or faculties.[53] Distinctions disappear for her, but not for the God in whom she is centered. One thinks of Plato's dialogue the "Ion," in which he describes the poet as mindless, since the poet must go out of his mind if inspiration is to enter it. In short, the poet can create only after losing his reason, much as the prophet must surrender to an outside power. In the *Dark Night of the Soul*, there is another apparent example of Christian monism. John describes God and the human soul respectively as a fire and a log, the former uniting with the latter in order to change it into itself. Of course, the divine flames consume evil humors rather than the true self; and it is clear from the context that purgation, not annihilation, of the self is thematic. Not surprisingly, the yearning for annihilation sometimes takes an explicitly aesthetic form. Describing her spiritual experience of a snow-covered landscape, under a full moon, the contemporary writer Nancy Mairs turns to aesthetic language when she speaks of "wishing for a kind of annihilation into all that beauty."[54] Often the same sort of phenomenon triggers religious experiences and aesthetic experiences: a serene meadow, a sunset, the ebb and flow of the ocean, mountainous terrain, the starry sky, and the desert. Still, even Thoreau did not vanish; he eventually returned to society, imparting the aesthetic delights and spiritual insights that he gleaned at Walden Pond. And, no matter how often she affirms the intimate union between God and herself, Teresa conscientiously insists upon preserving the distance between them: "That love which I know his Majesty [God] has for it [her soul] makes it forget itself, and think itself to be one with Him; and so, as being one with Him, and not divided from Him, the soul speaks foolishly."[55] In the end, for her, to unite with God is not to disappear into divinity forever, but to place one's will and spirit in harmony with God. According to John of the Cross, on the one hand, the "secret ladder of love causes the soul to become wholly assimilated to God," but on the other hand, one must distinguish between the two, because it is impossible for the soul to possess the capacity of God.[56] As a painting is a simulacrum that participates in its model, the soul participates in a spiritual exemplar.

Monism is problematic for aesthetics as well as for religion, because communication theories of art, such as Tolstoy's, presuppose an irreducible dualism between artist and spectator. He allows that, "A real work of art destroys, in the consciousness of the receiver, the separation between himself and the artist—not that alone, but also between himself and all whose minds receive this work of art."[57] From a phenomenological standpoint, any sense of separation dissolves, but ontologically the separate identities of artist and spectator persist, for the dualism of the artist who infects and the spectator who is infected remains however little it is noted. While the aesthetic appreciation of nature may seem to call for no psychical distance—"The more one can blend in with nature the better"—if one "becomes" the tree, can she still behold it? Francis and Buber insist that there is some ontological distance between the I and the Thou, even in the beholding of a tree. After all, if monism goes beyond all names and forms to an undifferentiated oneness and remains there, it cannot accommodate the aesthetic appreciation of nature in all its manifold expressions. Likewise, a unity that nullifies all distinctions or differences is inimical to art appreciation. Although monists urge one to go beyond all the multiplicities of sense data to what transcends perception—the universal One—they fail to show what is wrong with the thesis that the universal and the particulars interpenetrate, as when Taoists intuit the Tao amidst mountains and rivers.

One can only speculate about the effects of different metaphysical systems upon the history of world art. In Taoist paintings, landscapes abound. The character for "landscape" consists of the characters "water" and "mountain," representing respectively the yin and yang aspects of the Tao. In Taoism, outpourings from the Tao are not pseudo-entities, but full-fledged realities that manifest the Tao. If one identifies and interfuses with nature, one harmonizes with what is continuous with the Tao. By contrast, in the absolute monism of Advaita Vedantins, in which there is but one actual reality—everything else having the status of an apparition—the material world is decidedly penultimate; all plurality being reduced to the status of *maya* or appearance. As one might expect, landscape paintings play a relatively minor role in the rich gamut of Hindu art, but they preoccupy the Chinese artist, for whom the Tao is the mother of nature and the offspring are no less real than their source.

Buber criticizes monistic mysticism in which one loses his individuality: "What has to be given up is not the I as most mystics suppose: the I is indispensable for any relationship, including the highest, which always presupposes an I and You."[58] What one must give up is his false instinct for self-affirmation. Buber speaks at once aesthetically and religiously when explaining what he prefers over any purported union in which the I and You dissolve, " . . . what is greater . . . is the central actuality of an everyday hour on earth, with a streak of sunshine on a maple twig and an intimation of the eternal You."[59] In short, the artist or mystic who lives fully in the present moment will not crave annihilation. By definition, there must be an I or self for there to be a relation; moreover, there must be a relation for the I to be, to become, or to achieve actualization. Without mutuality the I remains stunted. Unlike Leibniz's monad, i.e., a self-enclosed mind that can unfold minus any commerce with others, Buber's I attains actuality only through reciprocity. Whether one loses herself in a finite Thou or an eternal Thou, the "loss" is at once a self-discovery, because to lose the ego is to find the self. The resultant harmony is one in which individuals participate in the universal, while still preserving their individuality. Reciprocally, the universal interpenetrates the particular. Teresa speaks to it when she urges people: " . . . to look upon our Lord as being in the innermost part of their soul."[60] The converse side of this interpenetration is evident in one of Augustine's prayers in which he asks if God might enter him and then realizes that he could not exist were he himself not already in God: "Is there anything in me, O Lord my God, that can contain Thee? . . . Or should I not rather say, that I could not exist unless I were in Thee, from whom are all things, by whom are all things, in whom are all things?" Teresa, who drew from Augustine, speaks of the two phases that sustain a harmony: "As water penetrates and is drunk in by the sponge, so, it seemed to me, did the Divinity fill my soul . . . and I heard Him say also, 'Labour thou not to hold me within thyself enclosed, but enclose thou thyself within Me.'"[61] In Catholic thought, the sacrament of communion literally embodies the interpenetration of the human and the divine. As the New American Bible reads: "The man who feeds on my flesh and drinks my blood remains in me, and I in him" (John 6:56). In such mutual dwelling there is intimacy, unity, continuity, in a word, there is communion, rather than monism.

Buber speaks pointedly to the mystic who reports that he disappeared into the void, i.e., that all duality between his self and what William James called the "more" dissolved into a commanding oneness:

> What the ecstatic calls unification is the rapturous dynamics of the relationship; not a unity that has come into being at this moment in world time, fusing I and You, but the dynamics of the relationship itself which can stand before the two carriers of this relationship . . . the relationship itself in its vital unity is felt so vehemently that its members pale in the process; its life predominates so much that the I and the You between whom it is established are forgotten.[62]

It is as if two dancers were to synchronize their steps and produce a single, flowing dance, but then project the singularity of their activity onto their separate beings. In other words, owing to the powerfully unified character of his experience, one may deny the irreducible duality of the dancers. Whenever the self and the other are acting in concert, there is always the danger that one will only affirm their oneness, not their individual natures. Similarly, the psychological intensity of the spectator's rapport with the aesthetic object can lead him to talk about becoming one with it. Because it feels as if all boundaries between the individual and the other or between the individual and God have vanished, it does not follow that this is true.

Clearly, there is no loss of identity when one "loses herself" in an artwork, immerses herself in the aesthetic enjoyment of nature, or identifies with a character in a drama. On a theistic account, dualism is true ontologically, but monism applies to the experiential quality of certain states undergone by some religious or aesthetic persons. The doctrine of monism is not false from a psychological perspective, but it is not literally true that the soul dissolves into God any more than it is true that the rapt spectator vanishes forever into the character Hamlet or that the lover literally becomes one with his beloved. One cannot hold da Vinci to his words when the master says: "He who cannot become the object cannot draw it." Reports of the soul's dissolution into God, artworks, or nature may be sincere, but they reveal the reporter's inner states, not the relationship in which he really stands toward the other.

For Buber, the fundamental union of self-integration does carry a risk, since one may rest content with this state rather than progress to a relation with God. Unless one goes beyond self-integration, he rests in solipsism—an unpopular philosophical option since the time of Parmenides. Concerning the origin of monism, Buber says, " . . . the soul may become one. This event occurs not between man and God, but in man."[63] From a subjectively true report: "I feel myself to be identical with God," the individual mistakenly infers a metaphysical conclusion: "There is no distinction whatsoever between God and me." Going further than Buber, Tillich equates monism with illness: " . . . participation is not identity. In participating in another being we are in the other one without losing our own identity, and only such a communion is worthwhile. Every other encounter is neurotic and perverted."[64] For Buber, self-unification is penultimate; it is a prerequisite for union with the other, but dwelling and remaining here turns a preface into a pseudo-ultimate.[65]

Two overlapping criticisms of monistic mysticism deserve special mention. First, monism is incompatible with dialogue, for mutuality requires two parties; and the unadulterated oneness of absolute monism would restrict discourse to the medium of the monologue. A second charge against monism is that it cannot accommodate love, a cardinal theme in art and religion. Sheer unity, in which no distinctions persist, seems to leave no room for the dualism of the lover and the beloved. Perhaps this is why monistic religions typically contain non-monistic offshoots. In any case, during monistic religious experiences, distinctions fall away; and one description is as good as another. It is no wonder that one then declares that aesthetic and religious experiences are indistinguishable.

Any discussion of union is incomplete without a consideration of love. Since the pre-Socratic thinker Empedocles, who said that the power of love was responsible for uniting the basic elements of the universe, Western philosophers have associated love with union. According to the Renaissance scholar Paul Oskar Kristeller, Marsilio Ficino held that: "By thinking and loving an object, the soul establishes a kind of unity with it, and in a sense acts upon it and transforms it."[66] Similarly, John of the Cross proclaims: " . . . it is love alone that unites and joins the soul with God."[67] Like art and religion, love is both a means and an end. Love is the way to reach union and is also inseparable from that end itself. A turn to love will often illumine art and religion—just as a turn to either of the latter two will often illumine the remaining two. All three, for example, flourish when the ego recedes. Undoubtedly the three possess affinities, because they tend to effect harmony. As in ordinary life, love is the most important emotion in the mystical life, whether it takes the form of *tz'u* in Taoism, *jen* in Confucianism, *agape* in Christianity, or *bhakti* in Hinduism. One can neither disengage religion from love ("God is love") nor wrest art from love. Consider the statement of the contemporary painter, Marc Chagall: "There's only one thing that guides my hand, and that's the urge to paint, and to offer love with my dreams and colors and shapes, and maybe with that something I was born with and don't really understand myself."[68] For him, love, art, and religion become difficult, if not impossible, to tease apart:

> As I grow older I see more clearly and distinctly what is right and wrong in our way of life and how ridiculous is everything not achieved with one's own blood and one's own soul, everything not infused with love. Everything can and will be transformed in life and art, if we speak the word love without shame. . . . In it lies true art: that is my technique, my religion; the new and old religion handed down to us from times long past.[69]

A literary artist as well as a saint, Teresa emphatically declares the priority of love over thought: ". . . the important thing is not to think much but to love much."[70] She would undoubtedly agree with the anonymous author of *The Cloud of Unknowing* who writes, "He whom neither men nor angels can grasp by knowledge can be embraced by love."[71] Again, in Ephesians 3:19, we find a prayer: " . . . to know the love of Christ which surpasses knowledge (RSV)." It was religious fervor, rather than erudition, which Francis brought to his love of nature. Tolstoy furnishes an aesthetic counterpart in his exclusion—however extreme—of the intellectual from art. He regards language as being uniquely suitable for the transmission of ideas and art as uniquely suitable for the transmission of the most laudable feelings: "By evoking under imaginary conditions the feeling of brotherhood and love, religious art will train men to experience those same feelings under circumstances in actual life . . ."[72]

Religion without love is, at best, a flight of the driven intellect, and, at worst, oppression; art without love is, at best, sheer technique and, at worst, soulless activity. In short, if reduced to mere means, religion becomes sheer magic and art becomes uninspired craft. As defended in Tolstoy's communication theory of art, all genuine art springs from love and culminates in love. After all, the artist can have no nobler purpose than to promote love among all of humanity. Linking love with God, Thomas à Kempis assigns the highest intrinsic value to love: "Nothing, therefore, is sweeter than love; nothing higher; nothing stronger; nothing larger; nothing more joyful; nothing fuller; nothing better, in heaven or on earth, for love descends from God, and may not finally rest in anything lower than God."[73] At Gauguin's retreat in the Marquesas were various carved and painted panels; among them, one read: "Love—and you will be happy." Another read: "Be mysterious and you will be happy." These sayings remind one that neither religion nor art can survive apart from love and mystery.

Since dialogue unfolds in time, Buber could not put stock in the notion of romantic love at first sight, but he did affirm the possibility of the immediacy of relationships when he said: "In the darkened opera-house there can be established between two of the audience, who do not know one another, and who are listening in the same purity and with the same intensity to the music of Mozart, a relation which is scarcely perceptible and yet is one of elemental dialogue."[74] Note that here an aesthetic context facilitates a spiritual engagement. While many deny the possibility of love at first sight, on the evident grounds that one requires time to cultivate love, and romantics insist that such instantaneous love is possible, Buber sets forth a compromise. One may kindle the spark of a relation in an instant, but the fullness of the relationship can only reach maturity through time. Indeed, if love were full-blown instantaneously, it would also be static or non-progressive. Likewise, the stirrings of the aesthetic may be sudden, but if one could appreciate, say, all the beauty of an object in a moment, then the aesthetic experience would be limited rather than boundless or inexhaustible. Correspondingly, the artist's direct inspiration hardly suffices to yield a masterpiece. Instead, the artist develops the inspiration; and, during the course of such elaboration, additions, subtractions, and other changes occur in response to impasses reached and further insights received. Hence, the completed work embodies the artist's "dialogue" with his model, theme, materials, and media.

Art, religion, and love coalesce in Tolstoy's definition of art as the transmission of religious emotions, i.e., feelings of brotherhood, solidarity, or love, through a public medium, to infect an audience. He concludes that all art worthy of the name is religious, because it has an overriding purpose: to communicate feelings that effect union among all humans. He states that only two sorts of feelings unite humans: (1) feelings that arise from an awareness of our sonship to God and of the brotherhood of human beings; and (2) "the simple feelings of common life, accessible to everyone without exception—such as the feeling of merriment, of pity, of cheerfulness, of tranquillity, etc."[75] Accordingly, Tolstoy recognizes two kinds of religious art that correspond respectively to the two sorts of feelings: religious art that communicates love of God and neighbor and universal art that conveys feelings common to all humans. While universal art seems too plain or simple to be deeply spiritual, it is really a mature expression of spirituality. Universal art stirs feelings of merriment, pity, or tranquillity, sentiments that punctuate the daily round of everyday existence and that regularly unite humans through their shared joys and sorrows. To have such feelings presupposes that one has already entered into union with one's fellows. Hence, Tolstoy says that a supposedly secular painting, *The Man with the Hoe* by Millet, can surpass in spiritual power an ostensibly religious work. This explains why a still life painting by Cezanne or a skeletal, ink wash, landscape painting by Ni Tsan moves one so deeply. Cezanne's mundane oranges raise questions about the ground of all being; and Ni Tsan's work invites one to discover the painter's spirit amidst the mountains and water. For Tolstoy, rapport among humans and rapport between humans and God are the loftiest spiritual goals; and love is the supreme example of the unions that constitute the varieties of harmonious experience.

"Harmony" is the term that some reserve for the ultimate form of union. After one recognizes the various common denominators between art and religion, she may wish to account for them. Not only is harmony the consummate expression of union in religion and art, but it also illumines their manifold affinities. Similarities between the aesthetic and the religious exist, because of their common aspiration for harmony. All humans feel the need for wholeness; and art and religion can promote harmonization, i.e., reconciliation of one's tensions, fears, struggles, and sorrows. In fine, religion and art find their deepest family resemblance in the yearning for harmony. A failure to yoke, harness, or harmonize one's thoughts, feelings, and willings undermines aesthetic as well as spiritual progress, resulting in half-hearted art and a diminished commitment to religion. No matter how tumultuous the artwork, if it is great, its point will be to effect harmony—whether through a catharsis that restores one's emotional balance or through communicating the solidarity that Tolstoy championed. To see that harmony is a primary goal of art, consider, for example, a satire that arouses one's indignation and leads him to an action that, in turn, resolves some tension. Time after time, significant art effects a harmony, as the Creator brought order out of chaos in Genesis. In addition, when an artist achieves coherency in an artwork, he may report a dividend of greater personal integration. While art wrings harmony from such mundane opposites as light and dark, loud and soft, or circle and square, religion wrestles with the supernatural opposites of the finite and the infinite. Of course, metaphysical art is content with presenting nothing less than a synthesis of the two.

An abiding value as an end in itself, harmony is always an expression of freedom, because harmony begins when one elects to put himself in accord with that which is natural. If one goes against the grain of nature, he meets obstructions, whether he is coming to terms with the media of art or seeking the divine. As a premier American architect, Louis I. Kahn, was fond of saying, "Without the approval of nature, nothing is possible." Religion also demands agreement with nature, because to act naturally is to promote harmony. The historical association between religion and art, in culture after culture, testifies to the fact that when the respective harmonies of each meet, they contribute to a greater harmony and one sees the highest soaring of the human spirit. From the perspective of Eastern and Western art, harmony serves as one of the most enduring paradigms of beauty. From the standpoint of religions, harmony represents the ideal form of happiness; and happiness is invariably a harmonious state, whether it is the unruffled bliss (*ananda*) of Hinduism, "the peace that passes all understanding" in Christianity, the stoic's repose, or the Buddhist's serenity. In addition, the restoration of harmony is always beautiful. Confucius's *jen* represents the supreme virtue and one may understand it as human-heartedness, benevolence, or fellow-feeling. The Chinese character itself suggests a union of two persons; this togetherness of persons is, of course, a sublime harmony. Emulating the Tao that reconciles all opposites, the sage attains tranquillity, a harmony in which he neither disturbs nor is disturbed. The artist works in order to achieve harmony between herself and her theme, between herself and her medium, between herself and ultimate reality, and between herself and her audience. In the West, philosophers have often likened artists to the Creator who brings order out of chaos. This order is not simply the opposite of chaos, i.e., a static order; instead, true order is an irresistible harmony that enchants artists and saints through its dynamic equilibrium. Hence, order, which is always minimally aesthetic, is a necessary but not a sufficient condition for the vital equipoise that constitutes harmony. In Zen, the ideal state of mind is not utter quiescence, but "rest amidst motion."

On the religious significance of harmony in antiquity, chapter seven of the *I-Ching* declares that when Heaven and Earth blend into a harmonious atmosphere, this will purify all things. In chapter seven of his *Hua-p'u*, Shih-t'ao finds such harmonious atmosphere to be an emergent from the fusion of brush strokes and ink washes: "When the brush strokes and ink washes are unified, this is called yin yun, that is harmonious atmosphere. . . . Apply it to painting a mountain, the mountain is spiritualized. . . . Apply it to human figures, and they are free from mundane defilements."[76] The subtle merging of brush and ink can create a spiritual effect that produces transcendental feeling. Since only a placid lake can reflect its surroundings without distortion, Chinese artists cultivate inner serenity in order to faithfully transmit their experiences. Of course, the tranquil artist is also poised, i.e., as ready to spring into action as a frog sitting on a lily pad.

Because art and religion are essential components of human nature, unless one nourishes both her aesthetic and spiritual sides, she is not a completely developed person. One who lacks either suffers from an impoverished "centeredness." If he were not off center, i.e., in a state of imbalance, he would not turn to art or religion. One drinks water, for example, because his lack of it causes a biological imbalance and only drinking can fill the void. Naturalists such as John Dewey would say that humans undertake all action, thought, and willing in order to effect such a restoration, completion, or harmonization. Theologians would add that humans are born out of balance and live to restore a balance, not the equilibrium of the womb as Freud would have it, but union with their source, i.e., the spiritual root, from which the embryo, womb, and all else derive.

A harmonious consciousness is intact, but one that lacks integration is scattered or dissipated. The attempt to yoke, harness or harmonize one's thoughts, feelings, and willings is crucial to the religious life. Kierkegaard gives us a foil for the religious individual when he relates the story of a man who glided across the surface of life, never introspecting, never questioning his own goals or values until one day he woke up and discovered it was too late for soul-searching, since he was dead. Likewise, the unsuccessful artist is one whose disintegrated art reflects a fragmented psyche. Harmony represents a desideratum whether in the self-integration of a person or the composition of a painting. In the aesthetics of Kandinsky, "To harmonize the whole is the task of art."[77] Stephen De Staebler and Diane Apostolos-Cappadona agree: "The obsessive quality of art is an attempt to reconcile opposites and keep an equilibrium, and, as in religion, this is art's validity."[78] Fundamentally, the relations between art and religion are grounded upon their common mooring in harmony. From antiquity to the present, philosophers have characterized art as a synthesis of opposites, e.g., colors, lines, forms, substances, and themes. Of course, there are opposite qualities within humans—good and bad, weak and strong, beautiful and ugly—that they must harmonize and balance. A like fusion of opposites is evident in religious experiences, as when Jonathan Edwards, after a walk through a pasture, remarked on the co-presence of God's majesty and grace, "I seemed to see them both in a sweet conjunction; majesty and meekness joined together: it was a sweet and gentle, and holy majesty; and also a majestic meekness; an awful sweetness, a high, and great, and holy gentleness."[79] Again, the Tao reconciles all opposites, including good and evil. Taoism enjoys widespread appeal, precisely because it celebrates harmony; the Tao itself is the great harmonizer; thus, humans flourish when they put themselves in accord with nature and thereby put themselves in accord with the underlying Tao, the reality that is both the way to harmony and the harmonious destination. Taoism finds the initial state of humans to be that they are born "out of step," in need of attaining attunement. Therefore, the problem of life—how to cultivate oneself—is aesthetic as well as spiritual in nature.

At times, the magnificent reconciliation of opposites in an artistic masterpiece finds a counterpart in the person of a saint. Accordingly, Reinhold Schneider recognizes that Francis " . . . unites so many contraries!—humility and power, innocence and experience, joy and bitter sorrow, audacity and scrupulousness, nobility and poverty . . . "[80] Again, viewing Francis as a fusion of various polarities, G.K. Chesterton hopes to shed light on such questions as: " . . . why the poet who praised his lord the sun often hid himself in a dark cavern . . . why the saint who was so gentle with his Brother the Wolf was so harsh toward his Brother the Ass (as he nicknamed his own body) . . . why the troubadour who said that love set his heart on fire separated himself from women . . . " [81] And

Friedrich Heer speaks of Francis as a "man who radiated both joy and sorrow, who united serenity and grief, quietude and turbulence, who rejoiced in all men, animals and things, yet was austere with the fortitude of the Desert Fathers . . . "[82]

The second precept from the rule of Augustine emphasizes fellowship or social harmony: "Above everything, live together in harmony." The I-Thou dialogue is another reference to social union or harmonization. As God has wrung order from the chaos of the physical universe, humans enter into dialogue in order to effect order in the social universe. Accordingly, Tolstoy argues that the whole point of art is communication and that what the artist seeks to transmit is fellow-feeling; thus, social harmony is the aim. For him, art captured the religious perception of his era and involved harmony: "The religious perception of our time, in its widest and most practical application, is the consciousness that our well-being, both material and spiritual, individual and collective, temporal and eternal, lies in the growth of brotherhood among all men—in their loving harmony with one another."[83] Of course, as Confucius emphasized, until one establishes inner calm, one cannot harmonize with others. Interestingly enough, the artist's or mystic's life has a kind of harmony, for she exhibits a rhythm or alternation in her stages; such waxing and waning are evident when periods of inspiration follow stretches of aridity. Evelyn Underhill states:

> The close connection between rhythm and heightened states of consciousness is as yet little understood. . . . Mystical, no less than musical and poetic perception, tends naturally—we know not why—to present itself in rhythmical periods. . . . Baron von Hugel adopted the presence or absence of rhythm as a test whereby to distinguish the genuine utterances of St. Catherine of Genoa from those wrongly attributed to her by successive editors of her legend.[84]

Analyzing the aesthetic principle of *k'ai-ho*, George Rowley captures the dynamic equilibrium that art and religion try to effect. Addressing *k'ai* (to open) and *ho* (to close) as the "unity of coherence," he elaborates:

> The most illuminating analysis of this creative process may be found in Shen Tsung-ch'ien, a writer of the eighteenth century. On the basis of the eternal flux of nature he described creation as *k'ai-ho*,—an "open-join" or "chaos-union" process. "From the revolution of the world to our own breathing there is nothing

that is not *k'ai-ho*. If one can understand this, then we can discuss how to bring the painting to a conclusion. If you analyze a large *k'ai-ho*, within it there is more k'ai-ho. Even down to one tree and one rock, there is nothing that does not have both expanding and winding up. Where things grow and expand that is *k'ai*, where things are gathered up, that is ho. When you expand *(k'ai)* you should think of gathering up (ho) and then there will be structure; when you gather up (ho) you should think of expanding *(k'ai)* and then you will have inexpressible effortlessness and an air of inexhaustible spirit. In using brush and in laying out the composition, there is not one moment when you can depart from *k'ai-ho'* " . . . in painting, when you expand *(k'ai)* you must think of gathering up (ho), "or else the composition will fly apart through the explosive tendency of creativity, and the structural unity of the whole will be lost"; when you pull the parts together *(ho)* you should think of the vital forces which gave them birth *(k'ai)*, "or else the result will be a dead, mechanical adjustment and the whole will have missed the life breath of the spirit."[85]

One thinks at once of the yogi's breathing with its parallel rhythm or alternation. Applied to art, *k'ai-ho* corresponds to yin and yang, the negative and positive aspects of pictorial composition. Broadly speaking *k'ai* and *ho* are the integrating, complementary powers or forces contained in all things. According to the Taoist law of reversion, whatever one takes to an extreme will produce the opposite of what she desires. Similarly, if one does not check the expanding aspect of creativity *(k'ai)* with the gathering aspect *(ho)*, the result is not creative painting at all, but a meaningless outpouring of energy; and, if one does not infuse the gathering or organizing phase of painting with *k'ai*, the work is frozen and lifeless. One might describe impulsive, unrestrained paintings as "all *k'ai* and no *ho*." Without limits, aesthetic value is just as impossible as ethical value. Painting in which excessive regard for structure extinguishes vitality is "all *ho* and no *k'ai*." When a painting does not issue from a continuous outpouring of spirit or *k'ai*, as checked appropriately by *ho*, the result is an artificial production. An expert observer should readily be able to detect the forger's work, assembled, as it is, part by part. In religion, if the religiously disposed is all *k'ai*, she is a fanatic; if all *ho*, she is dogmatic.

The principle of *k'ai-ho* makes clear that, in a painting, harmony refers to more than order; it refers to an order that is dynamic, i.e., possessed of the energy to evoke spiritual emotions, intuitions, and ideas in the beholder. Even the "charge" of a particular painting need not exhaust the energies that vitalize it. Mystics hold that all things interconnect and interpenetrate each other to yield a commanding oneness. Therefore, as an artist paints, his subject can gain power from every object in the universe. Hence, there is this Buddhist saying, "I raise my finger and the entire universe rises with it!"

Gauguin refers to the special harmony in a painting as a "magic accord" and as "the music of the picture" that seizes one's soul.[86] Suggesting the primordial status of such an ordered composition, he insists that such a seizure can even precede recognizing what the picture represents. Clearly, the ideal of harmony also attracted Matisse:

> What I dream of is an art of equilibrium, purity, and tranquillity, without disquieting or disturbing subjects, which could be for the mental worker, the business man, and the man of letters too, for example, a mental refreshment and relaxation, something analogous to a good easy chair in which one rests from his physical fatigue.[87]

Kandinsky speaks about the poetic use of a word in which repetition effects an inner harmony;[88] in effect, this is an acoustical *mandala*, with its oral "rings" radiating out and integrating the self. Illustrating the centrality of harmony in religious states of mind, James quotes from a Professor Starbuck's account of a profound spiritual experience: "It was like the effect of some great orchestra when all the separate notes have melted into one swelling harmony that leaves the listener conscious of nothing save that his soul is being wafted upwards, and almost burning with its own emotion."[89] With spiritual art, the creative act springs from the artist's state of harmony, issues in the harmonious whole of the artwork, and engenders harmony in the beholder. Therefore, such art and religion itself are best understood as universal efforts after harmony, within and without, which are inspired by the foundational harmony to which they point and from which all harmonies proceed.

5

Artistic Beauty, Natural Beauty, and Supernatural Beauty

A discussion of harmony leads quite naturally to the concept of beauty, for aestheticians have traditionally defined the beautiful in terms of the harmonious. Very often philosophers have described beauty in terms of a unity amidst variety. They have described this unity variously as an order, an arrangement of parts, a synthesis of elements, a balance, a proportion, a symmetry, or a harmony. Associating beauty with the classical canon of order or unity, Augustine declared that beauty exists when the parts of a thing "are so joined together as to form one harmonious whole."[1] Accordingly, to effect a harmony is also to bring about some measure of beauty. Not surprisingly, the concept of beauty is another important strand tying the spiritual and the aesthetic, for religious minds associate the unity of the invisible absolute with primordial beauty. Invariably, spiritually inclined philosophers interpret ultimate reality as either beauty itself (examples include Plato's Form of the Good and Augustine's God), as the ground of all beauties (as with the Tao), or as intimately related to beauty (according to the early Kabbalah, for example, beauty *(tif'eret)* is one of the ten *sefirot,* i.e., manifestations of the divine).

In Taoist aesthetics, beauty has a penultimate status, since the Tao is the root of beauty but is not beauty itself, just as the

Tao, although the ground of all being, is non-being or "nothing." As
the "mother" of opposites, Tao transcends the beautiful and the
ugly, male and female, good and evil. A Zen Buddhist anecdote
demonstrates that the formless beauty of the Tao and the perceptible beauty of physical things are complementary. To the ordinary
man, "Mountains are mountains and rivers are rivers." This means
that the uninitiated person can enjoy the physical beauties of
mountains and rivers, even though he takes them at face value and
cannot see beyond their surface qualities. But one who is on the
road to enlightenment reaches a second stage at which: "Mountains are not mountains and rivers are not rivers." The point is
that mountains and rivers are penultimate. This is because the
adept has shifted his focus from the multiplicity that constitutes
nature to the invisible, underlying oneness (*Dharmakāya* or Tao)
from which all such diversity emanates. Finally, at the highest
level of comprehension, the sage states: "Mountains are mountains
and rivers are rivers," as he simultaneously grasps the particulars
and the universal. Spiritual beauty appears when the sage detects
the interpenetrations between the universal Tao and particular
things, i.e., when he savors mountains as mountains and rivers as
rivers and both as rooted in the Tao. Evanescent beauty has its
charms and it arises from interaction between mundane particulars and the Tao. Therefore, perceptual beauty is not a finite expression of the infinite but a finite expression of how things are
grounded in the infinite. At this level, one discovers a more profound sense in which "Mountains are mountains and rivers are
rivers." One has a quickened appreciation of the physical beauty of
particulars, e.g., this mountain range and that river—and, at the
same time, a deeper awareness of the universal, spiritual reality
that is their foundation. In short, the One and the many are simultaneously appreciated. Particulars bring concreteness to aesthetic
experience and the universal renders it timeless. The perceptual
phenomena of phase one are affirmed, transformed, and elevated
in a higher intuitive realization. Here, the unity of things complements their particularity. It is no wonder that talk of the second
stage may put off nature lovers who prefer the third, more comprehensive realization. John Muir, for example, preserves the integrity
of particulars: ". . . as we study and mingle with nature more, the
pain caused by the melting of all beauties into one First Beauty
disappears, because, after their first baptismal submergence in
fountain God, they go again washed and clean into their individu-
alisms, more clearly defined than ever, unified yet separate."[2] Simultaneously appreciating the One and the many, Francis cherished

beauty on this third level at which "either or" gives rise to "both and." It is common to distinguish between two kinds of beauty—earthly and spiritual—and to assign the latter to God who is understood as the concrescence of truth, goodness, and beauty. Still, only a gossamer line may separate the varieties of beauty; indeed, Augustine describes the interpenetration between external and internal beauty:

> Late have I loved you, O Beauty, so ancient and so new, late have I loved you! And behold, you were within me and I was outside, and there I sought for you, and in my deformity I rushed headlong into the well-formed things that you have made. You were with me, and I was not with you. Those outer beauties held me far from you, yet if they had not been in you they would not have existed at all.[3]

Note the paradoxical implications of Augustine's mystical language: His "I" (ego) is outside and separated from his "me" (spiritual self); and God is in the latter, but if outer beauties can only exist or be grounded in God and if God is in Augustine's "me," then to appreciate outer beauties is to appreciate what is inside his "me"! More disposed toward the invisible than the visible, Augustine remained somewhat suspicious of outward beauties: "The eyes love beautiful forms of various kinds, brilliant and pleasing colors. Let these not possess my soul; that is for God to do."[4]

Typically, religious thinkers relegate physical or perceptible beauty to a plane beneath spiritual beauty. Christians, for instance, have held that changing, sensible beauties pale before the ideal beauty of God. Teresa believes that, measured against heavenly beauty, ". . . all the splendors of earth, so to say, are a daubing of soot."[5] Plato held that the more real a thing is the more beautiful it is. Therefore, the empirical horse that is always becoming something different is less beautiful than the form horse with its eternal being. Still, it does not follow that one should reject or condemn the beauty of artworks. Being ascetically inclined, Teresa reported that she had misgivings about possessing "painted pictures," until the Lord taught her that such mortification was not right, since she should not give up anything that kindled love in her.[6] While an introvertive mysticism moved St. Bonaventure to appreciate the beauties of the soul and God, an extrovertive mysticism moved Francis to love the beauties of nature and to discover his Creator therein. Obviously the two options are not mutually exclusive. For Francis, physical beauties are neither just points to deflect one to divine beauty, nor are they self-contained, resting points that are altogether disconnected from God's beauty.

Religious thinkers tend to repudiate the unmitigated subjectivism of the claim: "Beauty is in the eye of the beholder." They believe that beauty is no less objective than the divine beauty that addresses humans in the beauties of art as well as in the beauties of nature. In order to do justice to the facts of aesthetic experience, one needs a middle ground between subjectivism—which entails that Shakespeare's poetry is no more beautiful than the most banal greeting card poem—and objectivism—which places beauty in the unperceived object. Beauty is neither a strictly objective quality, i.e., one existing in the painting after everyone leaves the museum, nor a strictly subjective quality, i.e., one confined exclusively to human consciousness. Beauty is not in the work, irrespective of whether anyone beholds it, for beauty never exists unless the beholder brings the apt attitude or outlook. Instead of being strictly objective or strictly subjective, beauty arises when a subject meets an object and they coexist in relationship. Each is a necessary condition for the appearance of beauty, but only both yield a sufficient condition. In other words, beauty congeals only at the intersection of the receptive beholder and the object. And the same holds true with the category of the "holy." If an object is to be holy, it must be holy for someone; this is just to say that "holy," like "beauty," is a relational concept. Holiness is an emergent quality that surfaces in the relation between the human and the divine. In short, God unto himself, herself, or itself is not holy, for God is above the holy. God is simply all that God is—"I am what I am"—apart from any human predication.

Aesthetically speaking, the subjectivist holds that beauty begins and ends with his own internal states; and religiously speaking, the subjectivist finds no divinity beyond herself. Aesthetically speaking, the objectivist affirms the existence of unperceived beauty; and religiously speaking, the objectivist,who assigns all divinity to a wholly transcendental realm, embraces deism. The relationist agrees with the objectivist that beauty is not simply in the eye of the beholder, but also agrees with the subjectivist that the beholder's attitude is critical to aesthetic appreciation. For example, one should not approach a comedy in a glum frame of mind. Addressing the aesthetic and the spiritual, Evelyn Underhill writes that beauty is the real seen with love.[7] Approaching anything with the receptivity of love, the mystic finds beauty. Naturally, there is a reciprocity between such receptivity and beauty, for the beautiful can awaken, quicken, or deepen love.

That beauty exists only during the interchange between the I and the Thou is consistent with Part One of *I and Thou,* in which Buber holds that love exists neither in the self nor in the other but in the "between" which constitutes the relationship. It follows that beauty does not exist solely in the eye of the beholder, i.e., beauty is not merely subjective. Buber would also deny that beauty exists in a completely objective, independent way—apart from all human perception—as we suspect that the books continue to exist when there is no one in the library. In short, beauty is neither a sheer phantasm in the individual, nor an autonomous quality that inheres in an unobserved artwork. Since art appreciation involves a meeting between the beholder (the "I") and the artwork (the "Thou"), beauty exists when the I and the Thou intersect. Beauty appears between the two poles of subjectivity and objectivity—just as a shadow congeals when light meets mass. The actual and the potential converge as the I actualizes receptive consciousness and the Thou presents its potentialities for appreciation. Like love, beauty exists existentially, as experienced, or not at all. Just as love entails mutuality, beauty surfaces in the dynamics of such an I-Thou encounter. As sugar cannot be sweet without a taster, a painting cannot be beautiful without an appreciator. Rainbows appear only to creatures who have optical apparatus much like that of humans. Chuang Tzu proclaimed that the same beautiful woman who attracts men would cause fish to plunge to the bottom of the pond. If one defines "sound" as "waves of vibration," surely it can exist in a lifeless desert, but just as surely it cannot be beautiful music. Just as one may interpret beauty as a relational property between a subject and an object, he may contend that the numinous arises only in the interaction between the subject and the holy object or numen. It is not simply that art reveals or, as Otto says, expresses the numinous; rather, art brings the numinous into being.

One may take an objective approach to either art or religion. An institutional approach to beauty locates it in artworks themselves together with the institutions which house and exhibit them; and an institutional approach to religion locates it in religious pronouncements, encyclicals, edicts, or doctrines and in such structures as monasteries, convents, temples, churches, mosques, and other religious centers. One truth of objectivism is that value does not begin and end in the individual alone. One truth of subjectivism is that the individual "creates" beauty and such beauty "creates" her. In other words, the beauty of the artwork depends upon the conscious beholder; and the beauty of the work effects the self-actualization of the beholder. Similarly, for Buber there is no God without humans; God is a relational being and the individual participates in the creation of the I-Thou relation; moreover, the individual I is "created," i.e., achieves realization, in this very encounter.

Many thinkers emphasize the revelatory aspect of beauty. Aquinas, for example, defined beauty as that which illumines. Accordingly, one may call a sketch of an autopsy beautiful if it is highly instructive. True to his idealism, Coomaraswamy's concept of beauty, like his concept of art, is decidedly cognitive. He quotes approvingly from St. Bonaventure: "'It is knowledge that makes the work beautiful.'"[8] In short, he equates beauty with lucidity, intelligibility, illumination, revelation—concepts that apply to religious enlightenment, what Aquinas called clarity or enlightening radiance—and ugliness with vagueness, failure to communicate, or the inarticulate. Ugliness corresponds to the uninformed or shapeless, to whatever does not convey something of the essence or form upon which it is based. Plato's doctrine of recollection (anamnesis) is relevant to the concept of beauty as disclosure. Higher beauties of this earth, including paintings, call to mind or reawaken one to that eternal beauty that he beheld in a former state by means of a beatific vision (*Phaedrus*, 250–51). This suggests that we had a direct grasp or intuitive vision of ideal beauty in a past life. Like dialectical prodding, a series of perceptions can serve as the preface to a sudden realization. One remembers at once "the beautiful" with which she had a direct acquaintance in a previous existence.

Of course, natural beauties may be even more revelatory than artistic ones, for the former are more abundant, available to all, and sometimes issue in feelings of the sublime. Beauty here is inseparable from realization or actualization and requires that a thing be true to its own essence. Unless interfered with, natural objects develop in a necessary way. Every object in the universe, when it conforms to its own nature, or every person who conforms to his own character, is beautiful. Clearly, the fulfillment of a thing's being is also religiously significant, for the greater the actualization of an individual being the more it resembles the fully actualized absolute. Francis's "Canticle of Brother Sun" affirms that the natural creation, which "Genesis" repeatedly calls "good," is "beautiful." The first to be praised as beautiful is Brother Sun, the day itself, who brings light. Francis immediately adds that this Brother Sun bears a resemblance to the supreme Lord. Francis, however, does not relegate creatures and natural objects to the status of mere symbols of divine beauty. St. Bonaventure reports that Francis "beheld in fair things Him who is most fair."[9] Francis's appreciation of the earthworm shows that the saint also beheld in homely things

"Him who is most fair." For Francis, to ignore the splendors of creation would be a moral error as well as an aesthetic mistake, since recognition of and gratitude for the multifarious manifestations of God's fecundity are the appropriate and natural human responses to creation. Francis experiences nature as a kind of living scripture that deserves the same respect as does any sacred text. Other nature lovers, like Thoreau and Emerson, would agree that being interested in the beauty of nature is a sure sign of a moral soul.

The great leaps of Francis's projective faculty, by which he established rapport with animals, were aesthetic as well as spiritual triumphs. To embrace the spirit of a bird and enter into dialogue with it would be a supreme achievement in the training of any actor; and to appreciate the beauty of the simplest creature can elicit a spiritual feeling for its divine creator. Indeed, Paul Gallico asserts that there was an aesthetic foundation for Francis's eagerness to remove the earthworm from the path: "It has the great advantage of beauty over ugliness."[10] Francis beheld and was held by the manifold beauties of nature. He saw with a spiritual eye, with the intuitive penetration of the poet that he was, not with the rather intellectual eye that reads nature through categories or layers of symbolism and finds a creature that corresponds to every blessed attribute of God. Rather, Francis met animals one by one, just as the art collector savors each work individually. As Tolstoy elevated religious sentiment over formal education in art, Francis emphasized a spiritual knowledge—a synthesis of self-realization and dedication to God—over worldly knowledge. That Francis was not an intellectual is evident; that he was less aesthetic than one is less than evident.

While a Platonist recognizes a hierarchy of beauty in which earthly beauties ascend, like the rungs of a ladder, toward the absolute beauty of the Form of the Good, Francis seems to have a less hierarchical religious-aesthetic appreciation, for he relished the beauty of the plainest bird. Still, Bonaventure said of him: "He saw Beauty itself." Perhaps one can explain the last two points in terms of Francis's extraordinary emphasis upon the immanence of the divine. While the Platonist may make his ascent and leave the ladder behind and the pantheist never gets beyond the ladder, Francis adopts neither extreme. Creatures, as he sees them, are not just stepping stones to God, nor are they final resting places in themselves. Instead, each participates in a transcendental beauty; taken collectively, they are a tapestry of living, divine effluences. There is no need to deny that physical beauties are penultimate, for that is obvious to the spiritual mind. In *The Little Flowers of St. Francis,* a miraculously articulate statue urges Francis to adhere more to divine beauty "... than to the deceptive flowers of the world."[11] Clare, Francis's most ardent supporter, states that even the sun and moon admire God's beauty.[12] Like the artist who experiences the world in terms of concrete data, Francis shies away from abstractions. As the artist transforms the commonplace, Francis's appreciation of the natural world consecrates and renews it. His spiritual, aesthetic experience is at once a discovery and a transfiguration of nature. He never leaves nature, for it is precisely in and through nature that he meets his self and his God.

Like "beauty," "sublime" is a concept that appears in aesthetic as well as spiritual discourse. In Western aesthetics, the sublime means that which is boundless, unlimited, or infinite and therefore beyond one's grasp or control, e.g., the heavens, an approaching storm, or a mountain range. Thus, it is hardly surprising that thinkers often recognize a kinship—if not an identity—between the sublime and the holy. Otto makes one connection explicit: "In the arts nearly everywhere the most effective means of representing the numinous is 'the sublime.'"[13] Clearly, the aesthetic category of the sublime overlaps with that of the numinous. When the aesthetic majesty and mystery of the Great Pyramid at Giza dumbfound one, his experience invites comparison with Otto's apprehension of the *mysterium tremendum et fascinans* or "wholly other." Related expressions and terms that are mutually predicable of aesthetic and spiritual states include "absolute unapproachableness," "utterly unique," "uncanny," "mysterious," "terrible," and "awe-inspiring."

Of course, Otto's "wholly other" is just one attribute of the divine, for there is also the "ordinary" spirituality of van Gogh's painting *The Potato Eaters,* in which a homely meal becomes an ennobling event. Again, Mu-Ch'i's painting of six persimmons features commonplace objects in all their suchness, i.e., true nature, pointing beyond themselves. As Otto says, the aesthetic category of the sublime, like the spiritual category of the numinous, has a twofold, opposed nature, for it is both daunting and attractive.[14] The holy inspires awe and love; the former puts us at a distance and the latter draws us closer. Observing the moral import of these emotions, Teresa states: "With these two virtues, love and fear of God, we will travel the road to God in peace and quietness . . ."[15] Typically, the saint is someone who finds the holy in everything. Perhaps one can better express the content of Rudolph Otto's book *The Idea of the Holy* with the title: The Feeling of the Holy. Otto teaches that the holy has a twofold character: it looms over humans—keeping them at a remove—and it attracts them (the *mysterium tremendum et fascinans*). Great works of art also unite opposites, their excellence pulls us to them but their power humbles us and sets us back. One wonders if everything great has this twofold character. For example, when we appreciate nature, we try to become part of the landscape, i.e., to lose ourselves, but we also sense the daunting splendor of nature that can distance us. Human love is another obvious example; and, of course, self-discovery is at once attractive and intimidating. Closely related to the concept of the sublime is the idea of wonder. Both Plato and Aristotle say that philosophy begins in wonder; indeed, it is the first stirring of everything great, be it art, love, religion, or science. Childhood itself begins in wonder and endures as long as does any measure of wonder. In discussing Francis of Assisi, Armstrong identifies: "... wonder as among the saint's most striking and commendable virtues. It underlies his whole attitude to nature. Wonder naturally leads to worship ..."[16]

Buber's I-Thou relation is also germane to nature appreciation. To have the I-Thou orientation is to be receptive to a tree, to let it reveal its innermost nature or being. Explaining the reciprocity that can obtain between a person and a plant, Buber observes: "Our habits of thought make it difficult for us to see that here, awakened by our attitude, something lights up and approaches us from the course of being."[17]—what Buber called the "bestowing side of things." Francis's discourse with the universe takes the form of I-Thou dialogues, not simply with God, humans, animals, and plants, but with the inanimate elements of water, earth, wind, and fire. When his impaired vision required cauterization, Francis did not hesitate to ask Brother Fire to be considerate. Radically distinct from the objectivity of science, Francis's personal orientation welcomes even states of being, as when he greets "Sister Death."

As the I-It posture emphasizes predictability and belongs to science, the I-Thou perspective emphasizes spontaneity and belongs to art and religion. With the latter, one draws upon her imaginative faculty in order to empathize with and thereby meet the hidden aspects of things, animals, and, of course, people. To take up the aesthetic attitude is to suppress the ego, to curtail individual projections; it is to be open or receptive to the true character of an object. By contrast, the erotic attitude, which one may also apply universally, relates things to the ego, failing to view them as they are in themselves. For theists, to apprehend things as they really are is to uncover the inevitably personal side of nature, since all things, as creations of a personal God, are permeated by a personhood, just as a painting carries the personal stamp of its painter. Francis never finds anything to be "dead," a mere "It," since every object is effulgent with the Thou of the living Lord. Therefore, to aesthetically experience nature is a twofold event in which the particular and the universal interpenetrate; one appreciates the individual beauties of "Brother Sun" and "Sister Moon," but he also apprehends the invisible beauty of the divine from which all things flow. In short, the abstract (universal) and the concrete (particular) interfuse; there is no dichotomy between the sacred (universal) and the profane (particular). Of course, the sacred and the profane also interfuse in great art, for without the former, art ignores the transcendent; and without the latter, art ignores the immanent. Accordingly, Zen Buddhists speak about finding enlightenment—universal truth—in the midst of prosaic activities: "While carrying water and chopping bamboo."

That Francis was in the world but not trapped by it answers a question raised by one of his biographers: How can Francis's asceticism or renunciation of the world be squared with his ardent love of nature? His passion for the beauties of nature did not stop with these particulars, for they celebrate the supreme beauty of God from whom all other beauties issue. To be an ascetic is not to give up earthly pleasures and enjoyments, but to savor them without succumbing to them as ultimates. Asceticism entails appreciation without attachment or clinging. Craving natural objects is one extreme and being altogether alienated from them is the other. Buber forcefully decried the latter error: "But never should asceticism gain mastery over a man's life. A man may only detach himself from nature in order to revert to it again and, in hallowed contact with it, find his way to God."[18] Similarly, Chesterton has linked Francis's philosophy with "the ultimate recovery not the ultimate refusal of natural things."[19]

The universal and the particular are keys to the most exalted aesthetic experience of nature. By the scent of a rose or the taste of a berry, nature—unlike an artwork—is uniquely empowered to address all the senses. Nevertheless, to appreciate nature is not merely to recognize manifest perceptual qualities. To rest content with the delights of sensation would be to stop short of profound aesthetic experience. Apart from sensations, one can also detect physiognomic qualities, e.g., the cheerfulness of gibbons at play or the menacing tone of a storm, and capture them in his painting. If one is to go from a biological to a poetic appreciation of nature, one needs to apprehend such qualities. At this higher cognitive level, one can discover what is invisible to sheer perception, but what yields to intuition when one enters into rapport with natural objects. Bamboo becomes a representative of the Confucian gentlemen who is initially yielding but eventually springs back from any oppression. To personify nature as the Chinese and Francis do is to take up the aesthetic stance. To personify is to insist that the universe is never dumb and insensate; it is to affirm that nature is always ready to speak to the receptive artist or sage. To discern the "Thou" of anything is to depart from the literal or non-aesthetic as such. Ultimately, one identifies, empathizes, or unites with the natural object through an intuition of their common root. Ideally, as one appreciates the finite Thou of the tree or bird, her appreciation deepens and extends to the eternal Thou that gives rise to all. For Francis, the sun was "Brother Sun," because both he and the sun were members of the same divine family. In a similar vein, the Taoist Chuang Tzu once came upon a school of fish and exclaimed: "Look at the fish enjoying themselves!" But his companion objected: "You are not a fish; so, how do you know that they are happy?" To which Chuang Tzu replied: "You are not me; so, how do you know that I do not know?" Perhaps Chuang Tzu knew because he empathized with the spirit of the fish, their *ch'i* or Tao energy. The first canon of Chinese painting states: "spirit rhythm animates." The idea is that the painter should capture, not external appearances, but the inner reality or spiritual energy of a thing in order to animate his work. In other words, *ch'i* or spirit should pervade one's art. It follows that the highest appreciation of nature lies in apprehending the Spirit behind the myriad spirits that enliven natural things. One contemplates nature, not only to meet the soul of the flower, but to encounter the absolute All-Soul. Because the eternal Thou is present in every finite Thou, the poet speaks of being addressed by the soul of the flower.

Recently, the American aesthetician Allen Carlson has addressed the question: What are we to focus upon as the ingredients for an aesthetic experience of nature? In short, what do we concentrate upon?[20] He reasons that we cannot attend to everything, for such an impossibly-dispersed attention would yield "a booming, buzzing confusion." Instead, he recommends that one gain knowledge of the natural environment as the means for securing a unified aesthetic appreciation, because such knowledge enables one to detect relations that bring together otherwise disparate phenomena. He concludes that science and commonsense knowledge furnish the requisite foci for deriving aesthetic significance from the natural environment. Of course, the spiritually inclined, who do not separate appreciation of the universe from the appreciation of its origin, would regard this as a penultimate exercise. For them, the utmost aesthetic appreciation of nature obtains when spiritual insight supersedes or supplements intellectual knowledge. While Carlson's objective approach approximates an I-It posture, Francis constantly enters into dialogue with the animals and the elements, thereby engendering an I-Thou relation. Carlson's objectification of nature undermines the intimacy that many find to be essential to the most profound appreciation of nature. Therefore, two distinct models for the aesthetic appreciation of nature are evident: Carlson's intellectual approach, and the spiritual, intuitive, existential approach of figures as different as Martin Buber, Francis, and the Zen Buddhist D.T. Suzuki. In the first approach, a scientific, distancing, I-It orientation establishes a dichotomy between the spectator and natural objects. In the second, intuitive approach, rather than distance himself from nature, Francis passionately addresses nature in terms of "Brother" and "Sister." He invariably appreciates nature as personal, because God—the ground of nature—is personal and the divine energizes all things through his personhood. To fully appreciate an artwork, one wants to "meet" the artist who created it. Indeed, the traditional Chinese painter copies the works of the masters partly, at least, because he wishes to meet their spirits. Similarly, to fully appreciate our natural environment—with all its creatures, objects, and forces—one yearns to know something about its origin. There is spiritual as well as aesthetic merit in Chesterton's comment that one "sees more of the things themselves when he sees more of their origin; for their origin is a part of them and indeed the most important part of them."[21] Since a painting is a product of a personal agent, one must appreciate it accordingly; if the creatures and objects of the cosmos are creations of the divine, one must appreciate them as such.

Francis's emphatically personal, I-Thou orientation toward the variegated beings and objects of the natural world marks him off from the pantheist who conceives of the physical universe as a play of impersonal forces. The latter's rejection of the natural world as personal entails a significant impoverishment in his aesthetic experience of this world. Viewed personally, the sun becomes "Brother Sun," the moon "Sister Moon," because they are expressions of a personal God. Like the characters in a story, who point to a novelist, the created works are alive with a personhood that points to their divine author. In a related vein, Malcolm L. Diamond discusses an instructive difference between Spinoza and Buber: While Spinoza identifies extension and thought as the only two knowable attributes of Substance or God, Buber insists that these two are not exhaustive categories, for the personal is an irreducible third category of reality that one encounters as surely as she does physical objects and ideas; in short, the I-Thou is a "primitive" among life's givens or experiential fundamentals.[22]

From Francis's viewpoint, pantheism allows one to appreciate natural beauty, but it precludes one from apprehending the aesthetic splendor of divine creativity. In short, it leaves no room for beholding the universe as an artwork or the product of a designing mind. When one's aesthetic attitude incorporates a spiritual perspective, this infusion of purposiveness, intelligibility, or teleological significance enriches her aesthetic appreciation of nature. As things may work for an end in a drama, one beholds the diverse aspects of nature as constituents of a cosmic play, God being the dramatist. There is a parallel in the auteur theory of filmmaking, which invites one to look for the formal and conceptual hallmarks of a director in her film. By contrast, pantheism views nature as the play of powers that lack a coordinating consciousness and which themselves often have little or no consciousness. John Dewey clarifies this sort of difference by reflecting upon an aesthetic case in which one suddenly discovers that a supposed piece of "sculpture" is really a product of natural forces. He concludes that this discovery would justify moving any such "work" from a museum of fine art to a museum of natural history.[23] Surely, Dewey has a point. One's knowledge of a thing's origin affects how he regards and appreciates it, e.g., one does not criticize a painted rose for its failure to be fragrant. Moreover, if Francis is correct, the true beauty of nature will be opaque to those who do not behold the spiritual "root" with which nature is continuous. One related point, though not an emphasis of Francis, is that the pantheistic conception of the universe does not allow for the sexual language that a personal orientation toward nature encourages and which abounds among mystical writers. Of Francis himself, Chesterton says: "Notice, for instance, the sense of sex in inanimate things, which goes far beyond the arbitrary genders of grammar. It was not for nothing that he called fire his brother, fierce and gay and strong, and water his sister, pure and clear and inviolate."[24] It is precisely because Francis and Buber detected a finite "Thou" in natural objects that the two were able to enjoy the sort of intimate relation with nature that distinguishes them from pantheists.

Francis's God is no more equivalent to nature than is Lao Tzu's Tao, for each thinker understands his absolute as the ground of nature and, being more primordial than nature, as that which cannot be conflated with nature. It follows that a pantheist's enjoyment of the beauties of nature is incomplete when measured against that of Francis and the Taoists, for an awareness and affirmation of the absolute as the root of all such beauties enriches one's satisfaction. Thus, Edward A. Armstrong remarks that when one's appreciation of a lovely sight fuses with an apprehension of God as its source, ". . . a unique delight mingles with the mystic ecstasy" and an exceptional intensity stamps the experience, for there has been: ". . . the acknowledgment of a Power beyond things seen which creates, sustains, and cares."[25] D.T. Suzuki, in a discussion of the aesthetic appreciation of a flower, makes a related point: "If heaven and earth . . . issue from the one root which you and I also come from, this root must be firmly seized upon so that there is an actual experience of it; for it is in this experience that Nansen's flower in its natural beauty appealed to his aesthetic sense."[26] God is at the core of Francis's appreciation of nature; all natural phenomena finding their deepest beauty and coherency in the intuitive realization of the divine. It is not as if there can be no enjoyment of the beauty of an object unless one adopts a spiritual orientation, but to fully appreciate the beauty of anything one must realize its connection with its root. While Immanuel Kant thought one could know only the world as filtered and hence modified by the forms of his own intellectual apparatus, the mystic holds that the true self, as opposed to the ego, is capable of a direct insight into the ultimate, spiritual reality upon which all sensible things depend.

To believe that natural objects exhaust beauty is to endorse pantheism, but to appreciate things in terms of their origin is transcendentalism. The pantheist enjoys perceptual and conceptual beauties; but the transcendentalist's enjoyment goes further, because he intuits the spiritual beauty that grounds every perceptual beauty. This raises the paradox of incommensurate beauties: How can the absolute, invisible beauty of the One give rise to many visible beauties? With this problem the Platonic question of how particulars can participate in their universals reappears in aesthetic dress. If saints and artists are to address human needs, they must ground themselves in the physical world, but not be bound to it. Francis, for example, viewed nature as a theophany that, far from tying him to the material world, invited him to contemplate its transcendent ground. Similarly, an artist who writes satire needs a footing in the world, but she must not capitulate to the mundane—not if she wishes to express ideals or to create fantasies that transcend it.

Francis's profound aesthetic experience of nature depended upon how he experienced it as well as what he perceived. To be specific, Francis approached nature reverentially, as an outpouring or work in process—more like a performing art than a finished work—whose myriad, dazzling manifestations served as a conduit between humans and God. Through his poetry Francis reached for the divine; and, in natural beauties, he found God reaching for him. His aesthetic appreciation of nature is more inclusive than that of the pantheist or naturalist, because Francis celebrates not only physical beauties and their interrelations, but also the God that is beauty itself and that, as the locus of all beauties, provides the widest and most unified basis for any aesthetic appreciation. Even if atheism were true, spiritual aesthetic experiences of nature would contain something that is absent from secular aesthetic experiences of nature. The religious person's aesthetic experience of nature does not omit any of what the secular appreciator of nature experiences. Rather, the spiritual orientation is broader, more comprehensive or inclusive. One appreciates colors, sounds, tastes for their own intrinsic value, but she also appreciates them in the context of the cosmic root from which they spring. Here, one apprehends the patterns, schemes, and designs that mark the universe as moored in what William James called the "more," a unity of unities in which all things cohere. The religious appreciator experiences all that the pantheist can plus the "more." The Tao or God is no mere backdrop for all natural beauties; instead, the absolute permeates all things and thereby gives them significance. Like light penetrating a stained glass window, God's radiance brings out the beauty of the entire creation.

Rather than contradict the pantheist's vision, the spiritual perspective expands it. Aesthetic significance and spiritual significance are not mutually exclusive, for the same object can sustain and reward both orientations. In theism, unlike pantheism in which God and nature coalesce completely, God is transcendent as well as immanent, i.e., apart from as well as inherent in the universe. God remains neither fully available through nature nor completely exhausted by earthly categories. A kind of mystery belongs to theism that does not obtain for pantheism; this transcendent side of God is what Otto calls the "wholly other." Theologians or philosophers sometimes call this aspect of the divine "the Godhead" or the "God beyond god." And since mystery is an aesthetic quality in one's appreciation of nature, pantheism lacks one key aesthetic element for the aesthetic appreciation of nature.

The well-known pantheist Richard Jeffries, author of *The Story of My Heart,* enjoyed a sense of harmony with earth and sky, but he detected no God in nature. Concerning Jeffries's orientation, one might argue that a person cannot cherish nature with the ardor that humans reserve for each other, that a person cannot feel reciprocal love, and that contemplation of nature alone precludes the sexual tincture of many profound mystical experiences. The passion that Edna St. Vincent Millay expresses in her poem "God's World" is hardly compatible with the non-personal nature of pantheism:

> O world, I cannot hold thee close enough!
> Thy winds, thy wide gray skies!
> Thy mists that roll and rise!
> Thy woods, this autumn day, that ache and sag
> And all but cry with colour! That gaunt crag
> To crush! To lift the lean of that black bluff!
> World, World, I cannot get thee close enough!
>
> Long have I known a glory in it all,
> But never knew I this;
> Here such a passion is
> As stretcheth me apart,—Lord, I do fear
> Thou'st made the world too beautiful this year;
> My soul is all but out of me,—let fall
> No burning leaf; prithee, let no bird call.

Even Jeffries's pantheistic, aesthetic experience of nature may be parasitic upon religious experiences of nature in his culture. Perhaps he assimilated religious perspectives, concepts, or language from the poetry of an Emerson, the philosophy of a Thoreau, and the writings, teachings, and practices of religions with which he came in contact. For that matter, religious themes in literature, drama, music, painting, sculpture, architecture, and film may have shaped Jeffries's thought and experience. For example, if one appreciates Chinese landscape paintings, with their deeply spiritual import, this might influence the consciousness that he brings to nature. In any case, one's aesthetic appreciation of the natural landscape is always incomplete, since nature forever presents more than one can take in and absorb. Likewise, spiritual experience is such that one cannot plumb the depths of its inexhaustible foundation.

For the religious person to appreciate the many, she must appreciate the One, i.e., God, Tao, Brahman, or absolute reality. It is the mutual interpenetration between this One and the many that allows for the greatest relishing of the many. Taoists speak of the centipede with its multiple legs in order to illustrate the interfusion of the One and the many; those who see only the many legs miss the single centipede from which they emanate. The blur that marks our ordinary awareness of nature can yield to a unified, aesthetic-spiritual experience if one sees the falling leaf, the weathered rock, and the bird in flight as manifestations of a single underlying reality. For Francis, an intuition of the divine reality that underlies the universe arrests the "booming, buzzing confusion," furnishing the only suitable focus for the aesthetic savoring of the natural environment. It is difficult to overestimate the significance of the interpenetration of the One and the many, for if all things derive from and are continuous with the same source and if they are microcosms, to know the universe in its foundation is to know something of one's own true self.

Although one may find no logical or scientific necessity for the continued existence of the universe, religious nature lovers sometimes report that they sense an abiding dimension in their aesthetic experiences of the natural environment. If nature is merely contingent, there must be a reason why some experience a necessity in it. For them, the permanent is as much a part of the landscape as its impermanent colors, forms, sounds, aromas, and tastes. Taoists, for instance, speak about detecting "rest amidst motion," and, indeed, their ideal painting expresses both qualities. If one could find something enduring amidst the incessant changes of life, he might achieve repose, but this hardly seems possible, since nature is fragile, transitory, and may even be subject to entropy. Nevertheless, among those who seek calm, many join Francis and Lao Tzu in a turn toward nature. If only the unchanging can refresh, then perhaps nature succeeds by pointing to what transcends all transformations. Of course, it is not as though one merely observes the patterns, cycles, and other regularities and then extrapolates an idea of the eternal from the repeated play of natural phenomena. Intellectual abstractions about nature can scarcely establish the continuity or ongoing existence of the universe. Humans do not simply assign a continuing character to nature through reasoning by induction: "What has occurred will recur." Rather, they extract such a character from their deepest, intuitive, aesthetic encounters with nature. As lovers find a timeless moment in an I-Thou relationship, Francis's love of nature was, at once, a romancing of his unchanging Lord. For him, Lao Tzu, Thoreau, or Black Elk, only the spiritual hypothesis does full justice to one's most direct experience of nature. Neither in the transitoriness of the physical world nor in the shifting theories and concepts of science can one detect the enduring quality of religious truths as ageless and aesthetic experiences of nature and art as timeless. When nature lovers sense time standing still, one may interpret them as participants in the eternal moment of the mystics. To the spiritually inclined, only an invisible foundation, Tao, God, or Brahman manifested through nature, can yield "the peace that passes all understanding" or a sense of that which is utterly sublime. From a religious perspective, the aesthetically experienced permanence of nature then becomes a metaphor for the eternality of God. Nature can only appear as eternal, because through it one grasps what forever is, always was, and can never not be. To a mystic such as Francis, the universe is never a surd, never an inexplicable given about which one could ask: "Why does this universe exist rather than nothing at all?" After all, Francis believed that he had experiential grounds for knowing that the universe proceeds from God and that God's nature alone is self-sustaining.

A turn to the Taoist paradigm of beauty reveals affinities with various religious traditions and with philosophers such as Heraclitus, Plotinus, and Spinoza. Taoists cannot attribute perceptual beauty to the Tao, for it is invisible, inaudible, and intangible—in a word, imperceptible. Frequently, religions view sensory beauty as skin deep, with ultimate reality lying beneath such surface attraction. As the "form of the formless," the Tao possesses a transcendent, spiritual beauty that suffuses and beautifies the ten thousand perceivable things and that one can only intuit rather than sense. How might one describe this higher, spiritual beauty? As discussed earlier, many theoreticians characterize ordinary, perceivable beauty in terms of harmony; in fact, for both Eastern and Western cultures, harmony represents perhaps the most enduring paradigm of beauty. As a harmonization of parts is the basis for perceivable beauty, the ontological harmonization of all pluralities in the seamless Tao or uncarved block (p'o) is the basis of spiritual beauty. One argument in favor of the supremacy of spiritual beauty is simple:

1. To possess harmony, i.e., unity of parts, is to possess beauty.
2. The Tao unifies all things in a distinctionless oneness in which everything is latent and nothing is manifest. Its beauty is that of an undifferentiated whole, a higher unity or unsurpassed equilibrium; and, of course, no equilibrium is without aesthetic significance. Therefore, because the Tao

exemplifies the harmony or interfusion of elements to the greatest possible degree, one may speak of it as the highest beauty.

Drawing upon Guy Sircello, one could also argue that since: "... beauty ... is an extreme degree of a property ..."[27] and since the Tao actualizes the property of harmony or unity to the utmost, the supreme beauty belongs to the Tao. Ironically enough, when everything has been interfused, there is not, of course, any isolated individual remaining who can behold this beauty.

Of course, the imperceptible harmony of all potencies in the Tao necessarily constitutes a different sort of beauty from that of perceptual wholes or harmonies. Perhaps we get a better notion of this primordial harmony from C.Y. Chang, who quotes Alfred North Whitehead:

> The highest sense of peace is what we might call, in the words of Whitehead, "a deep underlying harmony," which is inherent in both man and the universe. It is the ground of all harmonies, from which emanates the all-expanding energy that constantly creates a new universe. Without it nothing that is real can be achieved. It is invisible and unfathomable, beyond the realm of discursive thinking.[28]

As *wu* or nonbeing, the harmonizer of all things, the Tao also possesses the beauty of perfect freedom, for: "The realm of nonbeing is absolutely free from limitations and distinctions."[29] This invisible beauty of the Tao is the "independent beauty" upon which all physical beauties are "dependent." To illustrate spiritual beauty, Chuang Tzu speaks of an ugly man who nevertheless attracted men and women as a magnet does filings. Such inner beauty, of course, rests upon the invisible, centered beauty of the Tao. Once apprehended such beauty is irresistible, but one can resist physical beauty. In chapter twenty-one of Chuang Tzu, people deny that a beautiful concubine is beautiful, because she is unduly conscious of her own beauty. Chapter twenty-six of the *Tao Te Ching* states that the sage is unruffled even when beholding a magnificent vista.

Religious thinkers are sometimes suspicious of physical beauty, because they deem it to be relative to the perceiver and therefore of little import. Chuang Tzu observes that men appreciate beautiful women, but eels like other eels, and monkeys like other monkeys. Against any unmitigated relativism, one could argue that a sensitive aesthete appreciates eels as well as humans. In addition, even if humans disagreed over the beauty of all finite objects, one or more could be correct in their aesthetic judgments. Finally, even if finite beauties were subjective, it would not necessarily follow that the beauty of the infinite is subjective. The man of Tao advocates returning to plainness, to the root, to the uncarved block that precedes all distinctions. Hence, the *Tao Te Ching* invites one to close the doors of perception and unite with the Tao, or, as Arthur Waley put it, exercise "a general perception not affected through particular senses."[30] What he calls "a general perception" is not a perception at all, but a mode of apprehension like the Buddhist's *prajñā,* i.e., a profound intuition, an immediate awareness as distinct from ordinary sensation. No normal sense faculty can be at work, for the Taoist sage "sees in total darkness and hears in total silence." This is not to say that intuition and sensation cannot work hand in hand, for clearly both animate the sage who proclaims: "Mountains are mountains and rivers are rivers."

Like Spinoza, Taoists view the natural universe as neither beautiful nor ugly in itself. To say that a thing is beautiful or ugly implies that it might have been different. If, however, the natural universe issues ineluctably from the Tao, then there was never any chance of an alternative universe, none relative to which one could judge this universe to be beautiful or ugly. Again, there can be no "beautiful" or "ugly" for any one who, rather than distinguish among things, unites with things, interfuses with things, and identifies with things. It is in this sense that the man of virtue: ". . . has no use for right and wrong, beautiful and ugly."[31] A passage from Chuang Tzu maintains that opposites or distinctions dissolve in the unifying flow of transformations: "The ten thousand things are really one. We look on some as beautiful because they are rare or unearthly; we look on others as ugly because they are foul and rotten. But the foul and rotten may turn into the rare and unearthly, and the rare and unearthly may turn into the foul and rotten."[32] Positing the universality of positive and negative qualities is another way to undermine distinctions:

> Choosing neither this thing nor that, but going along with all of them—there were those in ancient times who believed that the "art of the Way" lay in such things . . . each of the ten thousand things has that which is acceptable in it and that which is not acceptable. Therefore, they said, "To choose is to forgo universality. To compare things is to fail to reach the goal."[33]

It is by going along with all things, i.e., accepting their course, that one balances the shadows and lights and proclaims the resultant harmony to be beautiful.

One can better grasp Taoist spiritual beauty by contrasting it with Ronald W. Hepburn's contextualist theory of beauty: "Any aesthetic quality [from beauty to ugliness] is always provisional, correctable by reference to a different, perhaps wider context or to a narrower one realized in greater detail."[34] To illustrate, after a forest fire has destroyed the colors, forms, aromas, bird song, and creatures of the woods, one is apt to perceive the charred landscape as ugly. Nevertheless, beholding the burned woods from a fresh perspective—as affected by the elixir of moonlight—may restore aesthetic significance. After all, if the play of moonlight upon the Taj Mahal is aesthetically significant, may not such illumination have an aesthetic impact upon the gutted forest? The burned woods might present an austere beauty reminiscent of the striking arrangements of dead flowers at which the Japanese excel. About scorched forests, Holmes Rolston III states: "No one would feature these places in landscape paintings, they are not picturesque."[35] Still, some artists paint or photograph such scenes, because they present significant formal qualities.

If one is reluctant to judge a painting on seeing only a small part, perhaps she should not judge a natural object in isolation from its "frame," i.e., the wider natural setting or matrix of which it is a part and to which it contributes. Just as a wider setting can be relevant to aesthetic appreciation, a narrower scope, by which one examines sub-sets within an object, can be aesthetically rewarding. One might, for instance, appreciate the delicate veins of a stone that at first sight seemed uninteresting. Even fecal matter, viewed through a microscope, has aesthetic properties. When someone asked Chuang Tzu where the Tao exists, he stated that it is in urine and dung. Contextualists always regard beauty as relational; and what bestows beauty upon a whole can be conceptual as well as perceptual.

The rotting elk returns to the humus, its nutrients recycled; the maggots become flies, which become food for the birds. . . . Every item must be seen not in framed isolation but framed by its environment, and this frame becomes part of the bigger picture we have to appreciate—not a "frame" but a dramatic play. The momentary ugliness is only a still shot in an ongoing motion picture. . . . The usefulness of a tree in the

> ecosystem is only half over at its death; as an old snag or a
> rotting hulk it provides nesting cavities, perches, insect lar-
> vae, food for birds, nutrients for the soil . . .[36]

The decaying animal or plant that is repugnant in unreflective
experience becomes beautiful from the holistic perspective of biology. To adopt an ecosystemic perspective is to take up an aesthetic
outlook that transforms ugliness into beauty. To the discrimina-
tion-decrying Taoist, however, all such beauty would be penultimate,
depending as it does upon rational thought rather than immediate
insight or direct awareness. As resourceful as contextualism can
be, it cannot accommodate the beauty of a simple object. The paradox of simple beauty arises because everyone is familiar with such
beauties, say, the tone of a bell, but contextualism insists that
beauty is a function of a context, i.e., of plurality. Typically,
contextualists describe beauty in terms of a unity amidst variety.
They invariably equate beauty with order, an arrangement of parts,
a synthesis of features, a balance, a proportion, a symmetry, a
harmony, or an interdependence of components. Thus, one wonders
about the simple beauty of a blue sky, unmodulated by hues or the
leavening influence of any clouds, that completely occupies one's
field of vision. The contextualist regards beauty as a function of
relations; thus, he is mute before the simple beauty of a pure tone
or color patch. He always predicates beauty of a complex and never
predicates it of any simple part that contributes to the beauty of a
whole. According to Stephen C. Pepper's contextualistic theory of
beauty, "There is no such thing as a situation having a quality [e.g.,
beauty] without interrelated details to make it up."[37] To the contrary, the Taoist model—one representative of other religious traditions—explains how any object, no matter how plain, simple, or
homely, can reward aesthetic attention. If the Tao pervades all
things, then it irradiates even the simplest tone or color patch with
aesthetic quality; and there is a solution to the contextualist's problem of how the simplest entity can possess beauty. For a different
example of the simple, non-composite beauty that contextualism
cannot accommodate, one might consider the simplicity of the
uncarved block, i.e., undifferentiated Tao that is similar to the
unicity of God in Judaism, Christianity, and Islam.

From a spiritual perspective, a flower petal is a microcosm
within which the whole of nature vibrates. This makes the mystic's
model of aesthetic appreciation a more inclusive outlook—more
phenomenologically rich than that of the naturalist, who savors
only the perceivable phenomena, or the pantheist who supplements

her percepts with concepts of the interrelations between and among sensible phenomena. In addition, it involves the irony of starting with the isolated beauty of a tiny fragment of nature and ending with the most comprehensive kind of appreciation, for the smallest part of nature is like a monad that represents all that lies outside it. As Zeno's line was finite in extent but infinite in divisibility, even the most minute entity is inexhaustibly rich. Because a microcosm embraces all that there is, Thoreau could travel to Walden Pond and find himself, because his self was there, waiting to be discerned in the woods, clouds, pond, and creatures. Just as Thoreau could meet his true self in nature, he talks about discovering nature inside himself. Writing about the signs of spring, Thoreau says: ". . . there are as many within us as we think we hear without us."[38] It was precisely this inner world which Shih-t'ao claimed that painting can illumine, the artist being someone who "can embrace everything in miniature," i.e., reflect the entire universe on a microcosmic scale. Contemplation is the key to integration of the self with the universe; and the aesthetic concept of harmony again plays a role, ". . . the Taoist practitioner achieves a harmony of the microcosmic universe within and harmony in his relation to the macrocosmic universe without."[39] Here, the artist, like the Tao itself, becomes a seat of creativity and thereby produces transcendent beauty.

Recently, Sircello has developed a theory of beauty in which, for example, ". . . single notes in isolation can be beautiful . . ."[40] For him, that which is beautiful possesses one or more properties of qualitative degree (PQD)—an object can only be beautiful if it has such a property to a very great degree; thus, if the color of an object is beautiful, it possesses, for instance, considerable vividness.[41] On his last page, Sircello approaches the Taoist spirit: "In perceiving beauty we seem to be perceiving with a much greater degree of clarity than our ordinary perception has . . . we are filled, if only for a moment and if only in a limited respect, by a feeling of transcendent well-being."[42] A few pages earlier, however, Sircello declares, "I emphasize that, while the perception of beauty is necessarily clear perception, it is not perception that is, literally speaking, more clear than ordinary clear perception of ordinary, less-than-beautiful properties."[43] In the end, Sircello's is a naturalistic theory of beauty rather than a metaphysical theory of transcendent beauty. While he can appreciate the beauty of a vivid color, he is unable to enjoy "muddy colors."[44] Taoists, for whom the invisible Tao animates all things, can appreciate the "muddy" and even yearn to become one with the dusty world. In short, the Taoist's aesthetic experience of nature is rich, because muddy as well as vibrant colors possess full-fledged aesthetic value.

Contextualists often try to discover an artist's intentions in order to interpret or judge her work. Interestingly enough, Bernard Bosanquet appeals to a lack of intentions in order to argue that nature is never ugly: "If the intentional attempt at beauty is the main condition of ugliness, then in nature the main condition of ugliness is certainly absent, while immeasurable stores of form and order are as certainly present for those who can elicit them."[45] For him, without unfulfilled intentions, there can be no aesthetic failure. Since he will not impute to nature any conscious attempt at beautiful expression, so-called natural ugliness must follow from one's failure to detect beautiful forms amidst nature's boundless riches. Another contextualist, Stephen C. Pepper, also rejects the positive existence of ugliness, characterizing it in terms of unfulfilled intentions or unrealized value. As some theologians argue that there is no evil, since it is merely an absence of the good, Pepper argues that ugliness has the status of a privation: "Ugliness is moral disapproval of the absence of aesthetic value in a situation. It is an ethical rather than an aesthetic evaluation."[46] In this sense, ugliness is an absence rather than a presence, a nonentity rather than a positive reality.

Bosanquet's reasoning to show that nature is never ugly applies to the operations of the Tao, for the latter acts without intention. To intend is to calculate, deliberate, reflect, or desire, but any such ratiocination is at odds with the spontaneity of the Tao. Therefore, the *Tao Te Ching* warns: "When people become aware of beauty as beauty, ugliness is discerned." In other words, when people know beauty as an idea, then its correlative idea "ugliness" arises. Of course, such intellectual classification is quite different from the Taoist ideal of entering the distinctionless void. If one's intuitive perspective yields to the categorizing turn of mind, his direct grasp of beauty gives way to an indirect, inferential apprehension. Therefore, Pepper underlines the significance of intuition in grasping beauty, i.e., enhanced quality:

> Now, let us increase fusion, intuition, and quality, and decrease discrimination, analysis and relations. Let us carry this to a maximum where all details vanish and a rich quality takes full possession of the event. Here we have pure intuition. If the quality is very intense, it is sometimes called ecstasy.[47]

The intellect that identifies beauty, rather than savors it, also identifies the ugly. Conceptual understanding, with its analyses and distinctions, prevents one from enjoying a holistic grasp of the object. Wing-tsit Chan remarks: "In the philosophy of Lao Tzu, names, whether in the sense of analytical concepts or in the sense of fame and titles, break up original unity and simplicity and give rise to intellectual cunning and social discrimination."[48]

Nature cannot be ugly for the Taoist, since his intuitive, holistic appreciation of nature carries him beyond any superficial distinctions between the beautiful and the ugly. Abandoning intellectual classifications, the sage transcends relative distinctions in order to enjoy the invisible beauty of the Tao together with the perceivable beauty of all things that shimmer with its radiance. In the *Commentary on Lao Tzu by Wang Pi,* one finds: "Common folk see differences and are clear-cut; that means to differentiate and analyze (to make distinctions). I alone make no distinctions."[49] Applying this distinction-free consciousness to aesthetics, the text adds: "If one begins to distinguish or to divide, one cannot control the whole. Therefore that which has sound is not great music."[50] However paradoxical it may appear, Taoists believe that the greatest music is inaudible, for it contains the heavenly harmony of Tao. Audible tunes—no matter how delightful to the physical ear—remain of earthly or penultimate worth: "Where there is sound, there are parts..."[51] Chapter fourteen of the *Tao Te Ching* declares: "People listen to it [the Tao] but cannot hear it; its name is the inaudible."

The beauty of mundane objects is superficial or merely decorative—if one abstracts it from its metaphysical mooring in the Tao: "Drawing sustenance from Mother [Tao] is the root of life. All others reject the root which gives life to people, but honor the flower or unimportant ornaments."[52] Apart from their rootedness in the Tao, things possess only a sensuous, manifest beauty. Apart from its manifold offspring, the Tao, like the Judeo-Christian God, the Dharmakaya, or Brahman, possesses a spiritual beauty that one can intuit but not perceive. C.Y. Chang uses the terms "creativity" and "sympathy" in order to characterize the egress and reflux of the Tao,[53] for it is in their unimpeded emergence from and return to the Tao that all things express beauty.

As one learns from the "mountains and rivers" illustration, in aesthetic-religious experiences, the perceivable particulars and the imperceptible universal interpenetrate; physical beauty and spiritual beauty interfuse. To an individual who has attained this vision, no natural object is unmitigatedly ugly. Bosanquet observes that for Plotinus nothing is wholly ugly, for the beautiful is whatever expresses reason, law or principles; and everything, to some extent, does so: "... we know of nothing in which law is not revealed."[54] Of course, the Tao is a kind of logos or law of laws that ensures the harmonious flow of the universe. One who goes against the grain of nature acts unaesthetically, but any resultant "ugliness" belongs to human nature rather than nature as such. To equate the aesthetic with the lawful calls to mind the regularity, order, proportion, form, or balance that Greek aesthetics emphasized and which Nietzsche found to be desperately lacking in the natural world: "Imagine a being like nature, wasteful beyond measure, indifferent beyond measure, without purposes and consideration, without mercy and justice, fertile and desolate and uncertain at the same time ..."[55] In *The Future of an Illusion*, Freud also dwells upon the threatening aspects of nature. Rather than recoil from nature, Taoists have created archetypal landscape paintings and underlined their harmony with nature by depicting themselves in such scenes.

6

The Child-State and Revelation

All religions urge one to return to the child-state, i.e., to the beauty of the childlike consciousness that nourishes art as well as spirituality. Achieving a pristine mind is the objective, whether such innocence signifies a return to creativity or to holiness. Accordingly, the child symbolizes the ideal; and the sage of the *Tao Te Ching,* for example, returns to the condition of an infant. In a related metaphor, Taoism advocates return to the uncarved block, which represents the undifferentiated Tao, in order that one can create art that possesses childlike simplicity. Like an infant, the sage and the religious artist are receptive, flexible, and responsive to their surroundings. Their vision is free of prejudices, be they the mistaken dogmas of religion or the entrenched manifestoes of the art academy; therefore, they have the unlimited latitude for spiritual or creative action. In the *Tao Te Ching,* return is central to religion and art, because it leads to concord, oneness, or harmony. Again, Christ warned his disciples that unless they became as little children, they could not enter the kingdom of heaven. In the Confucian tradition, Mencius emphasizes that the great man retains the heart of a newborn babe. Part of the appeal of children is that they are generally less judgmental than adults, as artists are apt to be less judgmental than art critics and mystics less so than their detractors. Perhaps the fact that children have acquired fewer prejudices renders them more open, as in the story of the Emperor's New Clothes. Often the child, the artist,

133

and saint want to unite with the other rather than merely analyze
or evaluate it.

As noted previously, van Gogh sensed something of the divine
in the child at rest. In a letter, Gauguin recognizes the aesthetic
status of the child in Tahiti:

> I shall soon be a father again. . . . Good heavens, I seem to sow
> everywhere! But here it does no harm, for children are wel-
> come and are spoken for in advance by all the relatives. It's
> a struggle as to who should be the mother and father nurses.
> For you know that in Tahiti a child is the most beautiful
> present one can give.[1]

Of course, the child often epitomizes both purity of spirit and the
receptivity that is the foundation of all creativity. A childlike attitude has spiritual and aesthetic dimensions, for they both require
that one subdue the ego and see things with a fresh receptivity
that is unfettered by any exclusively practical considerations. When
one asks Hindus why God creates, they sometimes compare the
divine to a child at play. This is to suggest that God creates for
aesthetic instead of utilitarian reasons. Like the child or the artist,
God obeys no external rules, only those that he imposes upon
himself.

Scriptures sometimes recognize children for their special knowledge; thus Jesus thanks his Father for what he has hidden from
the learned but revealed to babes (Luke 10:21). Indeed, in the New
Testament, even the fetus may exercise insight. When Mary, pregnant with Jesus, visited Elizabeth, no one knew of Mary's condition, but the little unborn in Elizabeth leapt with joy, somehow
realizing that God was present. Children see more directly, because
they are unaware of the theories and abstractions that adults project
upon a situation. Free of preconceptions, the child has the latitude
to be creative and spiritual. Like the child, the mystic and the
artist put a premium upon immediate, intuitive experiences. Concepts, after all, are no substitute for concrete, lived existence, for
the vital reality that transcends all abstractions. Children at play,
with no thought of yesterday or tomorrow, participate in the "present
moment" that also nourishes the artist and the mystic.

The artist is characteristically more childlike than other adults.
Like Peter Pan, who never grows up, she persists in the activities
that others usually surrender with their youth: drawing, painting,
sculpting, dancing, singing, building, and writing. It is probably no

accident that fairy tales discuss "forever afters" as much as religions discuss immortality. Interestingly enough, the present Dalai Lama exhibits a childlike openness and a playful disposition. Still, the artist or saint is not someone who stays a child or refuses to grow up; rather, she incorporates her childhood into her growth. As Frank Barron notes, "Creative individuals retain qualities of freshness, spontaneity and joy, as well as a certain lack of cautious reality-testing—openness to the nonrational, if you will. They are in that sense childlike. But this is not regression, it is progression with courage. They bring their childhood along instead of leaving it behind."[2] In his exuberant paintings, Marc Chagall demonstrates such a carrying forward of one's early life. A childhood familiarity with farm animals influenced his tendency to juxtapose humans and animals in works such as *I and the Village,* in which man and goat meet face to face. Given the Hassidism of his parents, it is hardly surprising that Chagall's paintings are sometimes powerful expressions of the mystical, intimate link between humans and animals. Children's art invariably turns to animals and expresses affinities between humans and animals. For Francis, bridging the gap between humans and animals—an activity at which children excel—is surely a step toward reducing the chasm between humans and the divine. Reflecting the child's fascination with beings that are at once like and different from humans, the mystic has a tendency to regard humans and animals as interdependent, to seek harmony between the two, and in some cases to declare the indistinguishability or inseparability of the two. This continuity or identity between man and nature is nowhere more evident than in Taoism. Chuang Tzu once awakened from a dream in which he had been a butterfly and asked himself if he were now a butterfly who was dreaming that he was a man. A visual counterpart to this literary illustration exists in Shih K'o's tenth-century painting of a monk and tiger together at rest.

Describing his religious life as simple, Henri Nouwen speaks very appropriately of this kind of acquired simplicity as a "second naiveté,"[3] an expression that is just as applicable to the artist, because, as Belden C. Lane points out, this second naiveté involves the restoration of wonder.[4] First naiveté involves an unrestrained openness, but second naiveté brings an openness that experience enriches, a more scrupulous, rigorous receptivity. One now appreciates the truth, "Mountains are mountains and rivers are rivers," on a deeper level. While the second naiveté rekindles openmindedness, first-naiveté runs the risk of being empty-headed, i.e., altogether uncritical.

In the end, the hunger for return, which one finds in the literature of childhood, whether *Alice's Adventures in Wonderland* or *The Wonderful Wizard of Oz,* is a search for harmony, for return to one's origin, for this alone yields wholeness. Not only is it necessary to return, but she is not fully herself unless she does. Lane yearns for such a return, "How do I discover the second naiveté of which Paul Ricoeur speaks—the hard-won ability to reclaim the vitalities of myth on the far shore of critical suspicion? How can I be there again, without also denying all that I have since become?"[5] Next, Lane proposes that remembering is a way to retrieve religious states. Of course, one can interpret art as a way of recollection that is not simply a going back, but a re-collection of the self into a second naiveté.

Some thinkers attribute irrationality to the artist, saint, and the child alike. For a driven artist like van Gogh, who amputated part of his own ear, for Francis, who lived in a hole in the ground— not a cave but a cavity in the earth—there is a counterpart in the free play of children. Indeed, until a child is seven years old, society says that he has not attained the "age of reason." Moreover, one may compare the fantasies of a child with the wish-driven, irrational yearnings that Freudians attribute to artists and mystics alike. John M. MacGregor's *The Discovery of the Art* of the Insane, demonstrates that the art of the mentally ill has not yet found its way into the art world, i.e., the realm of art museums, prestigious exhibitions, fashionable galleries, critics, and art historians. Of course, one may say the same of the art of children.

The theme of returning appears in the second and third parts of *I and Thou*: "Return signifies the re-cognition of the center, turning back to it again."[6] One returns in order to rediscover what is central to all existence. One can only go so far away before he must try to come home again. As Alexander S. Kohanski states: "Return means complete, wholehearted turning toward the Thou."[7] According to Buber, each I is born with an innate Thou; and, until the individual's pristine, paired, and pairing nature is fulfilled, she will be greatly discontent. Because the congenital yearning to relate is universal, the artist also reaches back for the integrity of his original nature. Returning requires not just a different goal, but also a different sort of movement.[8] The manipulative, practical movement is superseded by the aesthetic, relational movement of the I gravitating toward and, ideally, being met by a Thou.

At times the child motif is inseparable from that of the noble savage. When a young Tahitian described Gauguin as "useful to others," the artist replied, "I indeed believe Totefa is the first human being in the world to use such words toward me. It was the language of a savage or a child, for one must be either one of these—must one not?—to imagine that an artist might be a useful human being."[9] Of course, some people would find it difficult to imagine that a religious figure might be a useful human being. Gauguin also unites the themes of "letting go" or eliminating the inessential—in Taoist terms, "losing day by day"—and the child:

> For my part I soon gave up all these conscious efforts [to grasp a Maori soul] which so interfered with the enjoyment of life. I let myself live simply, waiting confidently in the course of time for the revelations which the first moments had refused. A week went by during which I had a feeling of "child-likeness" such as I have never before experienced.[10]

As Gauguin's new life restored him to a childlike state, the medieval mystic, Hildegard of Bingen, found a taste of youth in her visions: "I see another light called the 'living light.' When and how I see it I cannot say but, during the time I see it, all sadness and anguish disappear, so that I seem to be an innocent young girl and not an old woman."[11] Cliff Edwards, author of *Van Gogh and God,* has observed that, following his spiritual rejuvenation, Charles Dickens's Scrooge declares: "I don't know anything, I'm quite a baby." Of course, a Taoist who divests himself of mundane knowledge becomes an "infant" again. When Lao Tzu says that the sage keeps people ignorant and thereby treats them as if they were children, such ignorance refers to simplicity and innocence, the absence of cleverness and guile. In place of conventional knowledge, the Taoist embraces "ignorance" or the "knowledge of no-knowledge." Ever suspicious of the limits of rational knowledge, he pursues loftier knowledge, i.e., an immediate, intuitive realization that surpasses discursive categories. Similarly, Tolstoy inveighs against the intellectualism or rationalism of the art schools; and a contemporary Hindu has observed that his school of Vedantic thought should be so free of intellectualizing that even a child could grasp it.

For the artist, return can trigger a spontaneous outpouring of creativity that is unrestricted by internal inhibitions and the external dictates of the academy. For the saint, return brings a grasp of what is and of who one is. Return also fosters the capacity for instantaneous forgiveness that is so evident in the love of children—a love that is pure and unconditional. Indeed, the person who is to love even his enemies must become like a child. If one becomes a child once more, he reexperiences a freedom and purity that are beyond concealment. Nothing less from the world of adults manifests the bliss, luminosity, and expressiveness of children's art. One recalls that Picasso was unable to produce childlike art until he himself had played with the exuberance of a child. If, like Tolstoy, one regards sincerity and the communication of fellow feeling as essential to art, the spirituality of children's art is incontestable. To a child every object is fresh, i.e., aesthetically arresting, since she has not yet consigned it to the oblivion of familiarity; and it is also fresh in the sense of being innocent, morally good rather than evil. A child takes things at face value until they prove to be otherwise. On a deeper level, a child can find every object to be spiritually significant, since it poses the mystery of its own origin and reason for being.

Return to a childlike state brings about a revelation, but revelations—according to Otto—are neither clear nor distinct: "God is approached more nearly in that which is indefinite than in that which is definite and distinct. He is felt in awe and wonder and worship rather than in clear conception. There is a sense in which darkness has more of God than lightness has."[12] Art and religion invite one to participate in the indefinite, the indefinable, or the ineffable. Anything more delimited could hardly inspire sublimity or worship. This indistinctness is not, however, tantamount to inarticulateness; the indefinite can be revelatory. The same Chinese characters, *hun t'un,* that one may translate as "unformed darkness" also suggest the "harmonious atmosphere" from which illumination issues forth. As in past ages, artists pursue art as a route to truth and ultimate reality; Chinese painting, for example, has long been directed toward disclosure of the Tao, but this is only possible if there is a true interpenetration of the artist and nature. In this exchange between the self and nature, one achieves a spiritual harmony and a taste of the Tao. Yen Yu, a prominent twelfth-century poetry critic, affirmed a revelatory kinship between religion and art: "Generally speaking, the Way of Buddhism lies on enlightenment. The way of poetry also lies on enlightenment."[13] Along with self-integration or union with the divine, a major purpose of aesthetic experience and religious experience is the revelation or uncovering of a profound reality. Union and revelation are reciprocal forces; every union reveals a fresh reality; and every revelation reinforces union with the divine.

With a metaphysical theory of art, i.e., one according to which art yields a glimpse of what is beyond the material world, art itself receives its full due, for it is revelatory of reality rather than a mere frill. According to Alfred North Whitehead, "Art at its highest exemplifies the metaphysical doctrine of the interweaving of absoluteness upon relativity."[14] Coomaraswamy quotes approvingly from Vishvanatha, who spoke of aesthetic experience as "the very twin brother of mystic experience . . . ," and concludes: "Religion and art are thus names for one and the same experience—an intuition of reality and of identity."[15] Just as revelation is a central theme in religion, it is a basic pursuit of art. Thus, Martin Heidegger held that the essence of art is: ". . . the setting-itself-into-work of the truth of what is . . ."[16] Art is disclosure, "disconcealment," truth released of all obfuscations and obstructions. Explaining how artworks can move one so powerfully, Clive Bell volunteers, " 'Because artists can express in combinations of lines and colours an emotion felt for reality which reveals itself through line and colour?' "[17] While many artists and religious figures seek insight or an unmediated realization, scientific knowledge requires the mediation of logical reasoning, whether by deduction, induction, abstraction, extrapolation, or speculation. By contrast, fundamental aesthetic and spiritual truths may arrive quickly—with the swiftness of an arrow hitting its target. Therefore, artists and saints talk of sudden illuminations, insights, inspirations, realizations, and enlightenments. The claim is that an instantaneous awakening can supersede time-consuming, inferential thinking. Of course, some question if such intuitions are veridical and demand proofs, arguments, or additional reasons to support the assertions of artists and religious figures. One reply to the skeptic invites him to contemplate artistic masterpieces in order to glean for himself their epistemological import. The believer can urge the skeptic to be an empiricist and to let his own aesthetic experience decide the case. This necessarily involves entering into an I-Thou dialogue with artistic masterpieces. Every I has the power to change the It of such a painting into a Thou; every such painting has the power to change the I, i.e., to engage and to actualize the I. Ideally, one's aesthetic encounter culminates in a communion with the eternal Thou. Of course, such an I-Thou moment demonstrates the revelatory power of art much more convincingly than could any intellectual proofs.

The limits of reason inspire a further response to the skeptic, for Immanuel Kant's discussion of antinomies, i.e., antithetical metaphysical assertions, demonstrates that some fundamentally opposed views are equally defensible. For example, even after centuries, philosophers continue to debate the existence of God. It is also clear that artists continue to disagree on the canons of great art. In short, the deepest truths of art and religion are beyond rational determination. Of course, this is not to diminish the awe-some powers of reason in its own domain. It is just that reason has limits and cannot set forth a formula for creating a great artwork, nor can it conclusively prove the truth or falsity of religious doc-trines. Given such limits, one may wish to consider the hypothesis that intuition can provide the way to foundational truths. Intu-itionism or super-rationalism, which elevates intuition over reason, is the view that ultimate truths are accessible by transcending reason through mystical experience or artistic inspiration. The main argument for super-rationalism has two premises:

1. Philosophical arguments, for more than two millennia, have patently failed to establish universal truths;
2. Some philosophers in the West, and especially in the East, advocate going beyond theses and anti-theses through di-rect knowledge, insight, or intuition.

From these premises, the intuitionist concludes that one should be enough of an empiricist to try the age-old path of direct experience or intuition. After all, philosophical arguments from Plato to the present have not settled one fundamental philosophical question. Moreover, many mystics, who have found success with their intui-tive approach, simply invite others to follow suit. Their point is that by emptying the mind of pros and cons, speculations, and proofs, one leaves room for the dawning of enlightenment. Often, mystics lead exemplary ethical lives and create artistic master-pieces that add weight to their case. After all, art is a quest for truths and the artworks of the world's mystics are often paradigms of aesthetic greatness.

One may also argue that imperfect humans could not possibly conjure up the lofty ideals of art and religion: aesthetic perfection and spiritual perfection. Moreover, for some, the ultimacy and ur-gency of such aims and their social significance—one may elevate either to the supreme, governing principle in one's life—count in favor of their legitimacy. Many, following William James, would add that one should judge the nature of people's interior states by their fruits or actions. Thomas Merton, for example, turned to the artistic productions of a people for evidence of their spiritual in-sight: "Could the Shakers do the perfect work they did (in their furniture, for instance) if their vision were not real? The witness of their craftsmanship is certainly most impressive."[18] Indeed, all the great religions appeal through their artistic contributions; these expressions strike a responsive chord in the beholder and point to more comprehensive truths.

Others argue that the empiricist habit of focusing upon outer experience, observation, and perceptions should not eclipse the significance of inner experience, introspection, and intuitions. One's interior life should be no less thematic than his sense perceptions. Surely an important test of the veracity of an inner experience lies in how well it coheres with other inner experiences. Religious and aesthetic insights should cohere with each other and with one's other profound experiences such as love. As one corroborates sense experiences by other sense experiences—"First I thought I saw a bird, but my flashlight revealed a bat"—one can only confirm his richest affective, interior experiences by means of other interior experiences. When a work of art elicits an aesthetic experience that reinforces one's fellow feeling, the moral value of the work is obvious. And when an artist's awakening gives rise to masterpieces, their aesthetic value counts in favor of their epistemological value for any who hold that truth and beauty are continuous.

Emphasizing that the artist is not a mere copyist, the painter Paul Klee has declared: "Art does not reproduce the visible; rather, it makes visible."[19] In fine, art delivers an insight into the metaphysical. Likewise, Coomaraswamy describes the artist of the *Upanishads* as one who, through the symbolic representation of Brahman, tries to render the invisible visible.[20] Hegel agrees that the end of art involves: ". . . the sensuous presentation of the absolute itself."[21] Chagall sympathizes, "The vital thing is to represent those elements of the world which are not visible, not to reproduce whatever we see in nature."[22] Gauguin, whom Chagall called "the only revolutionary" of his day, also views art as a bridge between the visible and invisible. An island lover once remarked: "Gauguin's paintings of islands are not really paintings of islands; the colors are too otherworldly for even the most exotic island setting." Asked what else Gauguin might be depicting, the traveller replied: "Images of heaven, shangri la, nirvana." Later, it did not surprise the traveller to read of the painter's spiritual interest. After referring to the forms and colors in his island landscapes, Gauguin asks, "To catch a glimpse of blessedness, is that not a foretaste of nirvana?"[23] All the above illustrate the metaphysical conception of art in which one conceives of art as a vehicle for reflecting spiritual reality, be it God, the Atman, or Nirvana. As previously noted, Schleiermacher refused to speculate on the connection between art and religion, but even he affirms a metaphysical theory of art. Speaking about "sudden conversions," people thinking about "lifting themselves above the finite," and the resultant "inward illumination," Schleiermacher remarks: "More than anything else a great and sublime work of art can accomplish this miracle."[24] In other words, even if theological discourse cannot communicate the infinite, artworks can do better. In any case, Westerners such as Schleiermacher understood art as a revelation of the infinite in the finite. To the spiritually inclined, the physical world does not exhaust reality; for they sense something "more." Kandinsky seeks an interior "more" and wants to communicate something other than the ego, namely, the soul that animates the body, the internal truth that only art can express.[25] Of course, the wider "more" is the absolute, and Kandinsky states that Matisse's pictures are attempts to reproduce the divine.[26] Here arises the aesthetic paradox of immanence and transcendence: although rooted in the material sphere, an artwork may transport the beholder to an ideal realm. While some artists and religious thinkers subscribe to the notion of art as revelation of the invisible and transcendental, others cry for a discovery of that which is perceivable and close at hand. Picasso astutely notes: "We always have roosters, but like everything else in life we must discover them. Just as Corot discovered the morning and Renoir discovered little girls. Everything must be discovered. . . . Roosters have always been seen but seldom so well as in American weather vanes."[27] Of course, the artist who represents visible forms may be doing so in order to convey something of the invisible— either the spirit of the artist or the necessarily invisible, inner force, or spiritual energy *(ch'i)*, which animates the thematic objects.

Another defense of super-rationalism concedes that there are no decisive arguments for it, but adds that one might expect this, since any intuition of the metaphysical is necessarily an ineffable experience. Art tries to convey what one can never fully convey. Great aesthetic experiences and profound religious experiences are always ineffable to some degree. One reason for their ineffability lies in the uniqueness of what one encounters—whether it is Clive Bell's one-of-a-kind aesthetic emotion, a state that he asserts is like nothing else, or Otto's "wholly other." A second reason lies in their inexhaustibility. No exposition of such experiences is ever complete, with all nuances articulated; indeed, what is central in such experiences is necessarily immune to explanation. Hence, ineffability is a universal hallmark of mystical states of consciousness. Of Monet's work, Chagall said, "There just aren't the words to talk about his painting."[28] In the classic article, "Aesthetic Concepts,"[29] Frank Sibley argues that however much one knows about a painting in advance of seeing it, however exhaustively someone describes it, one cannot judge the work aesthetically until he beholds it. The reason is that classificatory labels or concepts—no matter how many or how informative—are no substitute for the concrete impressions and feelings that arise on beholding a work as an aesthetic gestalt. Tillich agrees: "One cannot interpret a picture by stating its meaning in discursive sentences and then dispensing with the visual form. Every work of art—a poem, picture, piece of music—has something to say directly to its audience that cannot be expressed by scientific formulas or the language of everyday experience."[30] Suzuki submits that if one applies conventional language to the spiritual, such discourse, "... becomes warped and assumes all kinds of crookedness: oxymora, paradoxes, contradictions, contortions, absurdities, oddities, ambiguities and irrationalities."[31] Therefore, one purpose of religious symbols is to unite two worlds—the seemingly transparent domain of everyday life and the opaque realm that may be unknown but still posited, because spiritual and aesthetic experiences render one unable to believe that the ordinary world exhausts what there is. In the end, Sibley's essay underlines the significance of the experiential over the conceptual. Religious parallels abound; for example, the intellectual study of world religions is profoundly different from a vital participation in the rituals, prayers, and sacraments of a particular tradition. Otto's term "numinous" refers to the divine as transcendent of rational thought; and whatever one cannot intellectually grasp is ineffable. Of course, meanings that elude prose may yield to the artistic language of poetry and symbolism.

To affirm that which transcends ordinary discourse, some adopt negative language. Defenders of the way of negation hold that it is preferable to making false affirmations. Hence, Chagall called spiritual reality "unreality,"[32] Taoists refer to ultimate reality as *wu* or "nothing," and Zen Buddhists affirm that ultimate reality consists of: "vast emptiness with nothing holy in it!" As the first sentence of the *Tao Te Ching* states: "The Tao that can be spoken of is not the eternal Tao." In a similar vein, the Christian mystic Meister Eckhart speaks of the ultimate Godhead as nothing, but he also talks about the soul passing into this divine abyss of nothingness. Indian sages reply "neti, neti" ("not this, not this") when asked to describe Brahman. Of course, *śūnyattā,* the Buddhist term for "emptiness," does not refer to a literal vacuum. To the contrary, such "nothingness" pertains to an immeasurable plenitude, to an indescribably fecund reality. Similarly, the spaces in Sung dynasty landscape paintings make a positive contribution—they invite the viewer to "enter" the works and they also hint at an invisible reality. Moving from the visual to the auditory, silence holds a similar status. Discussing the tendency of Amerindian cultures to be more at ease with silence than Americans in general, Lane notes, "Silence, then, is not absence, but a different form of presence, a subtler expression of meaning."[33]

It is no wonder that so many soul searchers enter the vast emptiness of the desert, for the magnitude of its space is no less expressive of the divine than are the most soaring mountains. Again, not surprisingly, naturalists experience awe before the aesthetic power of the desert, with its haunting starkness, unlikely creatures, and subtle colors that stain even shadows. Nevertheless, the isolation of the desert or ivory tower is not always the ideal setting for contemplation. Suffering from distracted and dissipated thought, Teresa once remarked: "I . . . began to envy those who dwell in desert places; thinking that, as they see and hear nothing, they are exempt from distractions. I heard this: 'Thou art greatly deceived, My daughter, on the contrary, the temptations of Satan are more violent there.' "[34]

Some challenge the potency of art to disclose reality. "Art does not provide us with the meaning of human existence,"[35] Nicholas Wolterstorff insists, because he believes that it is the gospel of Christ which alone accomplishes that task. A critic of Wolterstorff might assert that it is precisely through artworks that the divine elects to "provide us with the meaning of human existence." After all, as discussed earlier, the religious aesthetics of Tolstoy and Tillich give preeminence to the meaning of life. Furthermore, a preoccupation with the meaning of existence is hardly foreign to artists such as Gauguin who ask: "Where do we come from? What are we? Where are we going?" In addition, Wolterstorff's claim raises the question of how non-Christian traditions might come to discover the significance of human existence. In his next sentence, he states: "Art is not a way of rising toward God." But how can one limit the means by which God raises up his children? In fact, art or aesthetic contemplation, from Plotinus to Tillich, is often understood as just such a ladder for ascending to the divine. The activity of religion always involves following a way, tao, *marga*, path, or highway; and art too is a way or road that frequently intersects with the religious route.

To assert that art and religion are revelatory is not to say that they are primarily intellectual pursuits. In truth, an anti-intellectual current runs through both. It was religious fervor, rather than erudition, that kindled Francis's love of nature. Accordingly, Julien Green has remarked that the youthful Francis learned little, as though he wanted to leave a void that only the Gospel could fill.[36] As Tolstoy elevated religious sentiment over formal education, Francis emphasized a spiritual understanding—a synthesis of self-realization and dedication to God—over worldly knowledge. It is here that Allen Carlson's thesis concerning the aesthetic appreciation of nature falters, for Francis, an exemplary appreciator of nature, does not rely upon the knowledge of a naturalist. Uneducated himself, Francis urged his brothers to be men of spirit rather than men of letters: "And those who are illiterate should not be eager to learn. . . . Instead let them pursue what they must desire above all things: to have the Spirit of the Lord and His holy manner of working."[37] Gauguin was of a like mind concerning artists: ". . . painters are never in need either of support or of instruction from men of letters."[38] Also disparaging intellectual abstractions, Tolstoy argues that art should be intelligible to all humankind, for if art is truly important, rather than a mere frill, it ought to be available to all. He defines art as the communication of feelings that flow from a religious perspective and concludes that such feelings can hardly be incomprehensible, ". . . because every man's relation to God is one and the same."[39] Earlier, he defends the universality of art: "Great works of art are only great because they are accessible and comprehensible to everyone. The story of Joseph, translated into the Chinese language, touches a Chinese. The story of Sakya Muni [the historic Buddha] touches us."[40] Tolstoy distinguishes between art and an act of intellect on the grounds that only the former can move people irrespective of their intellectual development and education: ". . . the charm of a picture, sounds, or of forms infects any man whatever his plane of development."[41] After emphasizing the preeminence of feeling in art, Tolstoy remarks:

> Professional schools produce an hypocrisy of art precisely akin to the hypocrisy of religion which is produced by theological colleges for training priests, pastors, and religion teachers generally. As it is impossible in a school to train a man so as to make a religious teacher of him, so it is impossible to teach a man how to become an artist.[42]

Tolstoy identifies a feeling, a sense of infection with another's feelings, as the essence of art. This feeling is familiar to the simplest people and even to children, but it is foreign to those who relish discussions of art.[43] The feeling, of course, is one of union with the artist and with others whom he similarly infects. Although Tolstoy mentions that ". . . the subject matter of Christian art is such feeling as can unite men with God and with one another,"[44] he tends to emphasize the latter sort of union.

The I-Thou perspective is inherently anti-intellectual. Of course, intellectual analysis may precede, but it never leads directly to the I-Thou relation. If one intellectualizes and abstracts, the other becomes an It, i.e., an object of analysis, but if one beholds, the other stands before the I as a Thou.[45] To know experientially is not to conceptualize or classify, but to directly encounter a unique Thou. This I-Thou awareness is concrete, direct, unmediated, and intuitive. By contrast, ratiocination is abstract, indirect, mediated, and conceptual. One who adopts an I-Thou perspective is beyond the distinctions of the analytic mind, as one must also be for the deepest art appreciation. Philip Wheelwright explains, "To speak significantly of God is not to talk about, but to address Him and (what is more essential) to be addressed by Him and respond to Him. God, in short, is not a he or she or it or they, but Thou."[46] Art lovers may think similarly in their encounters with masterpieces. Perhaps this helps explain why some flinch at the objectifying language of art criticism. In addition, the sale of artistic treasures can be disturbing, because "Thous" inhabit them, namely, the spirits of their artists who continue to address the beholder. One painting (*St. Eligius,* 1449, The Metropolitan Museum of Art, New York) by Petrus Christus, a follower of Jan van Eyck, dramatically testifies to the artist's regard for his work as a Thou, for the inscription reads: "Master Petrus Christus made me in the year 1449."

Buber's anti-intellectualism is evident in his claim that: "The world is not comprehensible, but it is embraceable: through the embracing of one of its beings."[47] It is equally true that although one's favorite artwork is never fully intelligible, she may nevertheless passionately appreciate it. Just as it is more important to encounter than to theorize about the divine, one should "meet" the great painting rather than merely interpret or analyze it. As with the highest flights of theology and philosophy, there is something incontestably penultimate about the best sort of art criticism. The I-It posture tries to analyze, explain, and quantify the world, but the live qualities of the world escape such a perspective. At their foundations, religion and art are beyond words. On this level, they lend themselves to being welcomed and appropriated rather than intellectually unravelled. Buber comments accordingly on the ultimate stance that we can adopt,

Only silence toward the You, the silence of all tongues, the taciturn waiting in the unformed, undifferentiated, prelinguistic word leaves the You free and stands together with it in reserve where the spirit does not manifest itself but is. All response binds the You into the It-world.[48]

To Chrysostom's declaration," He insults God who seeks to apprehend his essential being," one might reply: "He insults the artist who seeks to analyze the essence of his work."

Francis's anti-intellectualism toward the aesthetic experience of nature has its contemporary supporters. Edward Abbey's appreciation of the desert, for example, deprecates the conceptual: "I want to be able to look at and into a juniper tree, a piece of quartz, a vulture, a spider and see it as it is in itself, devoid of all humanly ascribed qualities, anti-Kantian, even the categories of scientific description."[49] The preeminent American naturalist John Muir sympathizes: "I have a low opinion of books. . . . One day's exposure to mountains is better than cartloads of books."[50] Indeed, even the critical rationalist Kant argues that the lay person's aesthetic judgment of a bird has a purity and an immediacy that is lacking in that of the ornithologist who engages in conceptual thinking, classifying, and evaluating according to standards of perfection. By contrast, the non-specialist is free to focus solely upon the formal qualities of the bird. Of course, Taoism enjoins one to "lose day by day," i.e., to slough off ratiocination, in order to harmonize with nature.

Illustrations of anti-intellectualism abound in the world religions. Representing Islam, Khaliq Ahmad Nizami comments: "The praise of illiteracy as the foundation of true or intuitive knowledge is frequent in South Asian Sufism."[51] Teresa reports that when she expressed regret, because she could not read some books that were in Latin, the Lord himself addressed and consoled her: "Be not troubled; I will give thee a living book."[52] A few days later, she observed: "I had little or no need whatever of books."[53] Of course, Thomas à Kempis and others would emphasize that there is nothing wrong with learning as such: ". . . but a clean conscience and a virtuous life are much better and more to be desired."[54] Augustine, a voluminous writer himself, praises: ". . . the just ones and the holy ones who rejoice in the word of God without reading, without letters. For whatever is written to us on pages, they discover through the Face of God."[55]

As religion distinguishes between the ego and the true self, it also acknowledges two corresponding kinds of knowledge, conventional knowledge and wisdom. Taoists contrast the "small knowledge" of the cunning and clever man with the "genuine knowledge" of the sage. To one degree or another, religions champion the latter over the former. Amish students conclude their formal education with the eighth grade, lest continued study nourish the ego. For John of the Cross, the role of faith is to darken ordinary understanding as a preparation for the union with God that alone can yield divine wisdom.[56] One thinks here of Zen Buddhist koans, i.e., puzzles that defy intellectual solution but facilitate meditation. The purpose of such conundrums is to serve as tools that bring ordinary, discursive thinking to a stop in order that enlightenment can dawn. Similarly, Frank Barron observes: "The artist often sees rational thought not, merely as an enemy but as a prison from which he must struggle to get free."[57] One achieves superior knowledge through an intuitive illumination that erupts only after one relegates discursive knowledge to its proper place. In a similar spirit, Teresa urges: ". . . when the soul is in the prayer of quiet, let it repose in its rest—let learning be put to one side."[58] She also reports that in the highest state of prayer, the senses and conception atrophy.[59] Discussing the union of the soul with God, Teresa explains why she is reluctant to intellectualize about her spiritual encounters. "During the time that the union lasts the soul is left as though without its senses, for it has no power to think even if it wants to . . . it is like one who in every respect has died to the world so as to live more completely in God."[60] Perhaps the artist is similarly reluctant to analyze her work, because during the creative act, something other than the routine intellect is at work. Moreover, the artist's all-consuming immersion in her project entails that she has died to the world of mundane distractions. Still, for Teresa, the intellect is not altogether out of the picture; instead, she speaks of it as a bystander during the union of the soul and God: "There is no reason for the intellect to stir . . . [but] through a small crevice it might observe what is taking place."[61]

Scholarship or erudition has long been suspect in artistic as well as religious communities. Witness Tolstoy's sustained and withering critique of art education in *What is Art?*. He charges that instruction undermines the artist's sincerity, i.e., disposition to feel the emotions that she transmits. Nevertheless, theoreticians from Aristotle to the present have recognized that there is a cognitive side to every art or craft. Surely, the painter must know his materials, the architect the laws of statics, the playwright the ways of human nature, but Tolstoy would insist that any such knowledge is a necessary rather than a sufficient condition for art production.

The art critic's knowledge is always penultimate, for what is great in a work tends to transcend explanation. While Plato characterizes the poet in the *Ion* as being out of his mind, Monroe Beardsley has shrewdly noted: ". . . the nonrationality of the poet may not be beneath, but above, reason itself."[62] In the *Meno,* for example, the diviner or poet is depicted as one who says many things truly, but knows nothing of what he says. Similarly, the Taoist speaks about the "knowledge of no-knowledge," i.e., insight that one receives through a mystical intuition.

One argument for cultivating intuition takes the following form: While reason is indispensable for activities from bridge building to rhetoric, it cannot address fundamental, metaphysical questions such as: Are humans free or determined? Applied to such questions, reason generates antinomies. Because the history of philosophy is the history of these unsettled questions, some urge a turn to intuition. Buddhists, for example, speak of *prajna* as superseding the senses and intellect. One stops believing either the thesis or the anti-thesis, because he reasons that by emptying his mind of both, he leaves room for the arrival of insight. In a story from Zen Buddhism, a priest pours too much tea into the cup of a visitor; and the guest blurts out: "The cup is full; no more will go in!" To which the priest replies: "Like this cup, you are full of your own preconceptions. How can I show you Zen if you don't first empty your cup?"

Prajñā, sudden realization, or *satori* is a kind of primordial consciousness as distinct from conventional thought. *The Cloud of Unknowing* speaks of such fundamental awareness in terms of "direct intuitions of truth" that arise without the aid of intellectualizing.[63] Rudolph Otto identifies *ahnung,* i.e., divination or intuition, as a key to grasping spiritual reality. Even the rationalist Immanuel Kant insisted that aesthetic judgments do not rest on the exercise of concepts, but rather on the free play of the imagination. That many people are unable to intuit "significant form" or to intuit the numinous is the most frequent criticism of intuitionism. Defenders of intuitionism counter that a person who cannot discern significant form is analogous to someone who is tone deaf. Concerning the person who cannot find God, Christians, for example, optimistically regard the searcher as someone who is still waiting for grace.

Teresa even goes so far as to say that truth or certainty dawns upon one after a religious experience, for during union with God, the soul neither senses nor understands; only later does it see the truth clearly.[64] So also, the struggling artist might proclaim, "How can I know what I am trying to achieve until I am finished?" In *The Principles of Art,* the aesthetician R. G. Collingwood sympathizes with this position and argues that one may distinguish art from craft on the grounds that a craftsman begins by knowing exactly where he is going and then proceeds accordingly. If the end is clear, then the means become mechanical and one's activity becomes a matter of technique. Like Aristotle's practitioner of *techne,* one who makes with a correct understanding of the principles involved is a technician or craftsman. By contrast, Collingwood's genuine artist realizes her truth only at the conclusion of the creative process, for it is only then that she has actualized the truth. Of course, the mystic can have no preconceived ideas concerning the absolute, because God, Brahman, or the Tao is altogether beyond conception. The passivity of William James's mystical states is also a safeguard against any attempt to exhaustively formulate ideas in advance. It is one of Thomas R. Martland's theses that: "Unlike craft and magic, which merely exposit or protect what men already know, art and religion distance from what they know and create in its place new understandings."[65] One who would meet a Thou, not an It, must be open to the unpredictable, the unexpected that also brings spontaneity to the would-be artist. Like art, rather than craft, religion is dialectical in that one confronts the other and is also confronted by the other. With craft, both the end and the means are already quite known. If one wishes to make a pot, she knows what is relevant for doing so, e.g., the correct temperature of the kiln. With art, the means and the ends cannot be completely foreknown—artworks sometimes emerge from an inchoate consciousness that experiments, free associates, "doodles," or plays. One may discard, supplant, or even reverse original notions. Again, with religion, one cannot completely know the end nor the means in advance. One cannot really know the end until he arrives at it. One cannot know the means until he forges his own individual path. Each must choose his own means (whether prayer, fasting, meditation, chanting, devotion, or action in the world) and reconstitute it, i.e., make it his own. With pseudo-religion, one purports to know both the means and the end. A fraudulent faith healer, for example, claims to possess the techniques required to heal any ailment. Like Kierkegaard's leap of faith or Buber's "narrow ridge," the artist's risk is unavoidable. It is only the magician and the craftsman who can rest in the definite. Obviously, some craftsmen do innovate, but by breaking new ground they become artists.

What one cannot explain may, nevertheless, be that to which one can point. Indeed, it is best to perceive the art critic and the spiritual mentor as pointers. A good critic is adept at pointing out important features in a work; she directs attention by gesturing toward the right areas and by giving verbal cues and clues. Buber, sounding like an art critic who seeks to help uncover the aesthetic qualities of an artwork that might otherwise go unnoticed, describes his contribution toward cultivating another's religious life: "I point to something in reality that had not or had too little been seen. I take him who listens to me by the hand and lead him to the window . . . open the window and point at what is outside. I have no teaching but I carry on a conversation."[66] Concerning the unique, numinous state of mind, Otto says,

> There is only one way to help another to an understanding of it. He must be guided and led on by consideration and discussion of the matter through the ways of his own mind, until he reach the point at which the "numinous" in him perforce begins to stir. . . . We can cooperate in this process by bringing before his notice all that can be found in other regions of the mind . . . "This X of ours is not precisely this experience, but akin to this one and the opposite of that other. Cannot you now realize for yourself what it is?" In other words, our X cannot, strictly speaking, be taught, it can only be evoked, awakened in the mind . . . [67]

Likewise, it is the role of the art critic to serve as a guide. She cannot adequately communicate her aesthetic experience of an artwork, but she can lead others to confront the work. Once she effects the confrontation, the critic seeks to elicit a certain experience in the spectator:

> Can't you feel the serenity in Mu-Ch'i's landscape painting? Look at the horizontal composition, the simple, soft ink wash as opposed to bright, possibly disturbing colors, the minimum number of brush strokes, the voids that invite, and the subtle ch'i, i.e., mist, that pervades the work. Don't they all contribute to a sense of tranquillity?

In religion there are gurus or spiritual guides, in art there are critics. Thinking about art, one can understand why the Greeks compared it to a mirror. Like a mirror held up to nature, art reflects the world, but it also reflects the self. Religion too needs this two-fold perspective if is to deliver a full-fledged revelation. Tillich, on seeing Botticelli's painting *Madonna and Child with Singing Angels*, characterized his experience as one of "revelatory ecstasy." As a soldier in World War I, Tillich relieved the darkness of his days by studying reproductions of classic paintings. At the end of the war, he visited the Kaiser Friedrich Museum in Berlin and stood before the original Botticelli: ". . . there was opened to me the meaning of what a painting can reveal. It can open up a new dimension of being, but it can do so only if it simultaneously has the power to open the corresponding level of the soul."[68] To discover something about reality is to discover something about oneself.

> [T]he arts do both; they open up a dimension of reality which is otherwise hidden, and they open up our own being for receiving this reality. Only the arts can do this; science, philosophy, moral action and religious devotion cannot. The artist brings to our senses and through them to our whole being something of the depth of our world and of ourselves, something of the mystery of being.[69]

Tillich also observes that, while science can speak volumes about a tree, the way of artistic creation penetrates directly to its hidden essence. "When we look at the pictures of Van Gogh we experience the power of being . . . which is effective in the life and struggle of the tree. We participate in it. We encounter a new quality. . . . Art makes us aware of something of which we could not otherwise become aware."[70] Tillich accused impressionist painters of veering away from being. Like others, he complained that impressionism rests content with dwelling upon outer surfaces rather than searching for inner reality. For example, he could find no substantiality in a painting of a boulevard by Monet.[71] Tillich further asserts that the impressionists capture fleeting color sensations, but do not penetrate "to the eternal, to the unconditioned content of reality which lies beyond the antithesis of subject and object."[72] Just as religions criticize one for resting content with sense pleasures, artists sometimes decry art that celebrates the sensory. Cezanne also faulted the impressionists for being preoccupied with superficial appearances, with surface rather than substance. Roger Fry states that, for Cezanne, "Reality, no doubt, lay always behind this veil of colour, but it was different, more solid, more dense, in closer relation to the needs of the spirit."[73] According to M.T.H. Sadler, Cezanne pursued platonic forms: "Cezanne saw in a tree, a heap of apples, or a human face, a group of bathing men or women, something more abiding than either photography or impressionist painting could present. He painted the 'treeness' of the tree . . ."[74] Taoist,

Ch'an and Zen Buddhist painters avoided the "veil of color" by avoiding colors as such, relying upon ink wash to point beyond the merely decorative or pretty to a deeper spiritual reality. Hence, Zen artists elevate a simple, monochrome landscape painting over an ornate, gold-leaf screen.

Of course, those who criticize impressionism for failing to disclose reality assume that there is an abiding reality. If one recognizes constant change as the real, then he will perceive an impressionistic art of shifting planes and flickering colors as a vividly concrete expression of that reality. Religions, however, tend to affirm four kinds of unchanging realities. First, there is the immutable absolute, whether it be God, the Tao, Logos, Brahman, or Allah. Second, there are universal moral imperatives, e.g., never treat a human being merely as a means rather than an end in herself. Third, there is an unending, blissful state or dimension, be it Nirvana or Heaven. Finally, there is the unchanging dimension of the individual: the soul, Buddha nature, or *atman*. Naturally this higher self can grow or develop, but its essence remains the same; one cultivates what is incipient. Hence Confucius's disciple, Mencius, speaks about the four roots of virtue that are innate in humans and only in need of being nurtured. Even Therevada Buddhism, which argued that constant change renders a permanent self impossible, soon gave rise to Mahayana Buddhism in which one distinguishes between the Buddha-nature, or true self, and the pseudo-self or ego.

Sometimes a philosopher or theologian claims that art does not merely symbolize the metaphysical, but that art can really deliver Kant's "thing in itself." Standing before the abovementioned painting by Botticelli, Tillich remarked, "In the beauty of the painting there was Beauty itself. It shone through the colors of the paint as the light of day shines through the stained-glass windows of a medieval church."[75] According to Otto, great art presents the numinous itself and this is most apparent in the Taoist and Buddhist paintings of the T'ang and Sung dynasties.[76]

Weiss raises what one might call "the paradox of artistic revelation" in this assertion: "Religious art embodies and points to Existence as affected by God."[77] His distinction between Existence and God is like that between creation and creator. Existence pertains to what is in space and time, but God, as spiritual rather than material, is non-spatial and, as eternal, is non-temporal. How then may existence, as influenced by God—a non-bodily reality—be embodied? That no intellectual solution readily presents itself will not greatly concern the mystically inclined. Of course, the paradox of the incarnation or avatar poses a related problem: How can the infinite become finite and remain infinite? It is through their revelatory powers that religion and art attempt to solve the paradox of the finite versus the infinite: How can a limited human being relate to an infinite other? In spite of the chasm between the spatial-temporal and the transcendental, a Schopenhauer finds that great music can deliver something of the infinite; and the sacrament of communion—a ritual with its own aesthetic qualities—enables another person to sense communion with the otherwise wholly other. Here are experiential responses, rather than intellectual answers, to the above paradox.

Remaining questions include: If Chinese and Western painters are both interested in disclosing the nature of reality, why are there great differences in their paintings? Are they all failures? Is any a successful disclosure of existence? Could all be successes, since each reflects a different aspect of reality? Of course, like questions apply to the world religions. Since they disagree on doctrines, are they all false? Is one true and supreme? Or are they, despite appearances, compatible? Rather than reject van Gogh or Shih-t'ao, Christianity or Taoism, one may embrace aesthetic as well as religious pluralism.

7

CREATIVITY

In traditional Judeo-Christian theology, God creates *ex nihilo,* i.e., "from nothing," in that he works alone; there is "nothing" else, nothing apart from him to direct his creation and no preexisting material from which to fashion the universe. Some thinkers, who wish to explain the paradox of creation, propose that God creates the universe out of himself, much as an artist draws her works from herself. Therefore, the divine creates from nothing, i.e., no thing, for he is no thing among things, but the origin of all things, and one should distinguish an ultimate from its effects. One should not confuse God with created things any more than one should confuse a painter with her paintings. In short, the universe pours forth from the absolute just as artworks issue from the prolific artist.

Divine creation is traditionally the model for artistic creativity, because both God and the artist wring order out of chaos; both bring about new universes, and both infuse life or animation into what was lifeless. Moreover, one may relate God's conjuring up of the universe from nothing to the artist's creating from "nonbeing," whether it be the painter who stands before an empty canvas or the writer who confronts a daunting, blank sheet of paper. Psychologically, artistic creation does involve a kind of production from "nothing," i.e., from an unknowable wellspring. One goes deeper than conscious concepts and principles. As C.Y. Chang states: "Creativity in the highest sense has its origin in nonbeing, or the void. . . . The great Chinese poets . . . penetrated to the void. . . ."[1] Of course, this void is not truly nothing; rather it is the ineffable

155

source of every thing. Understood immanently, the void is one's existential self that is not present in ordinary consciousness; understood transcendentally, the void is the source of all being, including the existential self. It is no thing, but the mother of all things. It is the primordial oneness, all plurality being a rupturing of this cosmic harmony. Taoists call it *wu* (nothing), *p'o* (the uncarved block), or the great simplicity. To them, the ultimate painter excels in manifesting childlike innocence; and his attainment is possible because he creates from a state of "nonbeing." Emptying himself of theories, theses, antitheses, prejudices, preferences, concepts, and hypotheses, the artist participates in a kind of "creation from nothing." Next, the artist transmits "nothing" that anyone could convey non-artistically. For that matter, the medium of an artwork is like nothing else. A water color exists nowhere else but in a painting. If the artist's work soars, it goes beyond all conventions and becomes a "nothing," one that is really a "something" that no previous artist has achieved. In addition, the artist should communicate "nothing," i.e., the ineffable Tao from which all things issue forth, as well as the "lesser nothing" which is the artist's ineffable true nature.

Creativity is obviously a touchstone if not the premier touchstone of contemporary art. Witness Picasso with his blue, rose, cubistic, and surreal periods. "Everything is still to be done, and not to be done over again," was his motto and a reminder that the so-called artist who merely repeats the past is a mechanic. It is less evident, but no less true, that creativity is also an important touchstone of religion. Buber, for example, trusts religion only insofar as it exhibits creativity: "Religion is true as long as it is creative."[2] When religion clings to the past, it reverts to magic, i.e., control or manipulation of the status quo. Conservatism, ever the enemy of creativity, is responsible for failed religion as well as failed art. If art or religion resists transformation, it suffers a loss in its power to transform the world. As Martland argues, bad religion or bad art tries to conserve rather than create.[3] A contemporary Trappist monk speaks of creativity, inspiration and spontaneity in the religious life:

> The monk's life is really very creative. Like a painter or a poet, he is inspired. He listens, combines what he hears with his own uniqueness, and produces something beautiful. Great paintings and poems cannot be produced by an assembly-line process. Contemplation can't be scheduled any more than you can open your arms and catch the wind. You can only stand and feel it on your face.[4]

John of the Cross compares the insecurities of art to advancement in the spiritual life as one enters "darkness" and leaves behind the traditional:

> [O]ne who is learning fresh details concerning any office or art always proceeds in darkness, and receives no guidance from his original knowledge, for if he left not that behind he would get no farther nor make any progress; and in the same way, when the soul is making most progress, it is travelling in darkness knowing naught.[5]

Obviously this is an overstatement. The Buddha, for example, did not break completely from his past; instead, he retained Hindu notions, such as *karma*, and integrated them into his own developing thought. Similarly, the most innovative artist remains indebted to her tradition. Indeed, the artist who breaks new ground also taps into his heritage. Thus, the bull motif of Picasso's early art eventually finds its way into the turbulent painting *Guernica*. Put generally, there never was a creative artist, religious figure, scientist, philosopher, or leader of any sort who did not do two things: draw from her tradition and depart from it. If she did not borrow from it, she would be rejecting the collective wisdom of her culture, but if she did not break away, she would be retarding progress. Individual reformers often produce societal reform that, in turn, sparks new reformers. Luther's break from Catholicism initiated the Protestant Reformation that itself soon motivated counter-reformation figures such as Ignatius Loyola. Certainly, the art world is not without its corresponding reformers. Impressionists such as Monet, who broke from a "weightier" style of painting, established an enduring vision, but Cezanne, a father of modern art, condemned the superficiality of impressionism and redirected the course of Western painting. The artist, who strains to create, feels the pain of detachment from the familiar. To veer from the established schools and conventions that a culture supports is necessarily to suffer the pains of the iconoclast. Creative artists and movements routinely face scorn; for example, some called Henri Matisse's group of young painters the fauves, i.e., the wild beasts. Religious reformers not only render themselves vulnerable to criticism, but they risk attack, assassination, incarceration, or execution.

Martland pinpoints tradition and innovation in Otto: "He calls man's religious interest in affirming his inherited structures the element of fascinosum, and his interest in transcending them the element of tremendum."[6] One may relate the retrospective (fascinosum) and prospective (tremendum) orientations to *k'ai ho* as well as to Nietzsche's Apollonian versus Dionysian tendencies, which also contribute to an equilibrium. One can identify the tandem actions of *k'ai* and *ho* in all the arts to varying degrees: jazz music celebrates *k'ai* and a sonnet is more expressive of *ho*. Fascinosum and tremendum operate in religious individuals, in religions, and in the arts. Martland concludes: "Though art and religion must reconcile and harmonize these two reactions, it is no easy matter."[7] Art and religion must always be on a narrow ridge between the security of tradition and the danger of innovation. For Buber, the narrow ridge lies between the confident, comforting systems of thought (the past) and genuine encounters (the eternal present). Such meetings are always unpredictable and uncertain excursions. In the landmark work of 1907, *Les Demoiselles d'Avignon,* Picasso at once borrows from traditional African art and propels painting into the twentieth century. Ironically enough, thirty years passed before a museum exhibited it. John Canaday indicates that the twenty-six-year-old Picasso was struggling toward the tremendum, since he painted "for the sake of increasing the scope and intensity of the art of painting."[8] A classic case of the coincidence of the retrospective and the prospective occurs in the Buddha's revolt against orthodox Hinduism. By rejecting the caste system, Gotama renounced the established order, but by carrying over *karma*, he affirmed a central doctrine of Hinduism. Religion and art both draw from and withdraw from their respective traditions. If either fails to transcend its roots, there is stagnation rather than creativity. If either fails to draw from its roots, the result is mere novelty and superficiality.

Uniqueness, a quintessential attribute of art, is also vital to religion, but it may be less apparent in the latter. Living the daily monastic life, Henri J.M. Nouwen found himself discouraged by the thought that nothing he did was new, he seemed to be making no contribution, but then it struck him that, "The mystery of God's love is that in this sameness we discover our uniqueness."[9] Rabbi Reuven Hammer explains how there can be newness in the recitation of a familiar prayer: "Of course, the main thing that is 'new' is oneself. Depending on my thoughts, my mood, my feelings, my existential situation of the moment, what I say, no matter how many times I have said it before, takes on new meaning."[10] Prayers, then, can be distinctive artworks. Just as every artist depicts a model from a unique perspective, each soul prays according to her own peculiar background, intentions, insights, and circumstances. Describing the abbot and novice master of a Trappist monastery,

Frank Bianco writes, "They believe God has called the monk-candidate to the monastery so he can hear that unique voice that was his from the moment of his creation. To adapt any other's voice, another's way, would be an imitation instead of the original that God intended."[11] Hasidism cautions that one cannot imitate another's praying anymore than one can imitate a tightrope walker's feat. Indeed, even the most cherished of ready-made prayers must be "recreated" in the chemistry of one's unique reading. Of course, one may borrow a prayer, as the artist learns a technique, style, or methodology, but she must then make it her own. Creativity, innovation, spontaneity, vitality, freedom, and flexibility also play a crucial role in prayer. Some insist that one must supplement traditional prayers with those that are new to the one who recites. As Hammer observed, the frequent recitation of traditional prayers can still be novel. Of course, even if every genuine prayer is a creation in which an individual expresses herself, prayer is not simply for the sake of self-expression—as Collingwood understands the role of art—but for the sake of communication with the divine.

Although copying the exact way of another would be a mistake, imitation of the divine is a different matter. According to Christianity, there is really nothing alien about the imitation of Christ, since to emulate Christ is to actualize one's true self, i.e., the "Christ" that is in oneself and all others. Ultimately, both art and religion require that any imitation of a model must transcend mere copying and culminate in self-actualization. After resting in Christ or the Buddha, one must cultivate her own autonomy. After the talented artist loses herself in the works of the masters, she must go beyond in order to release her own creativity. Inquiring about nothing less than the meaning of life, Thomas Merton asks: "Does God impose a meaning on my life from the outside. . . . Or am I called to create from within . . . ?"[12] Merton concludes that he forms his own life through a free response to God. By contrast, scientific formulas and discoveries lack the stamp of uniqueness of either one's personal prayer or the artist's signature. With science, the who is unimportant; it is the what that matters, the It rather than the Thou. While evolution may be evident in science, it is less at home in religion and art. As science speaks of predictability and necessity, art and religion speak of unpredictability and spontaneity. The creative power that is obvious in the flourishing of the artist is also manifest in the spiritual growth of the saint. As paradigms of spontaneity and vitality, artists and religious figures both meet their natural enemies in the form of mechanical actions and encrusted routines that promote enslavement to the past. Religion and art recognize naturalness as the standard of excellence. The ascetic strain in all religions represents an effort to avoid unnatural desires and unnatural pleasures; and the artist wishes to paint as naturally as clouds pass across the sky. Just as art woos the natural, religion pursues it. The Taoist, who recognizes the Tao as the root of nature, seeks to harmonize with it. Similarly, a Thomas Aquinas elevates divinely bestowed natural laws over civil laws, which are, after all, human conventions.

Of course, there are negative, as well as positive, shared features in the development of religion and art. The artist's "drying up of creative powers," i.e., writer's block, finds a parallel in Teresa's battle with "seasons of dryness" that frustrated her spiritual cultivation and prayer.[13] Corresponding to the demons that plague religious figures, Hughes Mearns, admittedly in lighthearted language, identifies an aesthetic counterpart in the form of a demon of inhibition:

> There is no doubt that something has a grip on our real self. . . . Every artist—painter, writer, or fabricator—generally knows about this unseen, unknown enemy; and every artist has, at some time or another, discovered a trick to throw it off that seemingly eternal guard. Some will smoke endless pipes and pretend to be thinking about nothing at all; and then, presto! They suddenly turn to work and have a lot done before the Thing (who is really a little stupid) can discover what's up.[14]

Tillich comments on the uncreative nature of the demonic: "Blasphemous imitations of the divine are extreme expressions of the demonic; things like witch sabbaths or black masses. . . . Even such art shows that the demonic does not have the imagination to create in and of itself."[15] Teresa accuses Satan of producing in her: "the aridity and indisposition for prayer."[16] Again, the *Dark Night of the Soul* contains frequent references to the painful but purgative aridity that the soul must endure on its spiritual odyssey. Of course, "writers' block" plagues painters, sculptors, and composers as much as it does writers. Thomas à Kempis emphasizes that self-seeking is the source of dryness: "If you seek yourself as the goal of your work in anything, you soon fall short in your activities, and become dry and barren of all the refreshment of grace."[17] Here, one should interpret "yourself" as "your ego." "Dryness" in the artist or saint arises when he focuses upon the superficial ego rather than the self that is continuous with its foundation. Dryness follows if one moves away from the fountain about which Thomas exclaims, "O Fountain of everlasting love."

Teresa's incapacity for prayer is uniquely frustrating, because, in all other cases of suffering, one can always pray for relief. But she cannot pray for assistance if she has lost the ability to pray. The paradox of prayer asks: How can one pray for the capacity to pray if one is unable to pray? Prayer involves a dialogue between the finite and the infinite, but the inability to pray signals a monologue. One speaks but fails to hear the response of the eternal Thou; and so one may wait, as the artist does, for intervention. Passivity, which is a kind of active waiting, is a part of the most dynamic lives in religion and art. If one cannot pray or create, she may pursue other activities and let inspiration take hold when it will. Zen Buddhism teaches: "One can attain enlightenment while carrying water or chopping bamboo," i.e., in the midst of ordinary work. The Eastern Orthodox Church has long emphasized repetitious prayer or chanting as a means to effect communion between the human and the divine. In a prayer by Kierkegaard, we find both the problem and a solution: "Oh, in the time of silence when a man consumes himself in the desert in which he does not hear thy voice. . . . Bless then this silence as thy word to man; grant that he never forgets that thou speakest also when thou are silent . . ." In aesthetic experience, such a situation would be less sanguine, because if art is communication and an artist cannot hear the muses, she cannot transmit their message through a work.

An insatiable appetite for the creative leads some today, as it does in all eras, to confuse sheer novelty with genuine creativity. Being unusual is not a sufficient condition for being creative, since there is such a thing as "original nonsense." After all, any would-be artist can do something bizarre. Witness Chris Burden, who, at the Los Angeles County Museum, fired a rifle into his arm—in the name of art. If a novelty is to be creative, it must be worthwhile, e.g., intellectually stimulating, emotionally rich, witty, ingenious, psychologically insightful, significantly formed, or eye-appealing. For a parallel to Burden in religion, consider the doctrines and practices of certain so-called religious cults, i.e., movements whose appeal may be in direct proportion to how sensational or weird they are.

Some have suggested that humans will never comprehend creativity, because the forces that are at work in one's creative process cease to operate as soon as she attends to the process itself. Perhaps if one introspects to discern creativity at work, he is like the man who sets an alarm clock in order to wake up and see himself sleeping! Possibly the creative process remains opaque because its wellsprings are so different from its fruits. Interpreting creativity as the product of divine madness, Plato offers another, admittedly extreme, reason for the unintelligibility of a creative process. Of course, religious thinkers would add that if a human creation is divinely inspired, one can never fully explain it. It also may be that the investigation of the creative process is necessarily analytic, but the process itself is irreducibly synthetic. Finally, the inspired artist may be unable to explain her creative activity owing to a kind of blindness. In the dark night of the soul, divine light penetrates the soul with such intensity as to blind it, as the earthly sun blinds the eyes. Just as the dark wellsprings of creativity can remain opaque to the artist, John of the Cross asserts: ". . . contemplation is secret and hidden from the very person that experiences it . . ."[18] It is no wonder that this experience is ineffable, since, in a way, one does not experience it. The same darkness that falls upon sense and reason is a light for the intuitive soul, a light that elevates sense and reason to new heights. Because the creative person's intuition transcends discursive reason, one cannot translate her insight into a conventional, rational explanation. For whatever reasons, creative processes have proved to be resistant to analyses. Neither artists, art historians, art critics, philosophers, nor psychologists have enjoyed much success in articulating any sequence of events that culminates in a creative product. Of course, some have rejected the idea of "the creative process," i.e., the notion that there is only one way to create rather than an open-ended list of procedures. While subject to considerable criticism, a four-part model of creativity—inception, incubation, inspiration, and work—serves to illumine certain relations between art and religion.

Inception

At the outset of creation, the artist becomes aware of a somewhat inchoate idea, emotion, image, or problem. For example, the bombing of the defenseless town of Guernica outraged Picasso, but he was not immediately certain about how to respond. Indistinctness prevails. Authors, for example, may not be able to explain precisely how the incept or germ of their story arises. An incident in the life of the prolific, short-story writer O. Henry demonstrates the point. Dining in a restaurant with O. Henry, a reporter asked him where his ideas came from. O. Henry held up a menu, declared that ideas were everywhere, and immediately created "Springtime à la Carte," one of his best-known stories. Of course, religious and aesthetic experiences can be spontaneous, something may suddenly induce a state of receptivity, as when St. Paul was thrown from his horse or someone is suddenly seized by the dramatic, formal qualities of a quickly approaching storm. Generally, however, neither grace nor artistic insight is likely to descend upon the undeserved. Spiritual or aesthetic moments usually occur only after some period of specialized preparation, be it a nun's novitiate or a sculptor's apprenticeship. The religious person may pray, meditate, morally reform, and follow a more ascetic life—all in order to enhance her likelihood of undergoing a spiritual experience. Typically, the artist masters the techniques and materials of her medium before creativity blooms. It is no accident that architects are the ones who usually make creative breakthroughs in architecture or that sculptors innovate in sculpture. Therefore, when a da Vinci is creative in science as well as in painting, people hail him as a genius. Naturally, what he accomplished would have been impossible were he not "doubly prepared." In short, incepts come to those who prepare themselves for them.

Without their respective preparations, neither the mystic's nor the artist's practices would constitute a discipline. Contrary to what their critics might suspect, preparation, rather than impulsive behavior, steers the artist as well as the religious agent. Preparation is also essential for the spectator who seeks an aesthetic experience of art or nature, since receptivity is a prerequisite for such appreciation. As John Dewey observes in *Art As Experience,* the diner who is best able to enjoy the art of fine cuisine is one who has sampled a great variety of foods and a great variety of preparations. Moreover, she should also be an accomplished chef, because one must be able to mentally reenact the production of a meal if she is to thoroughly enjoy it.

Shih-t'ao demonstrates preparation through identification when he reports that, while he studied the paintings of such past masters as Ni Tsan, he became united with them and was with them even when eating and sleeping. As important as it is for the student to appropriate past masters and masterpieces, his imitation of the masters must give way to a transformation of them. Of course, the artist may be able to identify with objects as well as with other artists. In Taoist thought, when the artist identifies with an object: "This interfusion initiates the process of creativity, which in turn establishes unity in multiplicity, the changeless in the ever-changing."[19]

Taoists emphasize preparation through repose and consider *hsu* (vacuity) or great calmness as the ideal frame of mind for the painter. One may speak of the "calm before the form" and of the serene and formless Tao as the root of all forms. Although painting freely issues forth from a tranquil consciousness, the painter rejects quietism, for this inner serenity is neither inert nor effete. The splendid paintings of a Shih-t'ao prove that it is a "dynamic rest," i.e., "a rest amidst motion" and "a motion amidst rest." Taoism recognizes such serenity as the wellspring of creativity. Here one thinks of Wordsworth's point that art is emotion recollected in tranquillity. When van Gogh notes that the seemingly effortless, unimpeded, artistic outpouring does not occur without prior effort, his remarks are equally applicable to the enlightenment experience of the mystic:

> [I]f the emotions are sometimes so strong that one works without knowing one works, when sometimes the strokes come with a continuity and a coherence like words in a speech or letter, then one must remember that it has not always been so, and that in time to come there will again be hard days, empty of inspiration.[20]

The artist goes dry again and the saint finds prayer to be dry as dust. Creativity requires not only sudden realizations, but the slow, thoughtful, cumulative acquisition and refinement of skills and techniques that render one capable of translating inspiration into art. Likewise, spirituality depends upon prayer, meditation, moral reform, breathing exercises, or ascetic practices as well as sudden illuminations.

Incubation

Incubation or gestation, in which the incept recedes from consciousness, marks a second possible stage. The poet Amy Lowell once compared allowing the seeds of a poem to slip into one's unconscious to dropping a letter into a mail box. Conscious, rational thought is hardly a sufficient condition for artistic or spiritual achievements. Relaxing or "letting go" is the saint's counterpart to the artist's gestation phase, since the activity of the rational mind suffices for neither spiritual nor artistic achievements. Teresa's biographer, Benedict Zimmerman, affirms the merit of passivity:

". . . she shows that the safest way for contemplation is not to lift up the spirit to high things, but to wait for God to lift it up."[21] William Ernest Hocking remarks,

[T]he mystic has not infrequently asserted, on the basis of his own experience, that there comes a stage of effort in which effort must be set aside in favor of a purely receptive attitude. . . . He recognizes the danger that his "trying" may be trying toward some preconceived goal and therefore impede his perception of the true goal, whose character is such that it cannot have been preconceived. He must render himself passive and wait in hope that God will vouchsafe to reveal.[22]

Collingwood insists that the artist cannot have a definite, preconceived end, because this is the sign of a mere craftsman. Such striving toward a fixed or preestablished end interferes with either aesthetic or religious spontaneity and insights. Accordingly, James holds that one achieves spiritual realization "by simply relaxing and throwing the burden down." Of course, the artist is well aware of the impasses so quickly reached through zealous, self-conscious exertions; hence, she also recognizes the value of "throwing the burden down." She is no more free to will or not will her aesthetic vision than the mystic is to will or not will her mystical states. Preparation and action can only take one so far; at this point, she must stand in readiness and wait for the "other" to complete her experience, be it the aesthetic incept or the religious "more." In short, passivity marks both spiritual and religious lives. Of course, such waiting involves a being-in-readiness, not a being-in-a-torpor. Speaking about the contemplation that refreshes, John of the Cross states: ". . . if a man have desire or care to experience it, he experiences it not; for, as I say, it does its work when the soul is most at ease and freest from care; it is like the air which, if one would close one's hand upon it, escapes."[23] John likens the "passive" agent who is receiving gifts from God to a model who is sitting before a painter: If the sitter were to move, because he wanted to assist the painter, this would interfere with the painter's activity and diminish the painting itself.[24] John underscores the importance of a wise passivity in remarking that if the soul in contemplation ". . . desires to work with its faculties, it hinders the work which God is doing in it rather than aids it . . ."[25] Still, it is important to note that the sitter is not inert; instead, even the seemingly motionless sitter is posing. As with a bow string that one draws and holds tight, the "resting" soul exerts energy, receives forces, and contributes to a dynamic state of being.

Art and religion, like the dreams that they both feed and draw from, sometimes involve loss of control. One thinks about the spiritual ecstasy of Teresa or the passion of Picasso. The artist may surrender to inspiration, to his materials, to a theme, or to the inevitability of emerging forms. Of course, there is usually more of an exchange, a reciprocity between the artist and his materials that resembles an I-Thou relation. An artist who refuses to succumb to the other is really a manipulator; and the supposedly religious individual who tries to prevail over the other is a magician. Invariably, the materials command the true artist's attention and she responds to their properties. The stone waits to receive the sculptor's impressions; and as she works, the stone's changing sounds and appearances move her. For a literary example, in the preface to *The Spoils of Poynton,* Henry James reports that a lady's allusion charmed and seized him, serving as a germ that became the original element of his novel. Of course, a spiritual person may abandon himself to divine providence. Humans forever attempt to accommodate their selves to the course of things, be it the galloping life process of the Tao or the natural properties of an artist's medium. Nevertheless, some people are suspicious of self-surrender—however significant it may be for religion and art. They are suspicious of any tendency toward submission or diminished self-control, because they conceive of the rational agent as someone who is self-sufficient, having no significant dependency upon others.

The relinquishment of self-control may have contributed to the stereotype of the artist and mystic as irrational, rendering both figures popular targets of criticism. People sometimes believe that saints and artists are mad, because of their unconventional appearance, demeanor, or actions. Francis, for example, wore such dirty, ragged clothing that people stoned him. Of course, the boundless optimism of the saint and the unrestrained imagination of the artist also raise questions about their sanity. That Francis heard voices and that Duchamp had a urinal exhibited in an art museum lead some people to categorize religious figures and artists as insane. In addition, other artists and religious individuals, who relinquish their self-control by a turn to alcohol or drugs, have gained the reputation of being mad. Some artists and mystics argue that the use of alcohol or other mind-altering substances reduces one's inhibitions and thereby helps him achieve a receptive consciousness. Naturally, one can only take such intoxicants in moderation;

and whatever state they induce is penultimate, since it lacks the noetic dimension of peak religious experiences. In addition, drug states possess a regularity or uniformity that is foreign to the spontaneity of the most exalted states of aesthetic or spiritual consciousness. That many artists and saints do not partake of drugs demonstrates that they are neither a necessary nor a sufficient condition for aesthetic or spiritual cultivation.

Perhaps meditation, chanting, breathing exercises, or prayer can duplicate or surpass whatever consciousness drugs can induce. If so, the ideal would be to avoid dependence on drugs. In addition, some contend that the drug-induced state is just a counterfeit experience, i.e., one that lacks any transformative power. Even those who approve of using drugs to promote religious consciousness emphasize that they serve merely as a means, not as an end.

Finally, critics who regard artists and saints as immature often confuse being childish with being childlike. To be childish is, for example, to be stubborn and petulant, but to be childlike is to be flexible and receptive. The former marks the very beginning of self-cultivation; and the latter marks achievement in moral, aesthetic, and spiritual development. Children may see only mountains and rivers, but to see them and celebrate them in the wonder of their invisible matrix is childlike. Here one returns to childhood and recovers the original joys of perceiving mountains and rivers, but now the experience is deeper, because one is fully aware of their metaphysical ground.

Inspiration

Continuing Amy Lowell's metaphor, the sender of the letter eventually receives a reply in the form of inspiration, a third phase of creativity. One now "sees" the way to continue and develop her incept. Perhaps one telescopes all the mystery of creation into this stage, since to define creativity in terms of inspiration is to define the unknown in terms of the ineffable. In any case, inspiration is evident in Teresa, who wrote quickly and without hesitation or editing, much as the Zen Buddhist executes his ink wash paintings with immediacy. According to one of Teresa's biographers, God allowed her to see at once her entire literary masterpiece, *The Interior Castle*. Not surprisingly, she wished that she could write with both hands in order to get down on paper all the ideas that were streaming into her head.[26] The spontaneous, untrammeled approach of Taoist and Ch'an Buddhist painters corresponds to the sudden enlightenment that mystics seek. One paints directly, as unhesitatingly as she writes her signature. Such moments of sudden illumination or enlightenment sustain both artistic creativity and spiritual development. Ideally preparation, complemented by receptivity, will culminate in inspiration.

To the Greeks, the artist was a mouthpiece or instrument through which the gods expressed themselves. Contemporary thinkers continue to attribute artistic creativity to afflation, i.e., divine intervention. Ben-Zion Bokser, for instance, observes: "Many students of creativity have indeed interpreted the experience which energizes the creative act as a mystical experience."[27] According to tradition, Francis's famous poem, "The Canticle of Brother Sun," came to him during a mystical ecstasy. And, on his death bed, William Blake asserted that all of his art depended upon celestial intercession. Teresa echoes the sentiment: ". . . if I manage to say something well the Sisters will understand that this does not come from me since there would be no foundation for it, unless the Lord gave it to me . . ."[28] Giving God credit for any eloquence (an aesthetic quality) in her remarks, Teresa speaks similarly of her prayer states: ". . . I see clearly that it is not I who speak."[29] Turning to an analogy, she concludes: "Thus I see clearly that all my gain has come through the revelations and raptures, in which I am nothing myself, and do no more to effect them than the canvas does for the picture painted on it."[30] Of course, Teresa more closely resembles a model who sits, projects an attitude, moves, and repositions herself, thereby influencing the outcome of the painting. Ironically, afflation at once diminishes the role of the messenger, who may disclaim being anything more than a conduit, and elevates the status of her message, since it comes from the divine.

From a religious perspective, the artist is as dependent upon the divine for inspiration as she is upon him for sustenance. Having been inspired, the artist is not in full control of her actions, i.e., she is not the sole influence upon the direction of the creative process. Likewise, when seized by love, one may also lose self-control. When suffering from demonic possession, one can exorcise the devil, but in cases of religious possession, one is powerless to "exorcise" God. Consider Nikos Kazantzakis's *The Last Temptation of Christ,* in which Jesus is being tormented, not by a devil, but by God: "It's God I tell you. No, there is no cure." Visions and sounds may also be involuntary, as when Francis hears the voice of God.

When an artist attributed his work to inspiration, a bystander asked, "If inspiration starts the creative process, how do you know when to stop?" "Inspiration," the artist replied. Perhaps creativity remains a mystery, because any explanation of a creative process depends upon generalizations and universal concepts, but each creative act, like every religious experience, is particular and unique. John of the Cross says that the Holy Spirit infuses secret wisdom—without the soul's knowledge or understanding. Such wisdom is ineffable, since one cannot couch it "in any form or image subject to sense."[31] That this wisdom is devoid of all sensible forms and images may point to its spiritual origin. With divine inspiration, the saint can "go beyond good and evil," for she does what is right spontaneously, without any need to ponder what is right or wrong. Augustine urged, "Love God and do what you will"; a mature Confucius did whatever he wanted to do without overstepping the boundaries of what was right. Of course, such unerring ethical conduct depends upon previous self-cultivation. Similarly, the artistic genius, who works directly, effortlessly, seemingly without the deliberations that preoccupy the beginner, draws upon extensive training and self-development. Ironically, the spiritual person's good deeds, which are impossible for others, seem to be effortless acts. Eckhart compares this phenomenon to the developed artist who appears to act without strain or exertion. Through great labor, both have developed a reservoir of excellence from which they may now draw with some ease.[32] The artist's goal is "artless art," art free of artifice. The saint seeks a goodness that, like Kant's good will, is uncontrived, i.e., uncontaminated by calculation.

Replying to someone who said, "God spoke to me in a dream," Thomas Hobbes's caustic reply was: "Oh, you mean that you dreamt that God spoke to you." Still, artists and religious figures often believe that the two possibilities are not mutually exclusive. The Native American Black Elk, for example, who recorded his dream encounters with the divine in ethereal, pastel, childlike paintings of Indians, horses, and buffaloes, interpreted his dream states as revelations, i.e., manifestations of the deepest possible contact with spiritual reality. For Black Elk, the fact that God had spoken to him through a dream in no way undermined the truth that God had actually addressed him. Indeed, humans have long reported receiving insights in their dreams. A poignant story relates that an artist woke from a dream with an inspiration, knelt and said a prayer of thanks to God, but never could remember the inspired idea once he stood up. The artist in this ironic anecdote might find consolation and sage advice in the remarks of Teresa:

Once our Lord gave me light in a matter that I was very glad
to understand, and I immediately forgot it, so that I was never
able to call it again to mind; and so, when I was trying to
remember it, I heard: "Thou knowest now that I speak to thee
from time to time. Do not omit to write down what I say; for,
though it may not profit thee, it may be that it will profit
others."[33]

Just as the artist's inspiration is fleeting, the saint's ecstasy is
transitory; in *The Varieties of Religious Experience,* William James
identifies transiency as one of the four hallmarks of mystical states,
the others being the incommunicability of the transport (ineffability), illumination (noetic quality), and receptivity (passivity). As
impermanent, spiritual experiences are more like the fleeting performing arts than the enduring plastic arts. Once completed, every
dance, concert, or drama is gone forever, like the short-lived cactus
flowers that bloom for only a day. Indeed, it is the evanescent
quality of some objects that lends them a special aesthetic poi-
gnancy. Of course, there will be more performances of *Hamlet* and
fresh desert flowers will renew the landscape, but this unique
Hamlet or that unique bloom can be no more. Like such botanical
epiphanies and mystical experiences, artistic masterpieces remind
one at once of his fragile status and of his yearning for immortality.
Indeed, while one beholds art, the ephemeral and the eternal are
never more in equipoise.

Work

Elaboration, work, or verification marks the final phase of creativity in which one develops the initial intuition and its
ramifications. As the reproductive metaphors of conception and
pregnancy apply respectively to the inception and incubation phases
of creativity, labor and delivery apply to the last phase of creative
activity. To the would-be poet who said, "I have ideas for poems,
but I just can't find the words," a critic replied: "Poems are not
written with ideas, but with words." Indeed, it is the work of a poet
to translate ideas and feelings into well-chosen words. Art entails
action, for after the insight comes the elaboration. When Buddha
received the four noble truths, the fourth was the activistic, eight-
fold path. We find a Christian parallel in the saying, "Faith without works is dead." In the Zen Buddhist monastery, there is a basic

rule to foster action: "No work, no eat." Genuine religion is always fruitful, productive, or constructive, as when religious figures establish hospitals, schools, libraries, and monasteries (altogether Teresa founded fourteen monasteries), feed the hungry, teach, preach, inspire, write, translate texts, undertake pilgrimages, and create art. Most importantly, religious leaders serve as role models in all the above capacities. On the essential nature of mysticism, which many regard as the essence of religion, Marc Chagall asks: "Without mysticism would there be a single great social movement in the world? Every organism—be it individual or social—if it is deprived of the force of mysticism . . . will it not wilt and die?"[34] Hinduism makes the dynamic component of religion explicit; alongside *jnana marga* (the way of knowledge) and *bhakti marga* (the way of devotion), there is *karma marga* (the way of action). Again, the would-be poet's notions, passions, and yearnings remain as stirrings unless he expresses them in actual art works. Of course, to be successful, they must inspire, stimulate, provoke, satirize, enlighten, or shape the conscience of a society.

At the end of an evening of entertaining, the poet Hart Crane sometimes excused himself for a short time and returned with hurriedly produced poems as going-away gifts for his guests. Since his friends found the poems to be of excellent quality, it appeared that Crane had found a way to avoid the "work" aspect of creative endeavors. But Crane eventually revealed his secret: he wrote the poems beforehand and only with all of the usual creative labor. There is no "easy art" any more than there is "easy religion," for as Spinoza remarked, "All things excellent are as difficult as they are rare." Hence, one sneers at paint-by-numbers "art" and disparages any just-follow-the-rules "religion" that preaches thoughtless adherence.

Of course, critics of the four-part model of creativity have observed that not every creator passes successively through all four phases in a lockstep fashion. One could, for example, receive fresh ideas during the elaboration phase or one might also receive an inspiration without any apparent gestation period, as in the case of improvisational art—much as one can have spontaneous religious experiences. Nevertheless, the account provides a general pattern into which many cases of creativity will fit. Just as the stages in creativity are reversible, as when elaboration sparks further inspirations, the mystic's stages of purification, illumination, and union with the divine are subject to reverses. To illustrate, illumination may lead one to renewed purgation. Moreover, union, which is epistemological as well as ontological, increases one's illumination and encourages further purification, e.g., through greater self-sacrifice. Three basic aspects of human nature—the volitional, cognitive, and affective—are at work in the three traditional stages of the mystic's odyssey. To begin with, purification requires reform of the will by a course of right action; next, illumination is the ultimate form of cognition; and, finally, union marks feelings of love, joy, or bliss. Not surprisingly, one can detect these three pulses in the artist: First there is the training, technique, or discipline that can rival the rigors of religious purification, second is inspiration, and finally fusion or identification with the subject, with all its attendant rapture.

Students of creativity sometimes ask if an original image or impression guides the artist from the incept to the completion of the work. If not, they wonder what could be "steering" her. Generalizations here are as dangerous as they are concerning the religious experiences that were non-imagistic for Bonaventure and imagistic for Francis. Perhaps the best record of artistic creativity lies in early efforts, just as the best record of spiritual cultivation lies in the deeds of the saints. Studying the drafts, preliminary sketches, prototypes, or notations of artists can facilitate understanding their final creations. Likewise, consulting the diaries, confessions, journals, and autobiographies of the saints can enrich our understanding of their religious pilgrimages.

Artists as different as Tolstoy and Kandinsky insist that art is a mere sham unless it is animated by the artist's inner necessity or emotion. Likewise, religion, no matter how impressive it may appear in its external expressions, is hollow unless it flows from the right inner states, intentions, aspirations, and feelings. In Kandinsky's view, "inner need" refers to the artist's yearning for spiritual expression.[35] In addition, if nothing in nature is in vain, such yearnings point to the objectivity of the spiritual dimension. Tolstoy stipulates one of the conditions for contagiousness in art: ". . . the artist should be impelled by an inner need to express his feeling."[36] As some have thought that the universal, human quest for the transcendent is sufficient evidence for the existence of the divine, Kandinsky thinks that the inner necessity to express oneself in art—as a drive at the depths of one's being—and the resultant art work verify the genuine spirituality of the artist's experience. Form, of course, is the outward manifestation of inner meaning and ". . . form-harmony must rest only on a corresponding vibration of the human soul . . ."[37] In other words, aesthetic order depends upon and flows from an ordered soul. The inner need consists of three mystical elements: the personality of the artist that calls for expression, the artist's drive to express the spirit of his age (it is a religious spirit that Tolstoy means), and the artist's need to further the cause of art, this being the element of pure artistry that endures in all ages and nations.[38] Whatever expresses one's inner need is beautiful; therefore, the ugly pertains to expressions of an inner need that remains stunted.[39] Asserting that dirt, as a physical substance, "has its own inner appeal," Kandinsky declares: "At the call of the inner need that which is outwardly foul may be inwardly pure, and vice versa."[40] The urgency to express one's inner need raises the topic of catharsis, an activity that can be as important to the religious individual as it is to the artist who finds great relief through the act of creation. Overwhelmed by the force of her mystical visions, Hildegard of Bingen was sick until she expressed them.[41] The spiritual and the aesthetic intermingle in the report of Maria Cheng, professor of dance theory at the University of Minnesota:

When I feel most profoundly moved, or when I've had a cathartic experience, it's an enlightening of the further complexity of life. Those have been the moments of true enlightenment if you will. A sense of wonder and awe, and the deeper understanding is not that you've found another answer—the deeper understanding is a deeper sense of wonder and awe at the complexity and that the basis of the complexity is a unifying simplicity.[42]

Tolstoy elevates sincerity to the status of a necessary condition for creativity. It is controversial to insist that only sincere art will infect others, since forgeries sometimes deceive beholders. Still, no artist receives a full measure of praise who is completely lacking in sincerity. Moreover, "insincere religious person" is an oxymoron. Even if the Donatists were wrong in claiming that the effectiveness of the sacraments depended upon the purity of the priest, it would remain true that their effectiveness depends partly upon the purity of the communicants themselves. Moreover, perhaps a Mass celebrated by a hypocritical priest is effective, because God works sacramentally through the flawed clergyman. Since sincerity is crucial to human relations, one would naturally expect it to play a role in the basic human projects of art and religion.

Taoist painting and poetry have a common source: the artist conveys his inner sublimity through the transparency of his outer expression. Freed from attachment to all things, the artist's true self is able to participate in an ontological identification with them.

Such ontological purity is the origin of both Taoist poetry and painting. This is evident when the poems of Su Tung–p'o move Shih-t'ao to a painterly response. While Shih-t'ao was skeptical as to whether or not his paintings did justice to the poems, other judges have been less critical. What is important is that the artist's serenity of spirit or harmony with nature be objectified—whether as painting, poetry, or calligraphy. As one art work may influence or inspire another, one spiritual experience may be the catalyst for another. To complicate matters, a spiritual experience that one records in an art work may, in turn, elicit another spiritual experience. In his literary masterpiece *The Confessions,* Augustine reports that he heard the voice of God; when Teresa read this account, it triggered a like experience in her, thereby yielding a case in which one spiritual experience produces another through the medium of an artwork.

Method

By definition, in any discipline, work proceeds according to a method, whether anyone acknowledges it or not. Still, the ways of art and religion are different from the procedures in other practices. Unlike science, with its single, fixed methodology (frame a hypothesis, gather data, perform experiments in order to confirm or disconfirm one's thesis, and share findings with one's fellows), art and religion draw upon multiple methods. Hinduism, for example, has three basic ways to spiritual cultivation: *bhakti* yoga—in which one approaches the divine through heartfelt adoration, *karma* yoga—in which spirituality takes the form of right action by a resolute will, and *jnana* yoga—in which one strives for perfection through cultivation of the mind. While scientific methodology is singular and formulaic, religious practices are manifold—running the gamut from a Zen Buddhist tea ceremony to Gregorian chants—and open-ended. Of course, artistic practices constitute an endless flow of approaches, schools, styles, genres, and techniques. Neither the artist nor the saint must submit to any single, determinate approach or methodology. Their methodological freedom and playful spirit are in sharp contrast to the stereotype of the scientist as sober and conservative.

As the American aesthetician Monroe Beardsley once observed, a problem-solving outlook marks science. Typically, the scientist seeks to solve a problem or answer a question. Similarly, religion begins when one finds the universe to be problematic. Hence, the Buddha asks: "What is the cause of suffering?" And theists ask: Why is there evil? It is, however, dubious that this problem-solving model of science and religion is as satisfactory for explaining the activity of artists. Although the artist may begin with a space problem (how to render a three-dimensional subject on a two-dimensional surface), a color problem, or a conceptual problem, she may also begin with no explicit problem in mind and simply "experiment." In this sense, the artist may enjoy greater freedom than either the religious figure or the scientist.

The Chinese principle of *wu-wei* is really a prescription against overdoing or doing anything unnatural. Among the "Elegant Sayings" of the Lamas in Tibetan Buddhism, one finds, "A hen when at rest produces much fruit." The emphasis is not upon literal or absolute stagnation, but upon natural movement as most productive. In an artistic or spiritual context, the Taoist speaks of allowing things to take their course; this is *wu-wei* understood as noninterference. Things are beautiful and good to the degree that one allows them to go on naturally. The naturalist John Muir supports noninterference when he says, "I have never yet happened upon a trace of evidence that seemed to show that any one animal was ever made for another so much as it was made for itself."[43] For a Christian counterpart to *wu-wei*, John of the Cross encourages others ". . . to allow the soul to remain in peace and quietness, although it may seem clear to them that they are doing nothing. . . . The truth is that they will be doing quite sufficient if they have patience and persevere in prayer without making any effort."[44]

When Shih-t'ao insists that "the perfect man [artist] has no method," he does not mean that the artist lacks any method whatsoever, but that "No-method is the method which is the perfect method."[45] His *wu-fa* (no method) is a direct application of the principle of *wu-wei* to the activity of painting. He renounces all established methods or techniques in order to break new ground with his own style. To differentiate it from conventional methods, he calls it "no method." An artist who practices it is free from method in a sense, because he is unbounded by traditional formulas or rules. Of course, Shih-t'ao is not an aesthetic anarchist who is categorically calling for the abolition of all methods. Instead, he rejects conformity to a fixed or preconceived method and advocates only that method that is born in the immediacy of artistic activity. Ideally, without enslaving forethought the method arises spontaneously. On the first page of the seventeenth-century *Mustard Seed Garden Manual of Painting*, one reads that the goal of every method is to appear to have no method. In Taoism, which urges one to "do without doing," the ideal is to act "without leaving traces," i.e., without artificial or excessive effort. While copying the masters, some Chinese artists settled for prettiness or superficial beauty instead of originality. By contrast, Shih-t'ao's innovative style, which included a form of pointillism, is a free from the shackles of tradition, because it is a natural outpouring of an untrammeled mind.

There are no mechanical rules or dogmas that govern the artist or the saint. Rigid rules restrict artists' creativity; indeed, by definition, artists are rule breakers. A similar iconoclasm is evident in religious agents. In *The Cloud of Unknowing,* one finds: ". . . techniques and methods are ultimately useless for awakening contemplative love."[46] At the command of God, Abraham was ready to break the age-old moral sanction against killing an innocent. One finds an aesthetic counterpart in Tillich's assertion: "Every academic rule ever formulated has been broken by creative artists."[47] Gauguin expresses the essence of *wu-fa*: ". . . others have honored me by attributing a system to me, I have never had one, and could not condemn myself to it if I had. To paint as I please, bright today, dark tomorrow. The artist must be free or he is not an artist."[48] Gauguin talks about his "method" as if it were no fixed approach at all: "It is a technique that changes constantly, according to the mood I am in. . . . Is there a recipe for the making of beautiful things? . . . the answer I have repeated so often: I am capricious."[49]

While rules facilitate religious cultivation, they are far from the core of lived religion. The early Kabbalah commands one "to make innovations in the Torah according to his ability."[50] Because the immaterial values of religion and art lie beyond the physical realm, ordinary rules do not necessarily apply to them. Stephen De Staebler and Diane Apostolos-Cappadona find that there is no rule-bound foundation for the evolution of the artist and suggest that there is none for the emerging religious individual: "Art training involves many nonsensical rules that are turned into dogmas. Once you evolve into your own artist you realize that it is highly arbitrary what you choose to discard and what meanings you attach to all the variables. . . . Well, if that is true in art, then why isn't it true in religion?"[51] Meister Eckhart observes that conventional ways are futile: "Whoever is seeking God by ways is finding ways and losing God, who in ways is hidden. But whoever seeks for God without ways, will find him as he is in himself, and that man will live with the Son, and he is life itself."[52] Similarly, in *Ascent of Mt. Carmel,* ii, 4, John of the Cross states that the soul, which achieves cultivation, is beyond ways or methods.

To those who criticized his technique, Chagall replied: "But these paintings are beyond technique: what counts is the love in the painting."[53] He added, "I've always done without theory or method."[54] Since every artist produces in some way—according to some method—Chagall can only mean that he worked without a static procedure; in effect, he worked directly, freely, or naturally. Accordingly, Tolstoy accuses art schools of teaching students to produce counterfeit art—works that are records of second-hand experiences—and he does not hesitate to extend his critique of art schools to "theological colleges."

Ascetics, who prefer naturalness over the ornate, flamboyant, or excessive, are prone to favor a kind of "austere aesthetic," as in the elegant simplicity of a Japanese tea house. In an extreme act, Francis once dismantled the roof of a friary, because he regarded it as too sumptuous. Undoubtedly he would have preferred the stark beauty of a simple tea house. Surely, he would have appreciated the low-set entrance that requires one to stoop, bend, "bow," and humble himself in the act of entering. The Trappist monk Thomas Merton has commented upon the aesthetics of monastic buildings:

> The purity of taste in a monastery is not merely a matter of aesthetic training. It flows from something far higher—purity of heart. The simple chaste lines of a monastic Church, built perhaps by unskilled hands in the wilderness, may well say infinitely more in praise of God than the pretentious enormities of costly splendor that are erected to be looked at rather than to be prayed in.[55]

Praising the homely lark, Francis noted that: ". . . Its plumage is of the same color as the earth and is an example to us that we shall not have fine and colored clothes, but simple and plain . . ."[56] Among Chinese painters, a popular saying reminds one that the plain and simple can indeed be beautiful: "The ink has all five colors." That a painter can derive unending gradations from ink is apparent in Mu ch'i's painting of six persimmons wherein the forms range from asphalt black to subtle grays to a nearly evanescent white. Connoisseurs place a premium upon paintings that produce a maximum effect from minimal elements. The Chinese artist has long known about the understated beauty of the prosaic object or scene. Exemplifying this spirit, Francis's art is the art of non-art, the creation of art without contrivance. One commentator, who asserted that Francis's words were "very simple and without art,"[57] was incorrect; instead, they were without artifice. After all, some regard him as the first great Italian poet. Francis's powerfully simple expressions ("I bless them as much as I can—and more than I can.") were integrated into sermons of the highest order, for they issued from the beauty of a sincere heart, one whose deeply felt emotions and simplicity of language allowed him to transmit his infectious love of God to the least educated of his brothers and sisters.

Every act of creation is simultaneously a revelation. Therefore, Mu chi's creation of a lyrical landscape painting is at once revelatory, for it expresses the spirit of the invisible Tao. As Martland makes abundantly clear, it is not enough to say that art reflects reality, for art is not simply a mirror held up before objects. Instead, genuine art makes a fresh contribution to reality. Rather than just uncover a pre-existing reality, the art work is a new reality that reconstitutes and illumines other realities. To illustrate, the artist's landscape painting reveals the nature of mountains in all their universality, but it also contributes new entities: "mountains as rendered by Shih-t'ao," in all their particularity. Such an innovator produces no "recycled" landscape painting; instead, his charged yet stable scenes expand the domain of what there is. The viewer is then free to immerse himself in the work and "wander" among the mountains that Shih-t'ao has created.

Every act of revelation is at once a creation. For example, the I-Thou encounter is not merely the revelation of each person to the other but the "creation" of two more fully actualized persons, beings who come to be through their dialogue with each other. In fine, such meetings are not simply epistemological but ontological as well. Given the inherent incompleteness of an I—humans are communal creatures who yearn for a Thou—one can become an I only by affirming a Thou. Spontaneity and individuality mark the I-Thou event, as they do the creative process. One can never duplicate an I-Thou relation any more than one can duplicate a masterpiece or two connoisseurs can have exactly the same aesthetic appreciation of a given work. Indeed, a forgery is offensive partly because the original artwork embodies a unique I-Thou encounter between the artist and whatever subject was thematic. Since each I-Thou relation is irreducibly individual, language—which is common stock in a society—necessarily fails to convey such relationships. Art, which reclaims particularity and uniqueness for the artist, is the only vehicle that can hint at such states.

Shih-t'ao's colorful words discourage those who would slavishly copy master painters: "Even if one closely resembles such painters, then he only eats their leftovers (spoiled soup or broth)."[58] Shih-t'ao categorically rejects blind adherence to the artistic preferences, approaches, or proclivities of one's contemporaries or predecessors. His point is that great artists should be teachers who inspire, not masters who rule or dominate. Tolstoy would agree that the artist, who simply takes from others, produces counterfeit art. Indeed, if a beholder becomes seized with false art, it can only be due to the appeal of associations, references, or the wider context that takes one beyond the work itself. Certainly, Shih-t'ao never discouraged artists from drawing upon the geniuses of the past; indeed, traces of Ni Tsan, Mi Fu, and others are plainly manifest in his works. He even speaks of becoming united with such past masters, "In my loneliness, I went to the study of an artist friend, and there I found on the table some genuine works by Ni, Huang, Shih, and Tung; and as I met with them (contemplated them) day after day, I became united with them, and after a few days more I was with them even while eating and sleeping..."[59] Naturally, Shih-tao insisted that one must reconstruct and reconstitute when he returns to the masters. The mistake is to mimic the superficial features, the likenesses or appearances of the masters, rather than to grasp their spirit and express it according to one's own style. In fine, one must assimilate and transmute. When Shih-t'ao urged artists to paint from actual scenery, it was absolutely necessary to reestablish this point, since some artists were copying works by the masters rather than addressing nature directly. One must recognize the masters' contributions, but he must also transcend them. As with a boat that one abandons on reaching the other shore, the artist must eventually leave the masters behind if she is to complete her own odyssey.

Freedom constitutes a common goal of art and religion, since each involves escape or liberation, as in the *moksha* experience of Hinduism. One is free when she is unimpeded or self-determined. Coomaraswamy elaborates upon aesthetic liberty: "The artist's theoretical or imaginative act is said to be 'free' because it is not assumed or admitted that he is blindly copying any model extrinsic to himself, but expressing himself, even in adhering to prescription or responding to requirements that may remain essentially the same for millennia."[60] Just as important as freedom from outside constraints, is internal freedom, i.e., freedom from the lesser self or ego. One can hold that God created freely because he acted independently of any external forces or guidelines in fashioning the universe. After all, there was nothing else but God before the creation. While the artist's freedom is obviously of a different order,

Kandinsky sees religious significance in it and emphasizes that no supposed canons of correctness should enslave the artist: "Absolute freedom, whether from anatomy or anything of the kind, must be given the artist in his choice of material. Such spiritual freedom is as necessary in art as it is in life. . . . This freedom is man's weapon against the Philistines."[61]

From a religious perspective, when an artist enters into rapport with her subject, she must respond to its dictates, but she can still be free, because what she resonates to in the object is a spiritual energy that is continuous with her own. If humans are made in the image of God and if they submit to his will, they are conforming to their own essences. Although apparently paradoxical, the only way to freedom, for the artist and the religious person alike, is through surrender. One must put herself in accord with that which is natural. Lest one interpret surrender as an abandonment to utter irrationality, religions identify the natural as the touchstone of rationality. To go against the grain of nature is to meet obstructions, whether one is coming to terms with the principles and media of art or struggling with divine laws. As the eminent American architect Louis Kahn insisted, no architecture is possible without the cooperation of nature. Similarly, no spiritual cultivation is possible without conformity to the logos, Tao, or God. Artists and saints are free if and only if they put themselves in accord with the inexorable. Freedom, in either case, is a thoughtful harmonization as opposed to an irrational rebellion. Accordingly, Walt Whitman's first poem in *Leaves of Grass* can speak of "freest action form'd under the laws divine."

To the spiritually disposed, freedom does not consist in resisting nature, for the laws of nature themselves have a divine origin. When one subscribes to them, she satisfies a prerequisite for the actualization of her own individual freedom. One should not confuse conformity to the "method of no-method" with bondage, for this method eliminates the restraints of standard methods and offers the purest freedom in which the artist can participate. Only painting that accords with this approach liberates the artist. Accordingly, the artwork progresses "like water flowing downward and flames burning upward." When one's painting is boundless, his execution is immediate, unhesitating, and powerful—an uninterrupted outpouring of spirit. Religions have long distinguished between natural and conventional law, teaching that adherence to the former yields freedom, for it is the way of one's own nature, but that conventional law can be arbitrary and enslaving.

Rekha Jhanji identifies two conditions for escape from bondage that obtain in art and religion:

> The similarity between aesthetic enjoyment and the supreme bliss of mystical experience is based on the following two psychic conditions: (a) transcendence of egocentricity; and (b) desirelessness. As a consequence of these two conditions, both the (ideal) beholder of art works (*rasika*) and the mystic experience a sense of liberation, and it is this liberty which generates the bliss.[62]

According to Jhanji, the objects and emotions that the artist conjures up, because of their imaginary status, are not ones with which he has a personal involvement. "This freedom from involvement gives him the joy which is associated with play. It is this purity of joy which led Abhinavagupta to see a parallel between mystical ecstasy and aesthetic enjoyment, for the mystic, too, sees the world as a play (*līlā*) of the divine creator."[63] Thus, the Hindu has an aesthetic answer to the perennial question: "Why did God create the universe?" The deity *Īśvara* created out of sport, from an innate tendency to play. Creation was aesthetic and spontaneous, arising from the sheer joy of creating, i.e., from creation for its own sake. Neither ego nor practicality was at work. Isvara's creation is divine play, i.e., a disinterested activity in which a kind of "purposeless purpose" yields great freedom and joy. Kant's aesthetics includes the related concept of "purposiveness without purpose." Thus, humans who wish to imitate the divine should emulate the playfulness of children, since their activity resembles divine activity. The pure play of the child participates in the untrammeled, creative activity of Isvara. This language of play invites a further comparison between the artist and the mystic, as fellow seekers of primordial innocence, and the child who excels at boundless, uninhibited play. The sheer joy of having no burden naturally issues in expressions of art, religion, and love. Creativity is free action as opposed to determined behavior; and when there is neither external constraint nor the internal slavery of selfish motives, spontaneity flourishes. A contemporary Trappist monk relates play—"activity that is done for pure enjoyment, nothing else"—to prayer: "What is important about play is that it is like prayer—we can only do it when we look to God. In prayer, we look to God for him to take care of whatever needs taking care of. In the spirit of play, we look to

God to be taking care of what needs to be taken care of—otherwise we can't play!"[64]

Chagall observes a measure of freedom in the beholder's activity: "The freedom of the spectator's eye in my picture is the freedom of the brush on canvas."[65] By following the artist's lines, movements, colors, and contours, one sets down the yolk of everyday actions and experiences new movement, feeling, and vision—in a word, she leaves the mundane world of cause and effect and participates in the timelessness of the aesthetic realm. To appreciate a Jackson Pollack painting is to discover that it is alive; its animation derives from the original dance, i.e., the footsteps, strokes, body movements, and gestures of the artist.

8

The Aesthetic versus the Spiritual

While the present study has emphasized similarities between the aesthetic and the spiritual, it is now appropriate to consider and evaluate proposed differences. Broader than the concept "artistic," "aesthetic" embraces the appreciation of natural as well as artistic beauty. Moreover, the aesthetic refers to whatever rewards the act of apprehension itself, be it perception or conception. Likewise, one may interpret the concept "spiritual" as being broader than "religious," the latter sometimes being relegated to the category of the institutional as opposed to the personal. Given that the aesthetic and the spiritual are both wide-ranging, deeply human, and universal categories, it is not surprising that there are manifold relations between them. Nevertheless, a number of thinkers have distinguished between the two. Some insist that the spiritual transcends the aesthetic, going "beyond name and form" or "beyond all images, symbols, or physical manifestations." After all, it would seem that one cannot capture a formless absolute in forms, irrespective of how aesthetic they might be. In short, the spiritual pertains to what is ultimate or supreme, while the aesthetic is penultimate. A prayer by Thomas à Kempis is illustrative when it characterizes the divine as, ". . . above all riches and arts . . . and above all that falls short of Thyself, O Thou, my God!" Here, one declares the supremacy of God over all other things. Of course, this would include the human institution of religion itself. If God is truth, beauty, and goodness, then divine beauty—not artifactual beauty—represents the summit of aesthetic perfection. Indeed, Moslems, Jews, and some Protestants refuse to depict the divine, because they hold that it is impossible and that any such efforts dispose one toward idolatry. If individuals have an aversion to the distorting power of art, they place preeminence upon the inward turn that disposes one toward introvertive mysticism, thereby elevating introspection, meditation, and reflection over perception. Since the *Dharmakāya* is invisible and the Tao is an imageless, superconceptual void, both would appear to be beyond the reach of all art and sense experience. According to Coomaraswamy, for the worshiper, "... the value of an image does not depend upon its aesthetic qualities." Coomaraswamy adds that the perfected yogin transcends all names and forms and worships the deity as he is in himself.[1] This, however, seems to be possible only for the *jivanmukta*, i.e., perfected soul. Apparently, art remains penultimate, since all forms issue from the ultimate and formless Brahman, God, or Tao. In response to this claim, the extrovertive mystic notes that the interpenetration of forms and the formless undermines any total dichotomy between the two and that a turn outward to the world of art and nature deepens the interior life. Sensing the formless amidst forms, i.e., the absolute amidst its manifestations, artists create paintings or poems to express this intermingling. Mountains and rivers do not just point to the invisible Tao; they participate in this foundational reality and are as inseparable from it as an effect is from a cause.

That art originates with humans, rather than with God, is another reason to regard artistic values as penultimate. Of course, the matter is not simple. If an artist receives divine inspiration, it will appear in her work and will stultify any efforts to altogether detach artistic from supernatural beauties. After all, philosophers inevitably regard God, Tao, or Brahman as beautiful, beauty itself, or the ground of beauty. Moreover, if the absolute is all-pervasive, it will be evident in nature as well as in artifacts. Indeed, Francis finds God in "Brother Sun" and "Sister Moon." In short, he found the universal in the particular. It may be more accurate to say that he found the universal and the particular simultaneously, the One and the many, much as the Zen adept grasps mountains and rivers together with their root. Thus, one can also argue that human beauties and divine beauty are inseparable, because of the causal relationship between them. With a divinely inspired artist, the resultant artwork is at once a manifestation of human skill and an intimation of divine beauty. Moreover, Francis does not regard the beauties of nature merely as visible means to an invisible end;

instead, he finds all of nature to be a kind of theophany or aesthetic incarnation.

Some have urged that religious experiences are supremely intense and that they command one's greatest loyalties. Accordingly, to be ultimately concerned is to reach a point at which one is willing to become a martyr. It appears that this disposition has been less common among artists than among saints. Still, even if there are fewer artistic martyrs, it would not necessarily follow that they are less passionate than religious zealots. Nevertheless, one wonders about the intensity claim. At the conclusion of chapter nineteen of the *Dark Night of the Soul,* the lover of the Lord must see the beloved or die. One might ask if there is a counterpart in art, an equal urgency, a comparable assessment of art as equally vital to life itself. Disposed toward a negative answer, Rudolph Otto regards the aesthetic category of the sublime as "a pale reflexion" of the religious category of the numinous.[2] Also affirming the uniqueness of religion, Tillich denies that religion is simply an area alongside, say, politics, philosophy, law, or art. Instead, he views it as: "... the experience of a quality in all of these areas, namely, the quality of the holy or of that which concerns us unconditionally."[3] Of course, the aesthete might argue that the aesthetic is also not just an area alongside others, but a pervasive quality of all of them. After all, the aesthete can discern aesthetic properties everywhere. Perhaps Tillich is on more solid ground when he uses the term "unconditionally," for the commands of religion are unconditional, but those of art are contingent or hypothetical. Surely, nothing less than God's unconditioned command moves an Abraham to decide to sacrifice his son. Abraham does not act because he wishes to get some desired result. He acts from a categorical imperative; he responds to God's dictate; and if there is any counterpart in art, it can only be the divine inspiration that steers the artist. In fine, both sorts of experiences are transmundane, i.e., involve a break from the prosaic. Against Tillich, one might argue that it is difficult to separate the spiritual from the aesthetic; one's appreciation of a Chinese landscape painting may involve an interfusion of religion and art. Indeed, no spiritual experience is devoid of aesthetic import, whether it takes the form of a unifying encounter or a dramatic moment. When, for example, a Teresa loses herself in communion with the divine, a consummatory, i.e., an aesthetic quality, is present—as it is in the coming to fruition of any activity. Otto observes that the aesthetic and the spiritual invariably interpenetrate, "So the idea of the sublime is closely similar to the numinous, and is well adapted to excite it and to be excited by it, while each tends to pass over into the other."[4] Again, Thoreau's appreciation of Walden Pond is surely a mixed experience in which he could scarcely abstract the aesthetic from the spiritual. To think that mystical experiences transcend aesthetic experiences is to assume that it is possible to completely disentangle these two varieties of experience. This is, however, dubious, because one can appreciate all of reality—including the religious life—for its aesthetic qualities. In a hymn, the religious import is apparent, but in, for example, a silent prayer, the inner calm that descends upon one is an aesthetic harmony; the "peace that passes all understanding" is as beautiful as it is spiritual. Given the multiple ways in which religion and art interrelate, it is not surprising that any proposed distinctions between the two are subject to criticism and qualification. While Tillich holds that religious experiences surpass aesthetic experiences in terms of urgency, their similarity impresses him: "I know that no artistic experience can match the moments in which prophets were grasped in the power of the Divine Presence . . . but. . . . In both cases, the experience goes beyond the way we encounter reality in our daily lives. It opens up depths experienced in no other way."[5]

In the Buddhist text, the *Milinda-pañhā*, Nagasena, who denounces distractions from the spiritual path, explains that fools take pleasure in the senses or the objects of the senses. Because art ensnares the senses, it threatens to misdirect one from spirituality. An anecdote from early Buddhism relates that a monk, after living in a cave for sixty years, received visitors who exclaimed over the loveliness of a painting on a wall of the cave. Demonstrating his single-minded commitment to spiritual cultivation, he replied that he had never looked up and noticed it. Moreover, at the mouth of his cave, there was a huge ironwood tree. He never looked up at that either, only knowing that it was in flower when he saw its petals on the ground each year. John of the Cross preferred a rosary made out of the bones of the spine from a fish, since, lacking in workmanship, these "beads" would hardly induce the user to form attachments to "visible instruments." In the mystical, Sufi school of Islam, many praised Shaykh Shihab ad-din for remaining oblivious to the powerful effect of music while he immersed himself in God.[6] Orthodox Jews, who maintain that it is wrong to listen to live music on Saturdays, believe that it will take one away from his proper spiritual pursuits. Even an art lover like Tillich warns: ". . . an easy identification of the two functions of man's spirit . . . leads to a replacement of religion by the arts."[7] Paul Weiss finds another possible point of tension between art and religion when he con-

tends that the excellence of an artwork may have no relevance for
its efficacy in promoting religion. Of course, one may wonder how
aesthetic excellence can ever be neutral or a disvalue. Weiss gives
no example, but he adds that appreciating the excellence of a work
may take time and attention away from the practice of religion.[8]
Discussing liturgical art, Wolterstorff asserts that if it is not infe-
rior to numerous other works in a culture, ". . . its aesthetic
magnificence tends to distract us from the liturgy."[9] Clearly, religious art may misdirect one from religion. However, it remains to
be shown that excellent religious art necessarily does so. Both Weiss
and Wolterstorff express concern explicitly about great art. But
Andrew M. Greeley maintains that outstanding art, rather than
misdirecting one from religion, can deliver one to it. Indeed, there
may be no better way to approach religion than through its artistic
expressions, whether as hymns, chants, paintings, poems, sculptures, the drama of the Mass, stories, parables, allegories, dialogues, myths, dances, or architectural works. Certainly, there are
numerous testimonials to artworks as vessels of revelation. So
interpreted, their aesthetic excellence renders them all the more
efficacious in advancing one's religious life. Art, rather than distracting one from religion, can immerse him in it. Hence, the more
elegant and beautiful the Japanese tea ceremony, the deeper may
be one's religious experience. Accordingly, one might ask Weiss to
elaborate on how a great work of art can frustrate the pursuit of
religion.[10] He does write: "Some objects and activities, which had a
religious role, may lose this precisely because they are so enhanced
aesthetically that they inhibit rather than promote religious activity."[11] But Weiss's claim is dubious and, again, he offers no example. Moreover, he ignores the fact that one's attitude helps
determine if an object plays a religious role.

The means-end distinction explains much of the uneasiness
between art and religion. In Judaism, Islam, and Christianity, for
example, one traditionally values art, because it contributes to the
experience of worship. Religions accept art as a means to ethical or
spiritual cultivation, but if one esteems art over all else, then he is
an idolater. In Tillich's terms, one is devoting ultimate concern
toward that which is not ultimate. According to such a "life-boat
theory of art," even masterpieces are vehicles that one should leave
behind after they have carried her to the other shore, i.e., to a taste
of the transcendent. In *Self-Consuming Artifacts: The Experience of
Seventeenth-Century Literature*, Stanley E. Fish writes about artworks that "self-consume" after they have served their religious
purpose. No longer useful, they are left behind and forgotten.

Nonetheless, one can challenge any such distinction between the sacred and the profane. Art, after all, is a part of religion. Singing hymns, for example, is not a mere means to religion; it is itself one aspect of a religious life. Even if the religious figure could detach art from religion, she cannot abandon the aesthetic, for one aim of religion is to attain spiritual consciousness, i.e., a state that is aesthetic (blissfully harmonious) rather than unaesthetic (discordant or incoherent). In short, even if, at its culmination, spirituality can exist without art, spirituality surely cannot exist without the aesthetic.

Of course, the aesthetic can have intrinsic value; it can attract as a self-contained phenomenon and not merely because it is conducive to promoting spiritual consciousness. Still, there is a hierarchy of intrinsic values in which some command greater allegiance than others. Seen from below, each is the end produced by some means, but viewed from above each is also the means to some further end. Only the spiritual is the ultimate good, for one does not turn to peak religious experiences in hopes of reaching loftier experiences. Thus, art is a means to the ultimate end of religious fulfillment. Of course, one can appreciate art as an end in itself, as in the cry "art for art's sake." But such an end—to promote enjoyment—is a lower end than enlightenment or spiritual rebirth and lower ends are means. Nevertheless, too sharp a distinction is being made when Coomaraswamy states: ". . . from a Christian point of view, the work of art is always a means, and never an end in itself."[12] One can appreciate the aesthetic qualities of an artwork for their own sake alone as well as for their contribution toward a religious end. Because art cannot be the end for a Christian, it does not follow that it cannot be an end. One can appreciate an artwork as an ingredient in a greater whole, i.e., as a means, but also as an end in itself. Not only can the two kinds of appreciation alternate, but subgression, i.e., the interfusion of both in a seamless experience, can occur. Indeed, this may help explain why Coomaraswamy refuses to distinguish between religion and art. In addition, an artwork is suitable for religious purposes precisely because it has autonomous, aesthetic value as opposed to, say, mere economic worth. When such art becomes a part of religion, it would not make sense to ignore its intrinsic value. In any case, it is dubious that a sensitive beholder could do so. Like religion, art is both a way or a means and the end to which the way leads.

According to Tillich, philosophy (with its concepts) and art (with its aesthetic qualities) are indirect ways to experience ultimate reality, religion being the direct way.[13] With religion, one may con-

front God directly, but in art, he meets God through the medium
of human fabrication. Paul Weiss agrees that in religious art: "God
is not faced directly, but only in the form of a qualification of existence."[14] Certainly, there is an immediacy to the religious encounter in which all language and imagery fall away and one meets the
"wholly other" without any such intermediaries. One may wish, for
example, to encounter the *Dharmakāya* behind the "mountains and
the rivers." From his idealistic perspective, Hegel explains that the
religious sphere as inner transcends the aesthetic as outer: "The
absolute is here removed from the externality of artistic production, and is received in a more spiritual way by the imagination, so
that the heart and the emotion, the inner life of the individual that
is to say, becomes its vehicle."[15] If art is a language by which one
speaks about reality, perhaps art cannot be a direct, unmediated
encounter with ultimate reality. It would seem that there is unmediated revelation only in spiritual experience as contrasted with
aesthetic experiences that are, given the media of the arts, inherently mediated. While Francis hears the voice of God without
mediation, the arts can only communicate through their respective
media. Art represents, depicts, imitates, expresses, refers to, sati-
rizes, or symbolizes; and, in doing so, it invariably reconstitutes its
object of attention. Of course, some defenders of the potency of art,
such as Clive Bell, believe that concentration upon significant form
can free one from representational data and enable her to intuit a
formless, metaphysical reality. As a pointing finger may lead one to
a direct vision of the moon, an artwork can lead one to a direct
apprehension of the thing in itself. Still, even if art can effect a
direct experience of ultimate reality, there remains an irony, for
just at the moment when art unites the human and the divine,
perception of that art may cease as one experiences an undifferentiated state of consciousness (one devoid of all ideas and sense
impressions). Nevertheless, if this is a condition of blissful equipoise—as it surely is—the aesthetic is present. Moreover, it is only
one form of spiritual-aesthetic experience. By contrast, Buber's
meeting of the I and the Thou is one that preserves both realities
in all their integrity and distinctness as well as their mutuality.

Another possible rift between the aesthetic and the spiritual
arises when one associates the former with the unreal. Some contemporary philosophers, such as Jean-Paul Sartre, deem art to be
an escape from the realities of life. One reply is that although art
sometimes involves escapism, it also delivers insights into reality.
In the *Republic*, Plato characterizes art as being at two removes
from the real, since the painter copies a physical horse that is itself

only a copy of the eternal and ideal form of a horse. Nevertheless, Plato's *Ion* leaves room for the inspired artist to intuit the metaphysical forms and convey some notion of them in his art. If things that one sees are fleeting and the things that he does not see endure (2 Corinthians 4:18), this would apparently relegate art to the status of superficiality. But a Christian could reply that just as the invisible Word was made flesh, divine inspiration can animate a painting. In addition, even if art cannot disclose the non-physical—and this may be conceding too much—art may excel at symbolizing it. At its most profound level, art is a quest for the real, a search for the ground of all existence. Even escapist art may deliver moral insights and express metaphysical truths in poetic or mythological language.

Some philosophers, who contrast spiritual activity with aesthetic passivity, assert that religion carries a practical urgency or impetus to action that is absent from art. This seems to follow from the fact that religion contains commands or imperatives that move humans to act. In particular, religious experiences lead to a commitment to action. In the final pages of *Psychology of the Imagination*, Jean-Paul Sartre distinguishes similarly between the aesthetic and the ethical by asserting that only the latter entails action in the real world. Also contrasting the moral with the aesthetic, Nicholas Wolterstorff maintains that to change one's moral character is to change how he is apt to act in the future, but aesthetic satisfaction pertains to what obtains ". . . while engaged in contemplation. It may or may not have consequences extending beyond the experience. But it itself is an experience of the moment."[16] Of course, one may contest any such distinction between the aesthetic as contemplative and the moral or religious as active. Tillich is living proof that aesthetic experiences do sometimes incline one to action; his study and appreciation of copies of artworks sustained him and enabled him to carry on in the face of wartime atrocities. To create or behold art is to engage in *wu-wei,* i.e., natural activity, rather than artificial striving or absolute inaction. At first glance, aesthetic appreciation appears to accomplish nothing, but it can foster self-cultivation; and nothing can be more natural than to develop one's nature. Therefore, aesthetic experience does culminate in action; indeed, it shapes the very self that is the only agent of human action. In a sense, a motion picture consists of a number of "rests," but the pauses in life that we call aesthetic experiences are only "pseudo rests," for amidst such respites there is the dynamic activity of enlightenment and psychic integration, a "collecting of the self" that is anything but stagnation. Art refreshes and liberates one, not because it temporarily puts an end to all her actions or motions, i.e., not because it immobilizes her, but because it offers her surcease from routine actions and reactions. As Coleridge points out, the artist not only creates works, but he recreates beholders. This is just to say that the poet transforms them into poets. "We know a man for a poet," says Coleridge, "from the fact that he makes us poets." Similarly, we can know that a man is religious from the fact that he makes us religious. As with other kinds of profound experiences, one would not call the aesthetic variety profound if it did not somehow change the individual. One reason that aesthetic experience is transformative is that it is illuminating; and what one knows influences her actions; thus one's encounters with art and nature can greatly influence her behavior. What Thoreau discovered at Walden Pond clearly reconstituted him. One might argue that Thoreau's rapport with nature was spiritual rather than aesthetic, but he himself would have resisted efforts to tease the two categories apart. Indeed, he was himself a confluence of both, not to mention the scientific. Underhill holds that the artist, unlike the mystic, whose states are ineffable, has the duty to act and thereby express what he perceives: "In his worship of Perfect Beauty, faith must be balanced by works."[17] Clearly, history belies Underhill's claim, for the mystic has a twofold duty, the first being to witness, i.e., to share her spiritual journey with others, and the latter being to find her self by expressing her self. Through writings, teachings, or actions, the mystic necessarily manifests something of her interior life—whether she expresses herself with the eloquence of a Teresa or the faltering efforts of one who is less artistically gifted. In short, the religious figure has as much obligation to communicate her deepest experiences as Underhill assigns to the artist.

Typically, philosophers characterize aesthetic experience as dualistic, since the subject or beholder and the object are two. Nevertheless, some thinkers characterize the highest spiritual experience as monistic, since they experience the individual self and the absolute as one and the same reality. Such monists sometimes distinguish between aesthetic and spiritual experiences on the grounds that only in the latter can one discover that she is identical with the absolute, as when the Hindu proclaims: "Atman is Brahman." The unity in aesthetic experience is psychological—one "loses" herself in the artwork, loses track of time, space, and whatever else is not thematic in the aesthetic object. In monistic religious experience, however, one believes that the unity is ontological, for she discovers her metaphysical identity with the divine. Of course, an artwork can awaken such an ontological experience. In any case, the distinction certainly does mark off some cases of spiritual experience—the monistic or non-dualistic variety—from aesthetic experiences. It does not, however, differentiate between theistic or dualistic religious experiences—whether in Hinduism, Judaism, Islam, Christianity, or Native American traditions—and aesthetic experiences. Indeed, Buber's inherently dualistic I-Thou orientation furnishes one paradigm for aesthetic appreciation. If the Hindu monist is correct, Buber's irreducible I-Thou dualism would seem to be wrong. Still, it remains to be shown why an omnipotent God could not appear to one person as that individual's very own self and to another as a separate Thou or even as the wholly other.

Some thinkers propose that spiritual experience is enduring, but aesthetic experience is fleeting. Underhill, for example, distinguishes between the mystic and the artist according to the duration of their experiences: the mystic lingers in the more real world, "... hovering like the six-winged seraph before the face of the Absolute," while the artist remains in this domain only fleetingly during her moments of creativity.[18] Of course, one may argue that religious experiences are just as evanescent; indeed, William James identified transiency as a feature of mystical states. Mystics are forever meditating, praying, chanting, practicing breathing exercises, and the like, all in order to reestablish the desired condition of consciousness. One might also challenge Abhinavagupta's distinction between aesthetic experience and mystical experience according to which the former catches only temporarily what the latter inculcates as a permanent disposition, namely, freedom from desire.[19] Again, this is dubious, because mystical states are transitory.

A more promising proposal for distinguishing between the aesthetic and the spiritual requires a turn to intentions. One might first consider the role of intentions in magic as opposed to religion. Magic is manipulative, because if the priest performs the sacrifice correctly, the gods must conform to his will. By contrast, religion requires conformity to the will of God. Although this distinction is surely subject to criticism and qualification, it does separate cases in which one's own character and intentions are relevant from those in which they are not. Intentions count in art and religion in a way that they do not count in science and magic, for a fiend could be a good scientist or magician, provided that his acts produced the desired results. If a fiend synthesizes the chemicals that can cure a deadly disease, he gets high marks as a scientist—even if he refuses to share his formula with the world. Similarly, if a man successfully performs a rain dance, he receives full credit as a magician—even if he danced in order to produce a devastating flood. One cannot be a hypocritical scientist or magician in the same way that one can be an insincere saint or artist. Indeed, Tolstoy held the romantic and popular view that the sincerity of the artist is a prerequisite for great art. By contrast, the character of the magician is irrelevant to his practice, since anyone who goes through the requisite actions, however mechanically, will effect the desired outcome. Neither art nor religion shares the routine, formulaic nature of magic. Of course, both the artist and the religious person run the risk of becoming as mechanical as the magician. If an artist becomes a mere imitator, he reduces his status to that of a lackluster craftsperson. To unreflectively "go through the motions" of, say, performing the Mass is to reduce oneself from a priest to a magician.

Before considering how intentions divide the spiritual from the aesthetic, it may be well to look at one way in which the two converge. According to the intentional fallacy in aesthetics, it is an error to interpret or judge a work of art on the basis of its creator's intentions. Unintended elements may turn out to be valuable features of the work and the creator's intentions are often unavailable. To illustrate, when someone asked T.S. Eliot, "Who is the 'companion' in your poem "The Love Song of J. Alfred Prufrock'?" Eliot conceded that he did not know. The questioner volunteered: "Could it be the other side of your self?" Eliot gratefully accepted this reading, learning something from it and thereby demonstrating that not even the poet himself can always be the definitive interpreter of his own poems. There is a parallel in the writings on spirituality of Henri J.M. Nouwen: "Someone might read what I wrote and discover something there that I myself did not see, but which might be just as valid as my original thought.... If I were to prevent people from drawing 'wrong' implications from my thoughts, I might fall into the temptation of thinking that I know what all the implications are."[20] Just as one might interpret an artwork differently from the way its originator does, the interpreter of spiritual remarks may understand them differently from the way their author does.

Despite the above similarity between art and religion, intentions function differently in one important regard; they can suffice in religion and ethics in a way that they cannot in art. For unrealized intentions—no matter how lofty—do not yield art. One may earnestly yearn to write the great American novel, but fail utterly at the task. In short, art begins on the other side of unrealized intentions. To the contrary, for Immanuel Kant, thwarted intentions in no way diminish the good will:

> Even if, by some especially unfortunate fate or by the niggardly provision of stepmotherly nature, this will should be wholly lacking in the power to accomplish its purpose; if with the greatest effort it should achieve nothing, and only the good will should remain (not, to be sure, as a mere wish but as the summoning of all the means in our power), yet would it, like a jewel, still shine by its own light as something which has full value in itself.[21]

It is noteworthy that this passage, which one might use to mark off the spiritual as well as the ethical from the artistic, is itself one of the most aesthetically stirring in Kant's writings. In a religious parallel, Teresa expresses the priority of intentions over results: "Don't think He [God] needs our works; He needs the determination of our wills."[22] Likewise, Thomas à Kempis states: "God . . . judges all things according to the intent of the doer, not according to the greatness or worthiness of the deed."[23]

Artists assume that intentions are necessary for creativity; thus, Tolstoy explicitly states that art is an activity in which an artist "intentionally transmits" a feeling to others.[24] Successful paintings, poems, dances, and sculptures all proceed from persons who have the appropriate intentions. Indeed, good results in religion, medicine, and law are scarcely accidental; they also follow from the proper intentions. However many there are, however ephemeral they may be, and however fast they succeed each other, intentions are all-important. Despite the cliché that says that the road to hell is paved with good intentions, good intentions are crucial in both art and religion as they are in all human endeavors. After all, from the fact that some power beyond one's control may prevent him from realizing his good intentions, it surely does not follow that he should adopt bad intentions. In the case of religion and morality, as opposed to art, intentions may be all that matters. Artists and religious figures agree that a good intention is a necessary condition for achievement, but Kant thinks that a good intention is a sufficient condition for moral excellence, provided only that one tries conscientiously to realize it. If circumstances beyond one's control prevent him from acting, he loses no ethical credit whatsoever.

There are, however, exceptional cases in which the agent's intention does not determine the outcome of a religious activity. In

Catholic doctrine, the performance of an *opus operatum,* e.g., a sacrament, is efficacious, regardless of the intentions of the priest who performs the rite. In a second kind of case, the Buddhist tries to empty his mind of all intentions or concepts in order that intuition can break forth. To illustrate, an eighth-century Chinese verse says that as wild geese fly, their reflection appears in the water below. Just as the geese do not mean to throw their image upon the water, the water does not mean to catch it. Nevertheless, it is at this instant, "that their beauty is most purely reflected."[25] Similarly, it is when an artist suspends all strained intentionality that she gives free play to her creativity.

Conclusion

Coomaraswamy's identification of art and religion is surely an overstatement; rather, they are irreducible, if often interrelated, expressions of the human spirit. As the tea ceremony demonstrates, the beautiful and the spiritual can arise and flourish as two, complementary aspects of a seamless experience. Indeed, they sometimes coalesce to the point that one may not be able to distinguish between them. Ideally, when the aesthetic and the sacred so interpenetrate, whether in a rain dance or a Gregorian chant, the beholder's unified experience will restore him to wholeness. Religion needs art to foster such wholeness or self-integration; and great religious art arises from just such personal wholeness. Of course, the non-religious art lover and the religious zealot, who rejects all art as idolatry, both deny this interdependence.

However often art and religion coexist, they need not do so in a peak experience. Teresa, for example, recognizes a moment at which one should turn from an artistic depiction of Christ in order to behold the divine presence itself:

> You may be in the habit of praying
> while looking at a picture of Christ,
> but at a time like this,
> do not turn away from the living image,
> the Person himself,
> to look at His picture.

> We do not carry on a conversation
> with a portrait,
> when the person we love is present.
> When a person is absent,
> and we feel his loss by our great aridity,
> then it is a great comfort
> to use a picture of the one we love.[26]

Like a raft that one leaves behind when he reaches land, one may leave art behind after it triggers spiritual states of mind. Of course, this hardly diminishes the crucial role that art plays in facilitating the onset of profound religious experiences. Moreover, there is a kind of mutuality, since spiritual consciousness is often a means to the creation of art. Relating the numinous to other states, Rudolph Otto declares: "It is a content of feeling that is qualitatively sui generis, yet at the same time one that has numerous analogies with others, and therefore it and they may reciprocally excite or stimulate one another and cause one another to appear in the mind."[27] One can only add that among the "others," it is the aesthetic that is preeminent. Art did not originate in religion nor did religion originate in art; neither preceded the other, for both are primordial, i.e., fundamental to human nature, and each nourishes and is nourished by the other. They are co-originating and co-transforming powers by which one becomes more human and expresses what is more than human.

Presumably, in the bliss of heaven, there would be no conventional, institutional religion as such. The need for rituals and symbols would drop away. Thomas à Kempis states: "When what is perfect shall come, all use of the sacraments will cease, for they who are blessed in the heavenly glory have no need of this sacramental medicine."[28] Perhaps traditional prayer also becomes superfluous for any one who enjoys the beatific vision of God, possibly creeds and commandments as well. Of course, even if there is no practical need for the sacraments, rituals, and prayers, they may endure because of their aesthetic value. Indeed, even if the institutions of art and religion are penultimate, surely aesthetic delight—which can, of course, be intuitive or conceptual as well as perceptual—and spiritual bliss would abide in any afterlife. Just as surely, the beauties of the beatific vision would endure as long as beings continued to enjoy their spiritual natures. Art is a means to spiritual states of mind, but the resultant spiritual consciousness is itself aesthetic. Thus, it would be a mistake to think that the aesthetic is left behind in a peak state. Whether or not one transcends art, the aesthetic remains an ongoing and ineradicable aspect of spiritual consciousness. Wherever there is harmonious consciousness and wherever there is the delight of uniting with the other, the aesthetic is present.

One may wonder if there is a common longing that drives religion and art; and one may wonder what gives them such urgency. While Nietzsche recognizes the will to power as the greatest human yearning and Thomas Hobbes identifies the will to live as the strongest human urge, poets and monks demonstrate that the will to find meaning in life can outstrip all other hungers. This is how art and religion gain their potency, for both are incomparably suited to communicate meaning, i.e., human significance and values.

Notes

Introduction

1. James Alfred Martin, *Beauty and Holiness: The Dialogue between Aesthetics and Religion* (Princeton: Princeton University Press, 1990), p. 166.

2. Roland Fischer, "A Cartography of the Ecstatic and Meditative States," *Understanding Mysticism*, ed. Richard Woods O.P., (Garden City, New York: Doubleday, 1980), p. 301.

3. William James, *The Varieties of Religious Experience* (New York: New American Library, 1958), p. 32.

4. See, for example, Thomas R. Martland, *Religion As Art: An Interpretation* (Albany: State University of New York Press, 1981); Hans Urs von Balthasar, *The Glory of the Lord: A Theological Aesthetics*, trans. Erasmo Leiva-Merikakis; ed. Joseph Fessio and John Riches (San Francisco: Ignatius Press; New York: The Crossroad Publishing Company, 1983–1991); Frank Burch Brown, *Religious Aesthetics: A Theological Study of Making and Meaning* (Princeton: Princeton University Press, 1989); Patrick Sherry, *Spirit and Beauty: An Introduction to Theological Aesthetics* (Oxford: Clarendon Press, 1992); and Andrew M. Greeley, *Religion as Poetry* (New Brunswick and London: Transaction Publishers,1995).

5. Friedrich Schleiermacher, *On Religion: Speeches to its Cultured Despisers*, trans. John Oman (New York: Harper & Brothers, 1959), p. 138.

6. Ananda K. Coomaraswamy, *The Transformation of Nature in Art* (New York: Dover Publications, Inc., 1956, as published by the Harvard University Press in 1934), p. 62.

7. Paul Weiss, *Religion and Art* (Milwaukee: Marquette University Press, 1963), p. 1.

8. Wassily Kandinsky, *Concerning the Spiritual in Art*, trans. M.T.H. Sadler (New York: Dover Publications, Inc., 1977), p. 7.

9. Clive Bell, *Art* (New York: Capricorn Books, 1958), p. 71.

10. Weiss, p. 15.

11. C.R. Leslie, *Memoirs of the Life of John Constable*, ed. Jonathan Mayne (London: Phaidon Press, 1951), p. 280.

Chapter 1

1. Seyyed Hossein Nasr, *Islamic Art and Spirituality* (Albany: State University of New York Press, 1987), p. 9.

2. John W. Dixon, "Painting as Theological Thought: The Issues in Tuscan Theology," *Art, Creativity, and the Sacred*, ed. Diane Apostolos-Cappadona (New York: Crossroad, 1984), pp. 293–5.

3. Nicholas Wolterstorff, *Art in Action* (Grand Rapids, Michigan: William B. Eerdman's Publishing Company, 1980), p. 62.

4. Paul Tillich, *What is Religion?*, trans. with an intro. by James Luther Adams (San Francisco: Harper and Row, Publishers, Inc., 1969), pp. 151–81.

5. Tillich, *On Art and Architecture*, ed. John Dillenberger and Jane Dillenberger, trans. Robert P. Scharlemann (New York: The Crossroad Publishing Company, 1987), p. 182.

6. Leo Tolstoy, *What is Art?* trans. Almyer Maude (Indianapolis and New York: Bobbs-Merrill Company, Inc., 1980), p. 15.

7. *Ibid.*, pp. 66–7.

8. George Dickie, *Art and the Aesthetic: An Institutional Analysis* (Ithaca: Cornell University Press, 1974).

9. Tillich, p. 172.

10. William E. Horden, *A Layman's Guide to Protestant Theology* (New York: Macmillan Company, 1973), p. 44.

11. Wassily Kandinsky, "Concerning the Spiritual in Art," *Art, Creativity, and the Sacred*, ed. Apostolos-Cappadona, p. 4.

12. Quoted by Cliff Edwards, *Van Gogh and God* (Chicago: Loyola University Press, 1989), p. 160.

13. Evelyn Underhill, *Mysticism: A Study in the Nature and Development of Man's Spiritual Consciousness* (New York: E.P. Dutton & Co., Inc., 1961), p. 174.

14. Andre Verdet, *Chagall's World: Reflections from the Mediterranean* (Garden City, New York: Doubleday & Company, Inc., 1984), p. 50.

15. *Ibid.*, p. 57.

16. Meister Eckhart, *Meister Eckhart: The Essential Sermons, Commentaries, Treatises, and Defense*, trans. and introduced by Edmund Colledge, O.S.A. and Bernard McGinn (New York: Paulist Press, 1981), p. 205.

17. *Ibid.*, p. 251.

18. Tillich, p. 54.

19. Chung-yuan Chang, *Creativity and Taoism: A Study of Chinese Philosophy, Art, and Poetry* (New York: Harper & Row, Publishers, Inc., 1963), p. 176.

20. Maurice Friedman, *Encounter on the Narrow Ridge: A Life of Martin Buber* (New York: Paragon House, 1991), p. 132.

21. Cecila Davis Cunnigham, "Craft: Making and Being," *Art, Creativity, and the Sacred*, ed. Apostolos-Cappadona, p. 11.

22. Tillich, p. 33.

23. *Ibid.*, p. 166.

24. *Ibid.*

25. *Ibid.*, p. 190.

26. *Ibid.*, p. 173.

27. Tolstoy, p. 143.

28. Tillich, p. 121.

29. Ananda K. Coomaraswamy, *Christian and Oriental Philosophy of Art* (New York: Dover Publications, Inc., 1956), p. 10.

30. Wolterstorff, p. 117.

31. Kandinsky, *Concerning the Spiritual in Art*, p. 28.

32. Sue Bender, *Plain and Simple: A Woman's Journey to the Amish* (San Francisco, New York: Harper & Row, Publishers, Inc., 1989), p. 1.

33. Tillich, p. 146.

34. Weiss, p. 60.

35. Tillich, p. 113.

36. John Dewey, *Art As Experience* (New York: G.P. Putnam's Sons, 1958), p. 9.

37. Wolterstorff, p. 170.

38. Coomaraswamy, *Christian and Oriental Philosophy of Art*, p. 102.

39. *Ibid.*, pp. 75–6.

40. Tolstoy, p. 67.

41. *Ibid.*, p. 95.

42. *Ibid.*, p. 53.

43. *The Cloud of Unknowing and The Book of Privy Counseling*, ed. William Johnston (New York: Doubleday, 1973), pp. 151–2.

44. Tolstoy, p. 72.

45. Paul Gauguin, *Gauguin's Letters from the South Seas*, trans. Ruth Pielkovo (New York: Dover Publications, Inc., 1992), p. 38.

Chapter 2

1. Underhill, *Mysticism: A Study*, p. 272.

2. Verdet, p. 87.

3. Emilie Zum Brunn and Georgette Epiney-Burgard, eds. and trans., *Women Mystics in Medieval Europe* (New York: Paragon House, 1989), p. 78.

4. Teresa of Avila, *The Life of St. Teresa: Of the Order of Our Lady of Carmel, Written by Herself*, trans. David Lewis, ed. Benedict Zimmerman, O.C.D. (Westminster, Maryland: The Newman Bookshop, 1944), p. 455.

5. James, p. 59.

6. Underhill, "The Essentials of Mysticism," *Understanding Mysticism*, ed. Woods, p. 38.

7. Teresa, *The Life of St. Teresa*, p. 252.

8. *Ibid.*, p. 366.

9. *Ibid.*, p. 429.

10. Teresa of Avila, *The Interior Castle*, trans. Kieran Kavanaugh, O.C.D. and Otilio Rodriguez, O.C.D. (New York: Paulist Press, 1979), p. 14.

11. Shin'ichi Hisamatsu, *Philosophy of Painting by Shih T'ao*, trans. Earle J. Coleman (The Hague: Mouton Publishers, 1978), pp. 15–16.

12. Bell, p. 54.

13. Rudolph Otto, *The Idea of the Holy*, trans. John W. Harvey (New York: Oxford University Press, 1969), p. 66.

14. Ralph Brown, *The Little Flowers of St. Francis*, trans. Raphael Brown (Garden City, New York: Doubleday, 1958), p. 196.

15. Johnston, p. 126.

16. Langdon B. Gilkey, "Can Art Fill the Vacum?," *Art, Creativity, and the Sacred*, ed. Apostolos-Cappadona, p. 189.

17. Bell, p. 33.

18. Verdet, p. 67.

19. *Ibid.*, p. 68.

20. *Ibid.*

21. Belden C. Lane, *Landscapes of the Sacred: Geography and Narrative in American Spirituality* (New York: Paulist Press, 1988), p. 159.

22. Thomas à Kempis, *The Imitation of Christ*, trans. Richard Whitford (New York: Doubleday, 1955), p. 231.

23. Tillich, p. 217.

24. Frank Lloyd Wright, *Conversations with Artists*, ed. Selden Rodman (New York: Capricorn Books, 1961), p. 48.

25. Bender, p. 136.

26. Otto, p. 29.

27. *Ibid.*, p. 69.

28. *Ibid.*, p. 70.

29. Kandinsky, p. 39.

30. Martin Buber, *I and Thou*, trans. Walter Kaufmann (New York: Charles Scribner's Sons, 1970), p. 54.

31. *Ibid.*, p. 113.

32. *Ibid.*, p. 125.

33. Teresa, *The Interior Castle*, p. 76.

34. Shih-t'ao, *Philosophy of Painting by Shih T'ao*, p. 102.

35. Bender, p. 49.

36. Buber, p. 125.

37. Ernest Hemingway, *The Green Hills of Africa* (New York: Charles Scribner's Sons, 1935), p. 12.

38. Buber, p. 58.

39. *Ibid.,* p. 173.

40. *Ibid.,* p. 57.

41. *Ibid.,* p. 59.

42. Black Elk, *Black Elk Speaks: Being the Life Story of a Holy Man of the Oglala Sioux*, as told through John G. Neihardt (New York: Washington Square Press, 1972), p. 167.

43. Buber, p. 61.

44. Chang, p. 188.

45. Jacques Maritain, *Creative Intuition in Art and Poetry* (New York: New American Library, 1953), p. 289.

46. Eckhart, p. 249.

47. Buber, p. 137.

48. Zum Brunn and Epiney-Burgard, eds. and trans., *Women Mystics*, p. 92.

49. Johnston, p. 96.

Chapter 3

1. James, p. 49.

2. Johnston, pp. 91–2.

3. Teresa, *The Interior Castle*, p. 96.

4. Vincent van Gogh, *The Complete Letters of Vincent Van Gogh*, Introduction by V.W. van Gogh, Preface and Memoir by J. van Gogh-Bonger, 3 vols. (Boston: New York Graphic Society, 1981), Vol. III., p. 58.

5. James, pp. 228–9.

6. Teresa, *The Life of St. Teresa*, p. 108.

7. *Ibid.,* pp. 465–6.

8. Augustine, *Augustine of Hippo: Selected Writings*, trans. Mary T. Clark (New York: Paulist Press, 1984), p. 28.

9. Buber, *I and Thou*, pp. 80–1.

10. *Ibid.,* p. 131.

11. Louis Z. Hammer, "The Relevance of Buber's Thought to Aesthetics," *The Philosophy of Martin Buber*, ed. Paul Arthur Schilpp and Maurice Friedman (LaSalle, Illinois, and London: Open Court Publishing Co., 1967), p. 616.

12. Buber, p. 60.

13. G.K. Chesterton, *St. Francis of Assisi* (Garden City, New York, Doubleday, 1955), pp. 87–8.

14. Walking Buffalo, *Touch the Earth: A Self-Portrait of Indian Existence*, compiled by T.C. McLuhan (New York: Simon and Schuster, 1971), p. 23.

15. Otto, p. 177.

16. *Ibid.*, p. 160.

17. Henri J.M. Nouwen, *The Genesee Diary: Reports from a Trappist Monasatery* (New York: Doubleday, 1981), pp. 140–1.

18. Lane, p. 45.

19. Edward Bullough, "'Psychical Distance' as a Factor in Art and as an Aesthetic Principle," *The British Journal of Psychology* Vol. 5 (1912): pp.87–117.

20. Edward Abbey, *Desert Soltaire: A Season in the Wilderness* (New York: Balantine Books, 1971), p. 14.

21. Underhill, "The Mystic as Creative Artist, *"Understanding Mysticism*, ed. Woods, p. 401.

22. Anthony De Mello, *The Way to Love: the Last Meditations of Anthony De Mello* (New York: Doubleday, 1992), pp. 97–8.

23. *Ibid.*, p. 108.

24. Eckhart, p. 285.

25. *Ibid.*, p. 288.

26. *Ibid.*, pp. 291–2.

27. F.C. Happold, *Mysticism* (Baltimore, Maryland: Penguin Books, 1963), p. 70.

28. Roger Fry, *Vision and Design* (New York: The New American Library, Inc., 1956), pp. 24–5.

29. Thomas R. Martland, *Religion As Art: An Interpretation* (Albany: State University of New York Press, 1981), p. 7.

30. Thomas Merton, *Contemplative Prayer* (New York: Doubleday, 1990), p. 112.

31. Underhill, *Mysticism: A Study*, p. 301.

32. Buber, pp. 112–113.

33. Immanuel Kant, *Critique of Judgment*, trans. J.H. Bernard (New York: Hafner Publishing Co., 1951), p. 65.

34. Buber, p. 57.

35. Happold, p. 208.

36. Thomas à Kempis, pp. 92–3.

37. Bell, p. 60.

38. *Ibid.*, p. 61.

39. *Ibid.*, pp. 62–3.

40. Bender, p. 61.

41. *The Early Kabbalah*, ed. Joseph Dan, trans. Ronald C. Kiener (New York: Paulist Press, 1986), p. 81. Kiener adds in a footnote: "Beauty is often linked with the Torah, especially the written Torah."

42. Nouwen, p. 94.

43. Teresa, *The Interior Castle*, p. 74.

44. Teresa, *The Life of St. Teresa*, p. 77.

45. Eckhart, p. 44.

46. Buber, p. 128.

47. Otto, p. 125.

48. Lane, p. 195.

49. Philip Wheelwright, "Buber's Philosophical Anthropology," *The Philosophy of Martin Buber*, ed. Schilpp and Friedman, p. 85.

50. Eckhart, p. 61.

51. Alexander S. Kohanski, *An Analytical Interpretation of Martin Buber's I and Thou* (New York: Barron's Educational Series, Inc., 1975), p. 85.

52. Buber, p. 85.

53. Teresa, *The Interior Castle*, p. 176.

54. Buber, p. 69.

55. Teresa, *The Interior Castle*, p. 7.

56. Teresa, *The Life of St. Teresa*, p. 492.

57. *Ibid.*, 496.

58. Johnston, pp. 162–3.

59. Teresa, *The Interior Castle*, pp. 115–16.

60. Teresa, *The Life of St. Teresa*, p. 265.

61. Bell, p. 67–8.

62. Lane, p. 76.

63. Teresa, *The Life of St. Teresa*, p. 266.

64. *Ibid.*, p. 267.

65. Andrew M. Greeley, *The Catholic Myth: The Behavior and Beliefs of American Catholics* (New York: Collier Books, 1990), p. 273.

66. Johnston, p. 82.

67. P. Pourrat, "His Passion: The Crucified One," *The Francis Book: 800 Years with the Saint from Assisi*, ed. Roy M. Gasnick, O.F.M. (New York: Collier Books, 1980), p. 92.

68. Otto, pp. 6–7.

69. *Ibid.*, p. 49.

70. Bell, p. 69.

Chapter 4

1. Chang, p. 121.

2. Frederick Buechner, *Telling Secrets* (San Francisco: Harper & Row, Publishers, Inc., 1991), pp. 44–5.

3. Thomas à Kempis, p. 178.

4. Tolstoy, p. 138.

5. Johnston, pp. 73–4.

6. Chang, p. 15.

7. Wolterstorff, p. 83.

8. Thomas Merton, *A Thomas Merton Reader*, ed. Thomas P. McDonnell (New York: Doubleday, 1974), p. 387.

9. Teresa, *The Interior Castle*, p. 43.

10. *Ibid.,* p. 75.

11. Augustine, p. 239.

12. Thomas Merton, *Conjectures of a Guilty Bystander* (New York: Doubleday, 1968), p. 19.

13. Thomas à Kempis, p. 235.

14. John of the Cross, *Dark Night of the Soul,* trans. E. Allison Peers (New York: Doubleday, 1990), p. 80.

15. Thomas à Kempis, p. 117.

16. Shaykh Nizam ad-did Awliya, *Nizam Ad-Din Awliya: Morals for the Heart,* trans. Bruce B. Laurence (New York: Paulist Press, 1992), p. 72.

17. Chang, p. 86.

18. Buber, *I and Thou,* p. 78.

19. *Ibid.,* pp. 77–8.

20. Richard Cartwright Austin, *Baptized into the Wilderness: A Christian Perspective on John Muir* (Atlanta: John Knox Press, 1987), p. 16.

21. Otto, p. 203.

22. Roger Fry, *Cezanne: A Study of His Development* (New York: The Noonday Press, 1958), p. 29.

23. Tillich, p. 132.

24. *Ibid.,* p. 151.

25. Teresa, *The Life of St. Teresa,* p. 500.

26. Chang, p. 77.

27. Martland, p. 50.

28. Jacques Maritain, p. 106.

29. *The World Treasury of Physics, Astronomy and Math*, ed. Timothy Ferris (Boston: Little Brown and Company, 1991), p. 831.

30. Paul Klee, "Klee on Modern Art," *Modern Artists on Art,* ed. Robert L. Herbert (Englewood Cliffs, New Jersey: Prentice-Hall, Inc., 1964), p. 77.

31. *Picasso on Art: A Selection of Views*, compiled by Dore Ashton (New York: Viking Press, 1972), p. 54.

32. Rekha Jhanji, *The Sensuous in Art: Reflections on Indian Aesthetics* (Shimla: Indian Institute of Advanced Study, 1989), p. 65.

33. Kandinsky, p. 2.

34. *The Upanishads: Breath of the Eternal*, trans. S. Prabhavanda and F. Manchester (New York: New American Library, 1957), p. 20.

35. Quoted in Austin, p. 83.

36. Buber, p. 59.

37. *Ibid.,* p. 70.

38. Black Elk, pp. 164–5.

39. *Ibid.,* p. 36.

40. Franz Meyer, *Marc Chagall* (New York: Harry N. Abrams, Publishers, Inc., 1961), p. 161.

41. Teresa, *The Interior Castle,* p. 20.

42. Augustine, p. 159.

43. Teresa, *The Life of St. Teresa,* p. 259.

44. Austin, p. 10.

45. James, p. 304.

46. Tolstoy, p. 50.

47. Underhill, "The Mystic as Creative Artist," *Understanding Mysticism*, ed. Woods, p. 401.

48. Gauguin, *Noa Noa: The Tahitian Journal*, trans. O. F. Theis (New York: Dover Publications, Inc., 1985), p. 11.

49. *Ibid.*, p. 17.

50. Henri Matisse, "Notes of a Painter," *Matisse: His Art and His Public*, by Alfred Barr Jr., "Notes d'un Peintre," trans. by Margret Scolari (New York: The Museum of Modern Art, 1951), p. 119.

51. James, p. 234.

52. Frank Barron, "The Creative Personality: Akin to Madness," *Understanding Mysticism*, ed. Woods, p. 319.

53. Teresa, *The Interior Castle*, pp. 174–5.

54. *The Search for Meaning: Americans Talk About What They Believe and Why*, ed. Phillip L. Berman (New York: Ballantine Books, 1990), p. 249.

55. Teresa, *The Life of St. Teresa*, p. 327.

56. John of the Cross, pp. 174–5.

57. Tolstoy, p. 140.

58. Buber, p. 126.

59. *Ibid.*, pp. 135–6.

60. Teresa, *The Life of St. Teresa*, p. 409.

61. *Ibid.*, p. 447.

62. Buber, p. 135.

63. *Ibid.*, p. 134.

64. Tillich, p. 16.

65. Martin Buber, *The Way of Man: According to the Teachings of Hasidism* (London: Vincent Stuart Ltd., 1963), p. 23.

66. Paul Oskar Kristeller, *Renaissance Thought and the Arts* (Princeton: Princeton University Press, 1990), p. 97.

67. John of the Cross, p. 166.

68. Verdet, p. 24.

69. Meyer, p. 591.

70. Teresa, *Interior Castle*, p. 70.

71. Johnston, p. 50.

72. Tolstoy, p. 190.

73. Thomas à Kempis, p. 110.

74. Friedman, *Encounter on the Narrow Ridge: A Life of Martin Buber*, p. 247.

75. Tolstoy, p. 150.

76. Shih-t'ao, *Philosophy of Painting by Shih T'ao*, p. 66.

77. Kandinsky, p. 3.

78. Stephen De Staebler and Diane Apostolos-Cappadona, "Reflections on Art and the Spirit: A Conversation," *Art Creativity, and the Sacred*, ed. Apostolos-Cappadona, p. 26.

79. Jonathan Edwards, "Personal Narrative," *The Works of President Edwards*, ed. Sereno B. Dwight, 10 vols. (New York: S. Converse, 1829), I, p. 61.

80. Reinhold Schneider, "Saint Francis in Art," *The Francis Book*, ed. Gasnick, p. 125.

81. Chesterton, pp. 12–13.

82. Friedrich Heer, *The Medieval World* (New York: Mentor Books, 1962), p. 223.

83. Tolstoy, p. 145.

84. Underhill, *Mysticism: A Study*, pp. 79–80.

85. George Rowley, *Principles of Chinese Painting*, 2d ed. (Princeton: Princeton University Press, 1959), pp. 48–9.

86. Charles Edward Gauss, *The Aesthetic Theories of French Artists: From Realism to Surrealism* (Baltimore and London: The Johns Hopkins Press, 1966), p. 56.

87. Gauss, p. 63.

88. Kandinsky, p. 15.

89. James, p. 67.

Chapter 5

1. Augustine, *Aesthetics: From Classical Greece to the Present, A Short History*, by Monroe C. Beardsley (New York: The Macmillan Company, 1966), p. 95.

2. Austin, p. 27.

3. Augustine, *Augustine of Hippo*, p. 144.

4. *Ibid.*, p. 151.

5. Teresa, *The Life of St. Teresa*, p. 320.

6. *Ibid.*, pp. 458–9.

7. Underhill, *Mysticism: A Study*, p. 258.

8. Coomaraswamy, *Christian and Oriental Philosophy of Art*, p. 102.

9. Edward A. Armstrong, *Saint Francis Nature Mystic: The Derivation and Significance of the Nature Stories in the Franciscan Legend* (Berkeley, California: University of California Press, 1973), p. 9.

10. Paul Gallico, "St. Francis and the Animals," *The Francis Book*, ed. Gasnick, p. 83.

11. Brown, p. 294.

12. *Francis and Clare: The Complete Works,* trans. Regis J. Armstrong O.F.M. CAP. and Ignatius C. Brady, O.F.M. (New York: Paulist Press, 1982), pp. 200–201.

13. Otto, p. 65.

14. *Ibid.*, p. 42.

15. Teresa of Avila, *The Way of Perfection*, trans. John Venard O.C.D. (Sydney: E. J. Dwyer, 1988), p. 136.

16. Armstrong, p. 240.

17. Friedman, *Encounter on the Narrow Ridge: A Life of Martin Buber*, p. 378.

18. Buber, *The Way of Man: According to the Teaching of Hasidism*, p. 19.

19. Chesterton, p. 57.

20. Allen Carlson, "Appreciation and the Natural Environment," *The Journal of Aesthetics and Art Criticism* XXXVII, No. 3 (Spring 1979): pp. 267–75.

21. Chesterton, p. 75. That knowledge of origins can affect one's aesthetic perceptions is evident in the phenomenological contrast between experiencing what we take to be a genuine masterpiece as opposed to what we regard as an imitation of it. For more on this issue, see part III of Nelson Goodman's *Languages of Art: An Approach to a Theory of Symbols* (Indianapolis: Hackett Publishing Company, Inc., 1976).

22. Malcolm L. Diamond, *Martin Buber: Jewish Existentialist* (New York: Harper & Row, Publishers, Inc., 1968), p. 45.

23. Dewey, p. 48.

24. Chesterton, p. 91.

25. Armstrong, p. 23.

26. D.T. Suzuki, *Zen and Japanese Culture* (Princeton: Princeton University Press, 1959), p. 353.

27. Guy Sircello, *A New Theory of Beauty* (Princeton: Princeton University Press, 1975), p. 85.

28. Chang, p. 89.

29. *Ibid.*, p. 35.

30. Arthur Waley, *The Way and Its Power: A Study of the Tao Te Ching and Its Place in Chinese Thought*, trans. Arthur Waley (New York: Grove Press, Inc., 1958), p. 210.

31. *Ibid.*, p. 137.

32. Chuang Tzu, *The Complete Works of Chuang Tzu*, trans. Burton Watson (New York: Columbia University Press, 1968), p. 236.

33. *Ibid.*, p. 369.

34. Ronald Hepburn, "Aesthetic Appreciation of Nature," *Aesthetics in the Modern World*, ed. Harold Osborne (New York: Weybright and Talley Inc., 1968), p. 53.

35. Holmes Rolston III, *Environmental Ethics* (Philadelphia: Temple University Press, 1988), p. 242.

36. *Ibid.*, p. 239.

37. Stephen C. Pepper, *The Basis of Criticism in the Arts* (Cambridge, Massachusetts: Harvard University Press, 1945), p. 62.

38. August Derleth, *Concord Rebel: A Life of Thoreau* (New York: Avon Books, 1962), p. 143.

39. Chang, p. 138.

40. Sircello, p. 58.

41. *Ibid.*, p. 39.

42. *Ibid.*, p. 138.

43. *Ibid.*, p. 136.

44. *Ibid.*, p. 103.

45. Bernard Bosanquet, *Three Lectures on Aesthetic* (Indianapolis & New York: Bobbs-Merrill Company Inc., 1963), p. 57.

46. Pepper, p. 58.

47. Stephen C. Pepper, *Aesthetic Quality: A Contextualistic Theory of Beauty* (New York: Charles Scribner's Sons, 1938), pp. 27–8.

48. *The Way of Lao Tzu*, trans. Wing-tsit Chan (Indianapolis: Bobbs-Merrill Company, Inc., 1963), p. 157.

49. Pi Wang, *Commentary on the Lao Tzu*, trans. Ariane Rump with Wing-tsit Chan (Honolulu: University of Hawaii Press, 1979), p. 62.

50. Wang, p. 126.

51. Wang, p. 125.

52. Wang, p. 63.

53. In his *Creativity and Taoism*, chapter one is entitled: "The Invisible Ground of Sympathy," and the second chapter: "Immeasureable Potentialities of Creativity."

54. Bernard Bosanquet, *A History of Aesthetic* (London: George Allen & Unwin LTD and New York: Humanities Press Inc., 1966), p. 115.

55. Friedrich Nietzsche, *Beyond Good and Evil*, trans. Walter Kaufmann (New York: Random House, 1966), p. 15.

Chapter 6

1. Gauguin, *Gauguin's Letters from the South Seas*, p. 29.

2. Frank Barron, "The Creative Personality: Akin to Madness," *Understanding Mysticism*, ed. Woods, p. 320.

3. Nouwen, p. 147.

4. Lane, p. 19.

5. *Ibid.*, p. 153.

6. Buber, *I and Thou*, p. 149.

7. Kohanski, p. 144.

8. Buber, p. 154.

9. Gauguin, *Noa Noa*, p. 18.

10. *Ibid.*, p. 31.

11. Hildegard of Bingen, *Women Mystics*, Zum Brunn and Epiney-Burgard, p. 23.

12. Otto, p. 220.

13. Chang, p. 186.

14. *Ibid.*, p. 237.

15. Coomaraswamy, *The Dance of Shiva* (New York: Noonday Press, 1957), p. 41.

16. Albert Hofstadter and Richard Kuhns, eds., *Philosophies of Art and Beauty* (New York: The Modern Library, 1964), p. 665.

17. Bell, p. 46.

18. Merton, *Conjectures of a Guilty Bystander*, p. 133.

19. Herschel B. Chipp, ed., *Theories of Modern Art: A Source Book by Artists and Critics* (Berkeley, Los Angeles, and London: University of California Press, 1970), p. 182.

20. Coomaraswamy, *The Transformation of Nature in Art*, p. 163.

21. Hofstadter and Kuhns, *Philosophies of Art and Beauty*, p. 425.

22. Verdet, p. 111.

23. Gauss, p. 54.

24. Schleiermacher, pp. 138–9.

25. Kandinsky, p. 9.

26. *Ibid.*, p. 18.

27. Ashton, pp. 34–5.

28. Verdet, p. 65.

29. Frank Sibley, "Aesthetic Concepts," *The Philosophical Review* 67 (1959): pp. 421–50.

30. Tillich, pp. 176–7.

31. D.T. Suzuki, "The Basis of Buddhist Philosophy," *Understanding Mysticism*, ed. Woods, p. 137.

32. Meyer, p. 15.

33. Lane, p. 63.

34. Teresa, *The Life of St. Teresa*, p. 497.

35. Wolterstorff, p. 196.

36. Julien Green, *God's Fool: The Life and Times of Francis of Assisi*, trans. Peter Heinegg (San Francisco: Harper & Row Publishers, Inc., 1987), p. 9.

37. Francis, *Francis and Clare: The Complete Works*, p. 144.

38. Gauguin, *Gauguin's Letters from the South Seas*, p. 99.

39. Tolstoy, p. 97.

40. *Ibid.*, p. 96.

41. *Ibid.*, p. 97.

42. *Ibid.*, p. 117.

43. *Ibid.*, p. 138.

44. *Ibid.*, p. 149.

45. Buber, p. 90.

46. Philip Wheelwright, "Buber's Philosophical Anthropology," *The Philosophy of Martin Buber*, Schilpp and Friedman, p. 85.

47. Hugo Bergman, "Martin Buber and Mysticism," *The Philosophy of Martin Buber*, Schilpp and Friedman, p. 298.

48. Buber, p. 89.

49. Abbey, p. 6.

50. Austin, pp. 62–3.

51. Shaykh Nizam ad-did Awliya, p. 376.

52. Teresa, *The Life of St. Teresa*, p. 231.

53. *Ibid.*

54. Thomas à Kempis, p. 35.

55. Augustine, p. 207.

56. John of the Cross, p. 180.

57. Barron, p. 312.
58. Teresa, *The Life of St. Teresa*, p. 120.
59. *Ibid.*, p. 145.
60. Teresa, *The Interior Castle*, p. 86.
61. *Ibid.*, p. 186.
62. Beardsley, p. 38.
63. Johnston, p. 95.
64. Teresa, *The Interior Castle*, p. 89.
65. Martland, p. 83.
66. Friedman, p. 382.
67. Otto, p. 7.
68. Tillich, p. 204.
69. *Ibid.*, p. 247.
70. *Ibid.*, pp. 15–16.
71. *Ibid.*, p. 61.
72. *Ibid.*, p. 68.
73. Fry, *Cezanne: A Study of His Development*, p. 37.
74. M.T.H. Sadler, *Concerning the Spiritual in Art*, p. xvii.
75. Tillich, p. 235.
76. Otto, p. 67.
77. Weiss, pp. 19–20.

Chapter 7

1. Chang, p. 184.
2. Sandra B. Lubarsky, *Tolerance and Transformation: Jewish Approaches to Religious Pluralism* (Cincinnati: Hebrew Union College Press, 1990), p. 84.
3. Martland, pp. 8–9.
4. Frank Bianco, *Voices of Silence: Lives of the Trappists Today* (New York: Doubleday, 1992), p. 202.
5. John of the Cross, pp. 154–5.
6. Martland, p. 34.
7. *Ibid.*, p. 42.
8. John Canaday, *What is Art?: An Introduction to Painting, Sculpture, and Architecture* (New York: Alfred A. Knopf, 1980), p. 126.
9. Nouwen, pp. 66–7.
10. Reuven Hammer, *Entering Jewish Prayer: A Guide to Personal Devotion and the Worship Service* (New York: Schocken Books, 1994), p. 100.
11. Bianco, p. 62.
12. Merton, *Contemplative Prayer*, p. 68.
13. Teresa, *The Life of St.Theresa*, p. 191.
14. Hughes Mearns, *Creative Power* (New York: Dover Publications, Inc., 1958), p. 101.

15. Tillich, p. 112.

16. Teresa, *The Life of St. Teresa*, p. 273.

17. Thomas à Kempis, p. 118.

18. John of the Cross, p. 66.

19. Chang, p. 207.

20. Vincent van Gogh, *The Complete Letters of Vincent Van Gogh*, Vol. II., p. 598.

21. Teresa, *The Life of St. Teresa*, p. 184.

22. William Ernest, "The Mystical Spirit and Protestantism," *Understanding Mysticism*, ed. Woods, p. 198.

23. John of the Cross, pp. 66–7.

24. *Ibid.*, p. 71.

25. *Ibid.*, p. 67.

26. Teresa, *The Interior Castle*, p. 10.

27. Earle J. Coleman, "Varieties of Mysticism," *The Menorah*, No. 3 (Spring 1985): p. 7.

28. Teresa, *The Interior Castle*, p. 34.

29. Teresa, *The Life of St. Teresa*, p. 112.

30. *Ibid.*, p. 441.

31. John of the Cross, p. 160.

32. Eckhart, p. 254.

33. Teresa, *The Life of St. Teresa*, p. 493.

34. Meyer, p. 448.

35. Kandinsky, p. 26.

36. Tolstoy, p. 141.

37. Kandinsky, p. 29.

38. *Ibid.*, pp. 33–4.

39. *Ibid.*, p. 36.

40. *Ibid.*, p. 40.

41. Zum Brunn and Epiney-Burgard, *Women Mystics*, p. 5.

42. Berman, p. 258.

43. Austin, p. 77.

44. John of the Cross, pp. 70–1.

45. Shih-t'ao, *Philosophy of Painting by Shih T'ao*, pp. 47–8.

46. Johnston, p. 92.

47. Tillich, p. 133.

48. Gauguin, *Gauguin's Letters from the South Seas*, p. 12.

49. *Ibid.*

50. Dan, p. 122.

51. Stephen DeStaebler and Diane Apostolos-Cappadona, "Reflections on Art and the Spirit," *Art, Creativity, and the Sacred*, ed. Apostolos-Cappadona, pp. 24–5.

52. Eckhart, pp. 183–4.

53. Verdet, p. 35.

54. *Ibid.*, p. 48.

55. Thomas Merton, *The Silent Life* (New York: Farrar, Straus, & Cudahy, 1957), p. 29.

56. Johannes Jorgensen, *St. Francis of Assisi*, trans. T. O'Conor Slone (New York: Doubleday, 1955), p. 155.

57. *Ibid.*, p. 60.

58. Shih-t'ao, *Philosophy of Painting by Shih T'ao*, p. 49.

59. *Ibid.*, p. 45.

60. Cooomaraswamy, *Christian and Oriental Philosophy of Art*, p. 36.

61. Kandinsky, p. 53.

62. Jhanji, p. 65.

63. *Ibid.*

64. Bianco, p. 206.

65. Verdet, p. 38.

Chapter 8

1. Ananda K. Coomaraswamy, "The Origin and Use of Images in India," *Art, Creativity, and the Sacred*, Apostolos-Cappadona, pp. 132–3.

2. Otto, p. 41.

3. Tillich, p. 206.

4. Otto, p. 42.

5. Tillich, p. 235.

6. Nizam ad-did Awliya, p. 119.

7. Tillich, p. 165.

8. Weiss, p. 16.

9. Wolterstorff, p. 188.

10. Weiss, p. 17.

11. *Ibid.*, p. 93.

12. Coomaraswamy, *Christian and Oriental Philosophy of Art*, p. 108.

13. Tillich, p. 141.

14. Weiss, p. 45.

15. G.W.F. Hegel, *The Philosophy of Fine Art*, trans. F.P.B. Osmaston, 4 vols. Vol. 1, (London, 1920), p. 142.

16. Wolterstorff, p. 174.

17. Underhill, *Mysticism: A Study,* p. 75.

18. *Ibid.*

19. Jhanji, p. 69.

20. Nouwen, p. 157.

21. Immanuel Kant, *Grounding for the Metaphysics of Morals*, trans. James W. Ellington (Indianapolis: Hackett Publishing Company, 1981), pp. 7–8.

22. Teresa, *The Interior Castle*, p. 59.

23. Thomas à Kempis, p. 48.

24. Tolstoy, p. 131.

25. Chang, p. 57.

26. Teresa, *The Way of Perfection*, p. 117.

27. Otto, p. 44.

28. Thomas à Kempis, p. 223.

Bibliography

Abbey, Edward. *Desert Solitaire: A Season in the Wilderness* (New York: Ballantine Books, 1971).

ad-did Awliya, Shaykh Nizam. *Nizam Ad-Din Awliya: Morals for the Heart*, trans. Bruce B. Laurence (New York: Paulist Press, 1992).

Apostolos-Cappadona, Diane, ed. *Art, Creativity, and the Sacred* (New York: The Crossroad Publishing Company, 1989).

Armstrong, Edward A. *Saint Francis Nature Mystic: The Derivation and Significance of the Nature Stories in the Franciscan Legend* (Berkeley: University of California Press, 1973).

Ashton, Dore, ed. *Picasso on Art: A Selection of Views* (New York: Viking Press, 1972).

Augustine. *Augustine of Hippo: Selected Writings*, trans. Mary T. Clark (New York: Paulist Press, 1984).

Austin, Richard Cartwright. *Baptized into the Wilderness: A Christian Perspective on John Muir* (Atlanta: John Knox Press, 1987).

Balthasar, Hans Urs von. *The Glory of the Lord: A Theological Aesthetics*, trans. Erasmo Leiva-Merikakis; ed. Joseph Fessio and John Riches, 7 vols. (San Francisco: Ignatius Press; New York: The Crossroad Publishing Company, 1983–1991).

Barr Jr., Alfred, ed. *Matisse: His Art and His Public* (New York: The Museum of Modern Art, 1951).

Beardsley, Monroe C. *Aesthetics: From Classical Greece to the Present, A Short History* (New York: The Macmillan Company, 1966).

Bell, Clive. *Art* (New York: Capricorn Books, 1958).

Bender, Sue. *Plain and Simple: A Woman's Journey to the Amish* (San Francisco, New York: Harper & Row, Publishers, Inc., 1989).

Berman, Phillip L., ed. *The Search for Meaning: Americans Talk About What They Believe and Why* (New York: Ballantine Books, 1990).

Bianco, Frank. *Voices of Silence: Lives of the Trappists Today* (New York: Doubleday, 1992).

Black Elk. *Black Elk Speaks: Being the Life Story of a Holy Man of the Oglala Sioux*, as told through John G. Neihardt (New York: Washington Square Press, 1972).

Bosanquet, Bernard. *A History of Aesthetic* (London: George Allen & Unwin LTD and New York: Humanities Press Inc., 1966).

———. *Three Lectures on Aesthetic* (Indianapolis & New York: Bobbs-Merrill Company, Inc., 1963).

Brown, Frank Burch. *Religious Aesthetics: A Theological Study in Making and Meaning* (Princeton: Princeton University Press, 1989).

Brown, Raphael. *The Little Flowers of St. Francis*, trans. Raphael Brown (Garden City, New York: Doubleday, 1958).

Buber, Martin. *I and Thou*, trans. Walter Kaufmann (New York: Charles Scribner's Sons, 1970).

———. *The Way of Man: According to the Teachings of Hasidism* (London: Vincent Stuart Ltd., 1963).

Buechner, Frederick. *Telling Secrets* (San Francisco: Harper & Row, Publishers, Inc., 1991).

Bullough, Edward. " 'Psychical Distance' as a Factor in Art and as an Aesthetic Principle." In *The British Journal of Psychology* Vol. 5 (1912): 87–117.

Canaday, John. *What is Art?: An Introduction to Painting, Sculpture, and Architecture* (New York: Alfred A. Knopf, 1980).

Carlson, Allen. "Appreciation and the Natural Environment." *The Journal of Aesthetics and Art Criticism* XXXVII, No. 3 (Spring 1979): 267–75.

Cary, Joyce. *The Horse's Mouth* (New York: Harper, 1990).

Caussade, Jean-Pierre de. *Abandonment to Divine Providence*, trans. John Beevers (Garden City, New York: Doubleday, 1975).

Chang, Chung-yuan. *Creativity and Taoism: A Study of Chinese Philosophy, Art, and Poetry* (New York: Harper & Row, Publishers, Inc., 1963).

Chesterton, G.K. *St. Francis of Assisi* (Garden City, New York: Doubleday, 1955).

Chipp, Herschel B., ed. *Theories of Modern Art: A Source Book by Artists and Critics* (Berkeley, Los Angeles, and London: University of California Press, 1970).

Chuang Tzu. *The Complete Works of Chuang Tzu*, trans. Burton Watson (New York: Columbia University Press, 1968).

Cloud of Unknowing and The Book of Privy Counseling, The, ed. William Johnston (New York: Doubleday, 1973).

Coleman, Earle J., *Philosophy of Painting by Shih T'ao* (The Hague: Mouton Publishers, 1978).

———. "Varieties of Mysticism." *The Menorah*, No. 3 (Spring 1985): 5–8.

Coomaraswamy, Ananda K. *Christian and Oriental Philosophy of Art* (New York: Dover Publications, Inc., 1956).

———. *The Dance of Shiva* (New York: Noonday Press, 1957).

———. *The Transformation of Nature in Art* (NewYork: Dover Publications, Inc., 1956, as published by Harvard University Press in 1934).

Dan, Joseph, ed. *The Early Kabbalah*, trans. Ronald C. Kiener (New York: Paulist Press, 1986).

De Mello, Anthony. *The Way to Love: the Last Meditations of Anthony De Mello* (New York: Doubleday, 1992).

Derleth, August. *Concord Rebel: A Life of Thoreau* (New York: Avon Books, 1962).

Dewey, John. *Art As Experience* (New York: G.P. Putnam's Sons, 1958).

Dickie, George. *Art and the Aesthetic: An Institutional Analysis* (Ithaca: Cornell University Press, 1974).

Diamond, Malcolm L. *Martin Buber: Jewish Existentialist* (New York: Harper & Row, Publishers, Inc., 1968).

Eckhart, Meister. *Meister Eckhart: The Essential Sermons, Commentaries, Treatises, and Defense*, trans. and introduced by Edmund Colledge, O.S.A. and Bernard McGinn (New York: Paulist Press, 1981).

Edwards, Cliff. *Van Gogh and God* (Chicago: Loyola University Press, 1989).

Edwards, Jonathan. "Personal Narative," In *The Works of President Edwards*, ed. Sereno B. Dwight, 10 vols.; Vol. I: chapters 5, 6, and 8 (New York: S. Converse, 1829).

Ferris, Timothy, ed. *The World Treasury of Physics, Astronomy and Math* (Boston: Little Brown and Company, 1991).

Fish, Stanley E. *Self-Consuming Artifacts: The Experience of Seventeenth Century Literature* (Berkeley: University Of California Press, 1972).

Francis of Assisi and Clare. *Francis and Clare: The Complete Works*, trans. Regis J. Armstrong O.F.M. CAP. and Ignatius C. Brady, O.F.M. (New York: Paulist Press, 1982).

Friedman, Maurice. *Encounter on the Narrow Ridge: A Life of Martin Buber* (New York: Paragon House, 1991).

Fry, Roger. *Cezanne: A Study of His Development* (New York: The Noonday Press, 1958).

———. *Vision and Design* (New York: The New American Library, Inc., 1956).

Gasnick, Roy M., O.F.M., ed. *The Francis Book: 800 Years with the Saint from Assisi* (New York: Collier Books, 1980).

Gauguin, Paul. *Gauguin's Letters from the South Seas*, trans. Ruth Pielkovo (New York: Dover Publications, Inc., 1992).

———. *Noa Noa: The Tahitian Journal*, trans. O. F. Theis (New York: Dover Publications, Inc., 1985).

Gauss, Charles Edward. *The Aesthetic Theories of French Artists: From Realism to Surrealism* (Baltimore and London: The Johns Hopkins Press, 1966).

Goodman, Nelson. *Languages of Art: An Approach to a Theory of Symbols* (Indianapolis: Hackett Publishing Company, Inc., 1976).

Greeley, Andrew M. *Religion as Poetry* (New Brunswick and London: Transaction Publishers, 1995).

———. *The Catholic Myth: The Behavior and Beliefs of American Catholics* (New York: Collier Books, 1990).

Green, Julien. *God's Fool: The Life and Times of Francis of Assisi*, trans. Peter Heinegg (San Francisco: Harper & Row, Publishers, Inc., 1987).

Hammer, Reuven. *Entering Jewish Prayer: A Guide to Personal Devotion and the Worship Service* (New York: Schocken Books, 1994).

Happold, F.C. *Mysticism* (Baltimore: Penguin Books, 1963).

Heer, Friedrich. *The Medieval World* (New York: Mentor Books, 1962).

Hegel, G.W.F. *The Philosophy of Fine Art*, trans. F.P.B. Osmaston, 4 vols. (London, 1920).

Hemingway, Ernest. *The Green Hills of Africa* (New York: Charles Scribner's Sons, 1935).

Hepburn, Ronald. "Aesthetic Appreciation of Nature." *Aesthetics in the Modern World*, ed. Harold Osborne (New York: Weybright and Talley Inc., 1968).

Herbert, Robert L., ed. *Modern Artists on Art* (Englewood Cliffs, New Jersey: Prentice-Hall, Inc., 1964).

Hofstadter, Albert, and Kuhns, Richard, eds. *Philosophies of Art and Beauty* (New York: The Modern Library, 1964).

Horden, William E. *A Layman's Guide to Protestant Theology* (New York: Macmillan Company, 1973).

James, William. *The Varieties of Religious Experience* (New York: New American Library, 1958).

Jhanji, Rekha. *The Sensuous in Art: Reflections on Indian Aesthetics* (Shimla: Indian Institute of Advanced Study, 1989).

John of the Cross. *Ascent of Mt. Carmel*, trans. E. Allison Peers (New York: Triumph Books, 1993).

———. *Dark Night of the Soul*, trans. E. Allison Peers (New York: Doubleday, 1990).

Jorgensen, Johannes. *St. Francis of Assisi*, trans. T. O'Conor Slone (New York: Doubleday, 1955).

Kandinsky, Wassily. *Concerning the Spiritual in Art*, trans. M.T.H. Sadler (New York: Dover Publications, Inc., 1977).

Kant, Immanuel. *Critique of Judgment*, trans. J.H. Bernard (New York: Hafner Publishing Co., 1951).

———. *Grounding for the Metaphysics of Morals*, trans. James W. Ellington (Indianapolis: Hackett Publishing Company, 1981).

Kohanski, Alexander S. *An Analytical Interpretation of Martin Buber's I and Thou* (New York: Barron's Educational Series, Inc., 1975).

Kristeller, Paul Oscar. *Renaissance Thought and the Arts* (Princeton: Princeton University Press, 1990).

Lane, Belden C. *Landscapes of the Sacred: Geography and Narrative American Spirituality* (New York: Paulist Press, 1988).

Lao Tzu. *The Way and Its Power: A Study of the Tao Te Ching and Its Place in Chinese Thought*, trans. Arthur Waley (New York: Grove Press, Inc., 1958).

———. *The Way of Lao Tzu*, trans. Wing-tsit Chan (Indianapolis: Bobbs-Merrill Company, Inc., 1963).

Leslie, C.R. *Memoirs of the Life of John Constable*, ed. Jonathan Mayne (London: Phaidon Press, 1951).

Lubarsky, Sandra B. *Tolerance and Transformation: Jewish Approaches to Religious Pluralism* (Cincinnati: Hebrew Union College Press, 1990).

MacGregor, John M. *The Discovery of the Art of the Insane* (Princeton: Princeton University Press, 1992).

Maritain, Jacques. *Creative Intuition in Art and Poetry* (New York: New American Library, 1953).

Martin, James Alfred. *Beauty and Holiness: The Dialogue between Aesthetics and Religion* (Princeton: Princeton University Press, 1990).

Martland, Thomas R. *Religion As Art: An Interpretation* (Albany: State University of New York Press, 1981).

McDonnell, Thomas P., ed. *A Thomas Merton Reader* (New York, Doubleday, 1974).

Mearns, Hughes. *Creative Power* (New York: Dover Publications, Inc., 1958).

Merton, Thomas. *Conjectures of a Guilty Bystander* (Albany: Doubleday, 1968).

———. *Contemplative Prayer* (New York: Doubleday, 1990).

———. *The Silent Life* (New York: Farrar, Straus, & Cudahy, 1957).

Meyer, Franz. *Marc Chagall* (New York: Harry N. Abrams, Publishers, Inc., 1961).

Nasr, Seyyed Hossein. *Islamic Art and Spirituality* (New York: State University of New York Press, 1987).

Nietzsche, Friedrich. *Beyond Good and Evil*, trans. Walter Kaufmann (New York: Random House, 1966).

Nouwen, Henri J. M. *The Genesee Diary: Reports from a Trappist Monastery* (New York: Doubleday, 1981).

Otto, Rudolph. *The Idea of the Holy*, trans. John W. Harvey (New York: Oxford University Press, 1969).

Pepper, Stephen C. *Aesthetic Quality: A Contextualistic Theory of Beauty* (New York: Charles Scribner's Sons, 1938).

———. *The Basis of Criticism in the Arts* (Cambridge, Massachusetts: Harvard University Press, 1945).

Prabhavananda, S., and Manchester, F., trans. *The Upanishads: Breath of the Eternal* (New York: New American Library, 1957).

Rodman, Selden, ed. *Conversations with Artists* (New York: Capricorn Books, 1961).

Rolston, Holmes, III. *Environmental Ethics* (Philadelphia: Temple University Press, 1988).

Rowley, George. *Principles of Chinese Painting*, 2d ed. (Princeton: Princeton University Press, 1959).

Schilpp, Paul Arthur, and Friedman, Maurice, eds. *The Philosophy of Martin Buber* (La Salle, Illinois, and London: Open Court Publishing Co., 1967).

Schleiermacher, Friedrich. *On Religion: Speeches to its Cultured Despisers*, trans. John Oman (New York: Harper & Brothers, 1959).

Sherry, Patrick. *Spirit and Beauty: An Introduction to Theological Aesthetics* (London: Oxford-Clarendon, 1992).

Sibley, Frank. "Aesthetic Concepts." *The Philosophical Review* 67 (1959): 421–450.

Sircello, Guy. *A New Theory of Beauty* (Princeton: Princeton University Press, 1975).

Suzuki, D.T. *Zen and Japanese Culture* (Princeton: Princeton University Press, 1959).

Teresa of Avila, *The Interior Castle*, trans. Kieran Kavanaugh, O.C.D. and Otilio Rodriguez, O.C.D. (New York: Paulist Press, 1979).

———. *The Life of St. Teresa: Of the Order of Our Lady of Carmel, Written by Herself*, trans. David Lewis, ed. Benedict Zimmerman, O.C.D. (Westminster, Maryland: The Newman Bookshop, 1944).

———. *The Way of Perfection*, trans. John Venard O.C.D. (Sydney: E. J. Dwyer, 1988).

Thomas à Kempis, *The Imitation of Christ*, trans. Richard Whitford (New York: Doubleday, 1955).

Tillich, Paul. *On Art and Architecture*, ed. John Dillenberger and Jane Dillenberger, trans. Robert P. Scharlemann (New York: The Crossroad Publishing Company, 1987).

———. *What is Religion?* translated with an introduction by James Luther Adams (San Francisco: Harper and Row, Publishers, Inc., 1969).

Tolstoy, Leo. *What is Art?* trans. Almyer Maude (Indianapolis and New York: Bobbs-Merrill Company, Inc., 1980).

Underhill, Evelyn. *Mysticism: A Study in the Nature and Development of Man's Spiritual Consciousness* (New York: E.P. Dutton & Co., Inc., 1961).

van Gogh, Vincent. *The Complete Letters of Vincent Van Gogh*. Introduction by V.W. van Gogh, Preface and Memoir by J. van Gogh-Bonger, 3 vols. (Boston: New York Graphic Society, 1981).

Verdet, Andre. *Chagall's World: Reflections from the Mediterranean* (Garden City, New York: Doubleday & Company, Inc., 1984).

Walking Buffalo. *Touch the Earth: A Self-Portrait of Indian Existence.* Compiled by T.C. McLuhan. (New York: Simon and Schuster, 1971).

Wang, Pi. *Commentary on the Lao Tzu by Wang Pi*, trans. Ariane Rump with Wing-tsit Chan (Honolulu: University of Hawaii Press, 1979).

Weiss, Paul. *Religion and Art* (Milwaukee: Marquette University Press, 1963).

Wolterstorff, Nicholas. *Art in Action* (Grand Rapids, Michigan: William B. Eerdman's Publishing Company, 1980).

Woods, Richard, O.P., ed. *Understanding Mysticism*, (Garden City, New York: Doubleday, 1980).

Zum Brunn, Emilie, and Epiney-Burgard, Georgette, eds. and trans. *Women Mystics in Medieval Europe* (New York: Paragon House, 1989).

Index

Abandonment to Divine Providence,
50
Abbey, Edward, 54, 147
Abhinavagupta, 181, 192
aesthetic
  all things are, xvii
  as passive versus active, xix, 190
  encompasses, xx
  versus "artistic," 183
  versus the spiritual, 183–95
aesthetic and spiritual
  and beauty, 107
  and triumphs, 113
  as ways of apprehending, 53
  as 'wholly other,' 68
  common denominators between,
    xviii
  interpenetrate, 185–86
  transcendence of time and
    space, 35
aesthetic attitude
  and a spiritual perspective, 119
  and suppression of the ego, 115
  and the I-Thou posture, 52
  and the objectivity of beauty, 64
  the prerequisite for aesthetic
    experiences, 53

aesthetic experience
  and action, 190
  and the I-Thou relation, xv
  as fleeting, 192
  lingers and shapes future
    experiences, 65
  purpose of, xvii, 138. *See also*
    religious experience
aesthetic experience of nature
  Allen Carlson's thesis, 145
  and a spiritual perspective, 119
  and permanence, 123
  as personal, 118
  as spiritual, 121
  as transformative, 191
  fewer write about, 54
  mystic's model of, 128
  of the pantheist, 118, 122
  Taoist's, 129–30
  two models for, 118
  universal and particular in,
    116–17
  utmost, 117–18
  wrong way to contemplate a
    tree, 59
afflation, 168. *See also* creativity
agape, 13, 97

221

ahnung, 149. *See also* intuition
and *prajna*
*Alice's Adventures in Wonder-
land*, 136
Amish, xviii, 18, 21, 42, 60, 79,
148
anamnesis, 112
ananda, xix, 100. *See also* peace
that passes all understanding
anatta doctrine, 73
Apostolos-Cappadona, Diane,
102, 176
Aquinas, Thomas, 112, 160
*Archetype and the Collective
Unconscious, The*, 84
Aristotle, 43, 76, 86, 115, 150
Armstrong, Edward A., 115, 120
art
abstract, 17, 19
all religious?, 11–21
Art and the Aesthetic, 8
Art as Experience, 163
as artless, 169, 177
as a way of recollection, 136
as counterfeit, 8, 177, 178
as escape, 189, 190
as religion, 20
as revelation, 15–16, 139. *See
also* revelation
bad, 51
bad and bad religion, 82
becomes uninspired craft, 98
communication theory of, 98,
74
defined, xx
essence of, 145
expressionist theory of, 7
formalist theory of, 8
great works of, 145
institutional theory of, 8
"is dead," xv, 2
"is religion," xiv
life-boat theory of, 187, 196
metaphysical theory of, 138,
141
nonrepresentational, 2, 17–18
religious, two kinds of, 99

representational theory of, 7–8
true value of, 4
art and religion
alcohol or drugs in, xiii–xiv,
43, 166–67
and a fresh vision, 57
and a total response, 40, 41
and love, xvii, 99
and metamorphosis of the self,
76
anti-intellectual current in,
144–54
approach one another, 36
as axiological, 11
as complementary responses,
xiv
as continuous with life, 11
as disparaged, xiii
as efforts after harmony, xviii–
xix, 105
as essential aspects, 25
as identical, xiv, 10, 139, 186,
195
as independent projects, xiv
as particular expressions of
universal truths, 5
as penultimate, 196
as primordial, 196
as reciprocal powers, xiii, 196
as revelatory, 144. *See also*
revelation
as ways of life, 43, 45, 47
audio-visual emphasis, 29
commingle in profound experiences, 10
common goal of freedom, 179.
See also freedom
"death" of, 3
draw from and withdraw from
tradition, 158
"dryness" in, xv, 160, 161, 164.
See also writer's block
economic well-being in, 46
like science, 8
naturalness in, 159–60
quest for self-realization, 71.
See also self, actualization

reluctance to distinguish
between, xiii
self-surrender in, 166
sex or reproduction in, 88, 122,
170
sincerity in, 173
ties between, xv, 8–11
versus science, xiv, 8, 51, 124,
139, 143, 152, 174. *See also*
science
art critic as pointer, 150–51
art criticism, language of, 146
artworks as intermediaries, xvi
Ascent of Mt. Carmel, 176
asceticism, 89–90, 116, 177
atman, 82, 153
"Atman is Brahman," 191
Augustine
and the baser self, 71
and the voice of God, 174
anti-intellectual side of, 147
knowledge of God, 75
on beauty, 107, 109
on loving God, 169
on self-integration, 86
on surrender to God, 50
Austin, Richard Cartwright, 78
auteur theory of filmmaking, 119
avatar, xvi, 23, 154

Barron, Frank 135, 148
Baum, Lyman Frank, 40
Beardsley, Monroe C., 149
Beatrice of Nazareth, 30, 47
beauties
higher, 112
physical, 108–109, 112, 116
supernatural, 184
beautiful
every object as, 112
from the holistic perspective of
biology, 128
Tao transcends the, 108
beauty
and intentions, 195
and subjectivism and objectivism, 110–111

and the intellect, 131
and the I-Thou relation, 111
as an extreme degree of a
property, 125
as illumination, 24
as indefinable, 68
as light, 61–62
as the real seen with love, 110
austere, 127, 177
"Beauty itself," 113, 153
contextualist theory of, 127–28
divine, 110, 183–84
eternal, 112
judgments of pure, 58
like love, 111
metaphysical theory of, 129
naturalistic theory of, 129
revelatory aspect of, 112. *See
also* revelation
spiritual, 108–109, 124, 125,
127, 131
Taoist paradigm of, 124
transcendent, 129
two kinds of, 109, 125
whatever exists has, xvii
*Beauty and Holiness: the Dialogue
between Aesthetics and
Religion,* 3
Bell, Clive
how art works can move one,
139
on aesthetic emotion, 142
on significant form, 34, 36, 69,
189
on the great ages of religion
and art, xv
on viewing objects as ends,
59–60
Bender, Sue, 18, 39, 60
Bergson, Henri, 89
Bernini, Gianlorenzo, 67
Bhagavadgītā, xvi, xvii, 6, 21
bhakti, 97
bhakti marga, 90
bhakti yoga, 174
Bianco, Frank 158–59
Black Elk, 31, 44, 85, 123, 169

Blake, William, 2, 168
Bodhisattva, xvi, 23
Bokser, Ben-Zion, 168
Bonaventure, St., 32, 109, 112–13, 172
Bonhoeffer, Dietrich, 2
Bosanquet, Bernard, 130, 132
Botticelli, Sandro 151
Brahman, defined xvi, 18, 38, 80, 191
Brother Giles, xviii
Buber, Martin
  every thing can appear as a you, 65
  I-Thou relation and one's whole being, the, 40–43
  narrow ridge, the, 158
  no God-hunting, 62
  on asceticism, 116
  on self-realization, 76
  on silence and the Thou, 147
  relation, purpose of, 58
  return to the Thou, 136
  versus a Hindu monist, 192
  versus Spinoza, 118–19
Buddha, 1, 90, 158, 170
Buddha-nature, 13, 153
Buddhism, xvi, 153
Buddhist Christian Studies, 4
Buechner, Frederick, 71
Bullough, Edward, 54

Canaday, John, 158
Canticle of Brother Sun, xvii, 112, 168
Cantique des Cantiques, Le, 30
Carey, Joyce 54
Carlson, Allen, 117–18, 145
catharsis, 173
Catherine of Siena, 87
Catholic Myth: The Behavior and Beliefs of American Catholics, The, 22
Caussade, Jean-Pierre de, 50
Cezanne, Paul, 152, 157
Chagall, Marc
  on love, 97, 177
  on Monet's work, 142
  on mysticism, 171, 182
  on negative language, 143
  on the invisible, 141
  praising Cezanne, 37
  refusal to disengage art from life, 11
Chan, Wing-tsit, 131
Chang, C.Y., 45, 73, 125, 155
Chesterton, G.K., 52, 102, 116, 118, 119
ch'i, 12, 37, 117, 142
child
  and harmony, xix
  and letting go, 137
  and receptivity, 134
  and the I-Thou outlook, 52
  as infant, 77
  in religion and art, xv
  van Gogh on, 10
  who addresses the trees and stars, 44
childhood, 85, 115, 135, 136
childlike, 81, 133–35, 137, 156, 167
children, 134, 181
children's art, 135, 138
Christ
  and the child, 12
  emptied himself, 73
  imitation of, 90, 133, 134, 144
  incarnation of, xvi, 9
  in one vision, 66
  picture of, 195
  present wherever, 89
  sacrifice of, 37
  suffering of, 68
Christianity, xix, 4–7, 9, 88, 192
Christo, 46
Chuang Tzu
  and the butterfly anecdote, 135
  on fish enjoying themselves, 117
  on opposites or distinctions, 126
  on the beautiful, 111, 125. *See also* beautiful

on the location of the Tao, 127
on the significance of a
mustard seed, 15
on the usefulness of uselessness, 60
poetry of, xvi
Cloud of Unknowing, The,
on art as penultimate, 59
on contemplation, 26, 66, 72
on empathizing with Christ,
68. *See also* Christ
on emptying the mind, 38
on forgetting time and place,
36
on love, 97, 176. *See also* love
on prayer, 47. *See also* prayer
on the receiver, 49
Coleridge, Samuel Taylor, 49,
191
Collingwood, Robin G., 150, 165
*Commentary on Lao Tzu by
Wang Pi,* 131
Concerning the Spiritual in Art,
2
Confessions, The, 174
Confucius, 1, 58, 103, 169
Constable, John, xvii
contextualism, 128, 130
Coomaraswamy, Ananda K.
all arts as representations, 17
his concept of beauty, 112. *See
also* beauty
identification of art and
religion, xvi, 10, 19, 139,
195
on aesthetic experience, 139.
See also aesthetic experience
on the artist, 141
"copying the masters," 178–79
craft, 150
craftsman, 150, 165
craftsmanship, 140
craftsperson, 41, 86, 193
Crane, Hart, 171
creation
and revelation, 178. *See also*
revelation

artistic, 58, 155
divine, 155
ex nihilo, 155
of artworks and the self, 82
paradox of, 155
creative act, 75, 148, 168
creative power, 49, 159, 176
creative process
analysis of, 103
artists transfigure things in,
62
as beyond comprehension,
161–62
conclusion of, 150
direction of, 168
idea of, 162
reciprocity in, 45
what motivates the, 89
creativity
and an original image, 172
and return, 133, 137. *See also*
return
and spirituality, 64
and sympathy, 131
artistic, 155, 176
divine, 119, 162
four-part model of, 162, 171
in Taoist thought, 163
moments of, 192
preparation for, 163, 164
seat of, 129
sincerity a necessary condition
for, 173
touchstone of art and religion,
156
true self rich in, 72. *See also*
self
uniqueness in art and religion,
158–59. *See also* art and
religion
versus novelty, 161
work in, 170–74. *See also*
afflation

Dark Night of the Soul, 66, 92,
160, 185
da Vinci, Leonardo, xviii, 96

De Mello, Anthony, 55
Demoiselles d'Avignon, Les, 158
demon of inhibition, 160. *See also* Satan
demonic, 160, 168
desert
  and God, 44
  Edward Abbey on the, 147
  only good for, 57
  praying in the, 78. *See also* prayer
  Teresa on the, 144
De Staebler, Stephen, 102, 176
detachment
  as "naked nothingness," 56. *See also* nothingness
Dewey, John, 20, 101, 119, 163
Dharmakāya, xvi, 23, 38, 108, 184, 189
dialogue
  between the I and the Thou, 9, 103, 118. *See also* whole being
  interfaith, 4–5
  in the act of creation, 44
Diamond, Malcolm L., 118
Dickie, George, 8
Discovery of the Art of the Insane, The, 136
disinterestedness, 55, 67. *See also* detachment
Dixon, John W., 2
Donatists, 173
Duchamp, Marcel, 2, 166

Ecstasy of St. Teresa, The, 67
Edwards, Cliff, 137
Edwards, Jonathan, 102
Einstein, Albert, 80
El Greco, 67
Eliot, T.S., 53, 193
Emptiness, 37–40, 73, 143. *See also* nothingness and the void
eternal moment, 124. *See also* eternal present and present moment

eternal present, 35–36. *See also* eternal moment and present moment
eternal Thou, 10, 41, 43–44, 71, 77, 89, 94, 117, 161
exclusivism, 5, 7
Existentialists, 14

Fauves, the, 157
Fellini, Federico, 12
Ficino, Marsilis, 96–97
finite versus the infinite, paradox of, 154
Fish, Stanley E., 187
forger, 76, 104
forgery, 11, 79, 173, 178
formalists, 19
"form follows function," 58
form of the formless, 39, 81, 124
For the Sake of Heaven, 54
Fountain, 2
Francis of Assisi, St.
  and animals, 55, 135
  and I-Thou relations, 41, 44, 46, 52, 115–19, passim. *See also* I-Thou relations
  and the stigmata, 31, 68
  and the voice of God, 31, 166, 168
  a unity of opposites, 102
  finds God everywhere, xvii, 184
  imagistic religious experiences of, 172. *See also* religious experiences
  on appreciating creation, 112–14, 121, 144–45
  on appreciating the One and the many, 108–109, 120, 123, 124
  one of his disciples, xviii
  on physical beauties, 109–110. *See also* beauties
  on the simplicity of, 177–78

freedom
  in art and religion, 51–52, 81,
    125, 174, 179, 180, 181, 192
  of the artist, 175, 176
  of the spectator, 182
Freud, Sigmund, 73, 101, 132
Friedman, Maurice, 14
Fry, Roger, 57, 59, 152

Gandhi, Mahatma, 7
Gauguin, Paul
  and fundamental questions, 16
  and the aesthetic capacity of
    humans, 27
  artist as useful, 136–37
  asceticism of, 89, 90
  on art and nirvana, 141
  on harmony, 105. See also
    harmony
  on love and mystery, 98. See
    also love
  on painters and men of letters,
    145
  on the child, 134. See also child
God
  as "good for nothing," 60
  "eclipse of," 3
  "is dead," xv, 1–3
God's World, 122
Greeley, Andrew M., 22, 68, 187
Green, Julien, 144–45
Grunewald, Mathias, 2
Guernica, 16, 157, 162

Hammer, Louis Z., 52
Hammer, Rabbi Reuven, 158
Happold, F.C., 56
harmony
  and aesthetic experience, xvii.
    See also aesthetic experience
  and chidren's literature, 136
  and freedom, 100. See also
    freedom
  and return, 133. See also return
  and the self, 74. See also self
  and union, 91. See also union

  as beauty, 107, 124, 125, 127.
    See also beauty
  as ordering of opposites, 101–
    105, passim
  between humans and animals,
    135
  cosmic, 156
  highest form of union, xviii, 99
  in art, religion, and love, 97
  of silence, 40. See also silence
  within and without, 129
  with nature, 132, 138, 174
Hassidism, 135, 159
Hawthorne, Nathaniel, 91
Heer, Fredrich, 103
Hegel, 31, 141, 189
Heidegger, Martin, 139
Hemingway, Ernest, 42–43
Hepburn, Ronald W., 127
Hildegard of Bingen, 137, 173
Hinduism, xvi, xix, 6, 174, 192
Hisamatsu, Shin'ichi, 33–34
Hobbes, Thomas, 169
Hocking, William Ernest, 165
Rolston, Holmes, III, 127
holy
  and the beautiful as omnipres-
    ent, xvii. See also beautiful
  and the numinous, 111. See
    also numinous
  a relational concept, 110
  as the unconditional, 185
  defined, 68
  for Tillich, 15–16
  its twofold character, 114–15
  Meister Eckhart on the, 64
Hommage à Apollinaire, 85
Horden, William E., 8
Horses Mouth, The, 54
hsu, 39, 164
Hua-p'u, 101
humility, 56, 80, 177
hun t'un, 138

I and the Village, 135
I and Thou, 136

I-Ching, 101
Idea of the Holy, The, 114
identity paradox, 19
I-It relations
  and science, 41, 51, 52, 115,
    159
  and usefulness, 58
  frustrate reciprocity, 45
  ownership and, 46
Imitation of Christ, 59
immanence and transcendence,
    paradox of, 142
Impressionism, 152, 153, 157
Impressionists, 152, 157
Incarnation, xvi, 153–54
inception, 162, 163, 164
incubation, 164–67
ineffable and negative language,
    the, 143–44
innate Thou, 76–77. *See also* I-
  Thou relations
inner need, 172–73
inspiration
  and active waiting, 161
  and emptiness, 73. *See also*
    emptiness
  and skills and techniques, 164
  and surrender, 166, 167
  as divine, 162, 168, 169, 184,
    185, 190
  as fleeting, 170
intentions, 172
  as irrelevant, 195
  everything hallowed through,
    65
  in art and religion, 192
  intentional fallacy, 193
  lack of, 130
  necessary for creativity, 194
  religion flows from, 172
Interior Castle, The, xv, 92, 167
intermediaries, 22–24
interpenetration
  between art and religion, 10
  between external and internal
    beauty, 109. *See also* beauty

  between humans and nature,
    87
  of all things, 105
  of the aesthetic and the
    sacred, xiv
  of the artist and nature, 138
  of the human and the divine,
    95
  of the One and the many, 123
  of the self and the other, xviii.
    See also self
  of the universal and the par-
    ticular, 34, 94, 108, 116, 131.
    See also universal and
    particular
intrinsic value, 58–59, 60, 188
intuition, 130, 139–40, 142, 149,
    162, 170
  arguments for, 140–41, 149.
    See also prajna
intuitionism, 140, 149
Ion, 92, 149, 190
irrationality, 36, 136, 143, 149,
    166, 180. *See also* Plato
Islam, xvi, 7, 147, 192
I-Thou and I-It relations, xv
  defined, 3
I-Thou relations
  and art, 139
  and nature appreciation, 115,
    118
  and one's total being, 46. *See*
    also whole being
  and painting, 139
  and the aesthetic attitude, 52.
    See also aesthetic attitude
  and the infant, 77
  and the self, 78. *See also* self
  and the spirt of the artist, 24
  and the unpredictable, 150
  and wholeness, 83. *See also*
    union
  anti-intellectual aspect of, 139
  as latent everywhere, 64, 119
  as receptive, 44, 51
  as trans-practical, 58

preserve distinctness and
mutuality, 189, 192
reciprocity between the artist
and materials, 166
revelation and creation, 178.
See also Buber, Martin
Īśvara, 181

James, Henry, 49, 50, 166
James of Massa, xviii
James, William
and the "more," 6, 121
judge interior states by their
fruits, 140
on drunkenness and art, xvi.
See also art and religion
on harmony, 105. *See also*
harmony
on mystical states, 65, 170, 192
on receptivity, 49. *See also*
receptivity
on sensible images, 30
on the artist and the religious
person, 90. *See also* art and
religion
on "throwing the burden
down," 165
on union, 87. *See also* union
Jeffries, Richard, 122
jen, 13, 97, 100
Jhanji, Rekha, 81, 181
jivanmukta, 184
jnana marga, 90, 171
jnana yoga, 174
John of the Cross, St.
against monism, 92, 93, 165,
169. *See also* monism
and lack of workmanship as
desirable, 186
"darkness" of the soul, 157
know oneself to know God, 75
love alone unites the soul with
God, 97. *See also* love
on contemplation, 165
on doing nothing, 175, 176.
See also Taoism

on the Holy Spirit, 169
on the role of faith, 148
on the two parts of the soul, 72
seeking God without stopping,
66
Judaism, xvi, xx, 4, 5, 6, 7, 9,
23, 192
Jung, Carl, 71, 84

Kahn, Louis, 180
k'ai-ho, 103–105, 158
Kandinsky, Wassily
his paintings, 18
inner necessity, 81, 142, 172,
173
on art and religion, xv. *See
also* art and religion
on form, xviii
on freedom, 179–80. *See also*
freedom
on harmony, 40, 102, 105. *See
also* harmony
on nonrepresentational painting, 2, 17
on the capacity of the artwork,
9
Kant, Immanuel
and aesthetic appreciation, 77
antinomies of, 139
art and the "thing in itself,"
153
categories of, 147
intentions and the good will,
194. *See also* intentions
on pure beauty, 58–59. *See
also* beauty
transcendental unity of
apperception, 82
karma, 82, 157, 158
karma marga, 90, 171
karma yoga, 174
Kazantzakis, Nikos, 168
Kierkegaard, Soren, 101, 161
Klee, Paul, 2, 13, 80, 141
koan, 148
Kohanski, Alexander S., 136

Krishna, xvi
Kristeller, Paul Oscar, 96
k'ung, 39. *See also* emptiness

Lane, Belden C., 37, 54
    anything as sacramental, 63
    on El Greco's paintings, 67
    on return, 136. *See also* return
    on "second naiveté," 135
    on silence, 144. *See also* silence
Lao Tzu
    and names, 131
    and the childlike, 12. *See also*
        childlike
    axial age of, 1
    distinction between Tao and
        nature, 119
    his turn toward nature, 123
    on ignorance, 137
Last Temptation of Christ, The, 168
law of reversion, 104
Leaves of Grass, 63, 180
lila, 181. *See also* play
Little Flowers of St. Francis,
    The, 36, 114
Living Flame of Love, The, 92
love
    and union, 96–97. See also union
    art, religion and, xvii, 40, 73, 98
    as disinterested, 55. *See also*
        disinterestedness
    Chagall on, 177
    inclusiveness of, 47
    of children, 137. *See also* children
    on contemplative love, 66
    religion without, 98
Love and Exile: An Autobio-
    graphical Trilogy, 12
Love Song of J. Alfred Prufrock,
    The, 193
Lowell, Amy, 164, 167
Loyola, Ignatius, 22, 157

MacGregor, John M., 136
Madonna and Child with
    Singing Angels, 151

magic, 51, 150, 156
magician, 166, 193
Mairs, Nancy, 92
mandala, 18, 21, 84, 85, 105
Man with the Hoe, The, 99
Marble Faun, The, 91
marga, 144. *See also bhakti*
    marga, karma marga, and
    jnana marga
Maritain, Jacques, 45, 79–80
Martin, James Alfred, Jr., xiii, 3
Martland, Thomas R., 150, 156,
    157, 158
Marx, Karl, xiv
Master of Flemalle, 2
Matisse, Henri, 79, 90, 142, 157
maya, 94
meaning
    and value of life, 13
    in life, 35, 197
    of existence, xx, 144
    of life, 16, 144, 159
means and ends, 150, 187, 188
Mearns, Hughes, 160
Meister Eckhart,
    and prayer, 45. *See also* prayer
    and the Godhead as nothing,
        37, 143
    and the holy, 64. *See also* holy
    even in evil, 62
    on seeking God, 176
    on the being of a stone, 12
Mencius, 133, 153
Meno, 149
Merton, Thomas
    and being over knowing, 75
    and Chuang Tzu, 7
    and the meaning of life, 159.
        See also meaning
    and transformative power of
        prayer, 57. *See also* prayer
    art and the self, 74. *See also* self
    art as evidence for the spiri-
        tual, 140
    on the aesthetics of monastic
        buildings, 177

method, 174–184 passim
"of no-method," 175, 180. *See also* wu-fa
Meyer, Franz, 85
Michelangelo, Buonarroti, 2, 12
microcosm, 128–29
Mi Fu, 179
Milinda-pañhā, 186
Millay, Edna St. Vincent, 122
Millet, Jean-François, 99
Mohammed, 61
moksha, 179
Monet, Claude, 78
monism
    and spiritual experiences, 191–92
    as problematic, 93
    described, 91
    of Advaita Vedanta, 94
    origin of, 96
    Teresa and John on, 92
    versus communion, 95
Mother Teresa of Calcutta, 53
Mu Ch'i
    painting of six persimmons, 33, 114, 151, 177, 178
Muir, John, 81, 87, 108, 147, 175
Mustard Seed Garden Manual of Painting, The, 175
mysterium tremendum et fascinans, 114, 115. *See also* wholly other
mystery, 121, 138, 152
mysticism
    extrovertive vs. introvertive, 109, 184
    stages of, 171–72
Mysticism: A Study in the Nature and Development of Man's Spiritual Consciousness, 30

Nagasena, 186
Nasr, Seyyed Hossein, 1
Native American, 10, 53, 85, 169, 192

nature, to personify, 117
"neti, neti," 38, 143
Newman, Barnett, 17, 73
Nichomachean Ethics, 76
Nietzsche, 1, 88, 132, 158
Nirmānakāya, 23
Ni Tsan, 46, 163, 179
Notes of a Painter, 90
nothing
    creation from, 155, 156
    doing, 42, 175
    Existentialist's question, 14
    Tao as, 108
    ultimate reality as, 37, 38, 39, 143
nothingness, 37, 38, 39, 42, 72–73, 143. *See also* emptiness and the void
Nouwen, Henri J.M., 54, 62, 135, 158, 193
numen, 39
numinous, 14, 18, 19, 30, 38
    and art, 111, 153
    and the sublime, 185, 186
    as "that which is nothing," 39
    as transcendent of rational thought, 143
    catalyst can be routine, 62–63
    criticism of, 149
    defined, 68
    described by Otto, 151, 196

objectivism, 110, 111
O. Henry, 162–63
omnipresence, 61–66 passim
    irony of, 63
    of beauty, 61. *See also* beauty
    of Christ, 61. *See also* Christ
    of light, 61
    of positive value, 62
    of the divine, xv–xvi, 12, 13, 16
    paradox of, 65
opus operatum, 195
Otto, Rudolph
    on receptivity, 53. *See also* receptivity

Otto, Rudolph *(continued)*
  on revelation as indefinite, 138
  on the art of China, Japan,
    and Tibet, 34
  on the element of fascinosum
    and the element of tremen-
    dum, 157–58. *See also*
    wholly other
  on the numinous, 18–19, 62–
    63, 68, 114, 151, 153, 196.
    See also numinous
  on the sublime, 185. *See also*
    sublime
  on the wholly other, 69, 121,
    142. *See also* wholly other

pantheism, 119, 120, 121, 122
pantheist, 52–53, 113, 118, 119,
  120, 121
passivity, 49, 150, 161, 164–66
  passim, 170. *See also*
  receptivity
peace that passes all understanding, 124, 186. *See also*
  ananda
Pei, I.M., 39
Pepper, Stephen C., 128, 130
personal, the, 119
personhood, 115–16, 118
Phaedrus, 112
Picasso, Pablo
  and children's art, 79
  and Guernica, 16, 157, 162
  and humility, 80
  and *Les Demoiselles d'Avignon*,
    158
  economic well-being, 46
  on creativity, 156
  on discovery of the perceivable,
    142
  on emptiness, 40
Plato
  and divine madness, 162. *See
    also* irrationality
  and the real, 109, 189–90
  on forms, 17, 18, 107
  recollection, doctrine of, 112

play, 134, 181. *See also* līlā
Plotinus, 132
pluralism, 4, 5, 6, 7, 35
p'o, 32, 38, 40, 124, 156
Pollack, Jackson, 182
Pourrat, P., 68
practical orientation, 57, 58, 59
prajñā, 126, 149. *See also*
  intuition and *ahnung*
prayer
  as aesthetic, 21
  as unique, 158, 159
  creativity in, 159
  highest state of, 148
  of one's whole being, 45, 47
  paradox of, 161
  perpetual, 54, 65, 66
  persevere in, 175
  traditional, 196
  two ways of, 32
present moment, 134. *See also*
  eternal present and eternal
  moment
Principles of Art, The, 150
psychical distance, 45, 54, 93.
  See also aesthetic attitude
Psychology of the Imagination, 190

quietism, 164

Ramakrishna, Paramahamsa, 12
rasika, 181
Ray, Man, 57
receptivity, 49, 50. *See also*
  passivity
relativism, 125. *See also* objectivism and subjectivism
religion
  and the art form of humor, 9
  as artistic, xvi, 21–24 passim
  becomes magic, 98. *See also*
    magic
  defined, xx
religious experience, 32, 185. *See
  also* aesthetic experience
Republic, The, 189
return, 133, 136, 137

revelation
  a quest for the real, 190
  art and the possibility of, 8
  child-state and, the, 133, 138
  in art, 139, 151–52, 187, 189
  in dream states, 169
  of the finite in the infinte, 142
  paradox of, 153
Roiphe, Anne, 5
root, 118, 119, 120
Rowley, George, 103
Ryder, Albert Pinkham, 2

sacred and the profane
  all things as sacred, 13, 62
  in art, xix, 62
  no dichotomy between, 116, 188
Sadler, M.T.H., 152
Sambhogakāya, 23
Sartre, Jean-Paul, 189, 190
Satan, 144, 160. *See also* demon of inhibition
Schleiermacher, Frederich, xiv, 8, 141–42
Schneider, Reinhold, 102
Schweitzer, Albert, 12
science
  God and art replaced by, 3
  objectivity of, 115
  "second naiveté," 135, 136
sefirot, xvi, 23, 107
self
  actualization of, 159
  and nature, 78
  finding one's, 74, 75
  one's true, 71–72, 73, 156
Self-Consuming Artifacts: The Experience of Seventeenth-Century Literature, 187
Shakers, 21
Shihab ad-adin, Shaykh, 186
Shih-t'ao
  no method as the perfect method, 175
  on copying the masters, 178–79

on doing nothing, 42
on "harmonious atmosphere," 101
painting the entire universe, 129
preparation through identification, 163
Sibley, Frank, 142–43
silence, 39, 40, 126, 144, 147, 161
simple beauty, paradox of, 128
sincerity
  as essential to art, 138, 193
  of the artist, 81, 193
Singer, Isaac Bashevis, 12
Sircello, Guy, 125, 129
Slivka, Rose, 15
Smith, Houston, 9
space, 35–40 passim, 143
Spinoza, Baruch, 118, 171
spiritual consciousness, the
  aesthetic as an aspect of, 196–97
spiritual versus the religious, xx, 183, 188
Spoils of Poynton, The, 49, 50, 166
Springtime à la Carte, 163
St. Eligius, 146
Stations of the Cross, 17
stigmata, 31
Story of My Heart, The, Richard Jeffries, 122
Strada, La, 12
subgression, 188
subjectivism, 110, 111
sublime
  and natural beauties, 114. *See also* beauties
  and peace, 124. *See also* peace that passes all understanding
  and wonder, 115. *See also* wonder
  in art, 36, 39
  straddles the aesthetic and the religious, 14
  versus the numinous, 185. *See also* numinous

suchness, 15
sui generis emotions, 49, 66–69
    passim, 196
śūnyattā, 38, 84, 143
super-rationalism, 140, 142
Suzuki, D.T., 118, 120, 143

Taoism
    and harmony with nature, 102,
        135, 147
    and return, 133. See also return
    creative process in, 79. See
        also creative process
    "do without doing" in, 176. See
        also John of the Cross
    its spiritual masterpiece, 6
    Tao is in even urine and dung,
        62
Taoist painting and poetry, 173–
    74
Tao Te Ching, xv, 6, 38, 39, 42,
    71, 81, 88, 90, 125, 126, 130,
    131, 133, 143
"Tat tvam asi," 80
techne, 150
Tennyson, Alfred, 8–9
Teresa of Avila, St.
    against monism, 92. See also
        monism
    and the paradox of omnipres-
        ence, 65. See also omnipres-
        ence
    anti-intellectualism of, 147,
        148, 149
    finds the sacred in everything,
        62
    humor of, 9
    identifies two kinds of visions,
        32
    on art, 109, 195
    on divine inspiration, 168,
        169–70. See also inspiration
    on harmony, 94, 95. See also
        harmony
    on intentions, 194. See also
        intentions

on joyful suffering, 67
on knowledge of God and the
    self, 75
on loss of self, 79
on love, 97, 114. See also love
on not striving, 42
on passivity, 164–65. See also
    passivity
on receptivity, 49. See also
    receptivity
on Satan and prayer, 160, 161.
    See also Satan and prayer
on the desert and Satan, 144.
    See also the desert
on "the greatest freedom," 50,
    62, 65. See also freedom
on union with God, 76. See
    also union
spiritual experience in, 174
tactile sensations of, 30
visions and artistic master-
    pieces, 86
theophany, 184–85
Thomas á Kempis, St.
    aesthetic as penultimate, the,
        183
    distinguishes between two
        wills, 72
    knowledge of self and God in,
        75. See also self
    on emptiness, 38. See also
        emptiness
    on intentions, 194. See also
        intentions
    on learning, 147
    on love, 98, 59. See also love
    on self-seeking, 160–61
    on "those who love Jesus," 59
    "use of the sacraments will
        cease," 196
Thoreau, Henry David
    against monism, 93. See also
        monism
    as a confluence of the spiri-
        tual, aesthetic, and scientific,
        191

experience of nature, 6, 123, 186

on the self in nature and nature in the self, 129. *See also* interpenetration

Tibetan Buddhism, 175

tif'eret, 107

Tillich, Paul

aesthetic experiences and action, 190. *See also* aesthetic experience

against monism, 96. *See also* monism

and revelatory ecstasy, 151–52. *See also* revelation

art as ineffable, 143

art as religious, 14, 15, 16

art as the direct way to ultimate reality, 188

on "Beauty itself," 153. *See also* beauty

on creative artists as rule breakers, 176

on non-art and non-religion, 3

on non-objective artists, 18, 19

on the demonic, 160

on the subjectivity of the artist, 78

religion as the experience of the holy, 185. *See also* holy

religion described, 8

religious experiences versus aesthetic experiences, 186

Tolstoy, Leo

against exclusivism, 5, 7

art and spiritual union, xviii, xix, 4, 9, 13, 26, 88, 89

art and the ego, 79

art defined, 97, 99

art, essence of, 72

art, purpose of, 103

counterfeit art, 8, 177, 179. *See also* forgery

on art schools, 81, 145, 148, 177

on intentions, 172. *See also* intentions

transmission theory of art, 74, 87, 98. *See also* art, communication theory of

total response, 49, 40–47 passim. *See also* whole being

tradition and innovation, 157

transcendental unity of apperception, 82

tsadik, xvi, 23

tz'u, 97

ugliness

and moral action, 113

as the unformed, 24, 112

ugly

as stunted expression, 173

as unexpressed form, 24

charred landscape as, 127

nature is never, 130, 131, 132

"there can be no 'beautiful' or 'ugly,' " 126

Underhill, Evelyn

on beauty, 110. *See also* beauty

on rapport with things, 89

on spiritual perception, 57–58

on the artist and disinterested love, 55. *See also* love

on the artist and the saint, 29, 191, 192

on visions and voices, 30. *See also* visions and voices

rhythm in mystical as well as musical perception, 103

union

and God, 83, 86

and harmony, 102. *See also* harmony

and the union of communion, 89

as a prerequisite, xvii

in art and religion, 84

in one's object of attention, xviii

of communion, 87, 89

of relationship, xviii

of self-integration, 195. *See also* self-integration

union *(continued)*
  religion needs art to foster, 138
  three senses of, xvii, 83, 91
  with all things, 76
  with God, 76
  with the absolute and aes-
    thetic experience, xiv. *See
    also* 83–105 passim
universal and particular
  coincidence of, 33–35, 94, 184.
    See also aesthetic experience
    of nature
Upanishads, 21, 81, 141

van Eyck, Hubert and Jan, 2
van Gogh, Vincent
  and an I-Thou relationship
    with nature, 65, 77. *See also*
    I-Thou relations
  a painting of a peasant's
    shoes, 13, 62
  on inspiration, 164. *See also*
    inspiration
  on passivity, 49–50. *See also*
    passivity
  on the infant and the eternal,
    10. *See also* child
  "ordinary" spirituality of, 114
  Tillich on, 152
Van Gogh and God, 137
*Varieties of Religious Experience,
  The*, 170
via negativa, 37
visions
  as inexhaustible, 87
  beatific, 112, 196
  of Hildegard of Bingen, 173
  of Teresa of Avila, St., 65–66,
    67, 85, 86
  of the artist and the saint, 29
  two kinds of, 32
Vivekananda, 5
voice(s)
  "does not hear thy," 161
  heard by the artist or the
    saint, 29, 166
  of God, 168, 174, 189

voices and visions, 30, 31
void, the,
  and space, 37
  and the Lord, 38
  as self and source of every-
    thing, 155–56
  as superconceptual, 184
  disappearing into, 95, 130
  identify with, 84
  in a Chinese painting, 39, 87.
    See also emptiness and
    nothingness

Walden, 46
Waley, Arthur, 126
Walking Buffalo, 53
Weiss, Paul
  on abstract painting as appro-
    priate for religious art, 19
  on all religions, xvi
  on religious art as embodying
    existence, 153
  on tension between art and
    religion, 186–87
What is Art?, 148
Wheelwright, Philip, 64, 146
Whitehead, Alfred North, xiv,
  125, 139
Whitman, Walt, 63, 180
whole being
  action of, 41, 45, 46, 51
  and dialogue. *See also* dialogue
  Buber on, 42, 52
  Tillich on the arts and, 152
wholly other
  and aesthetic emotion as
    unique, 142
  and significant form, 68–69
  and the religious encounter,
    189
  as the *mysterium tremendum
    et fascinans*, 114. *See also*
    Otto, Rudolph
  as the transcendent side of
    God, 121
  like musical feeling, 68
  or numen, 39

Wittgenstein, Ludwig, 9
Wolterstorff, Nicholas
   abstract art and the holy, 17.
      See also art
   art and the meaning of existence,
      144. *See also* meaning
   art as distracting from liturgy,
      187
   moral versus aesthetic, 190
   on anti-art, 2–3
   on finding the self, 73–74. *See
      also* self
wonder, 115, 135, 138
Wonderful Wizard of Oz, The, 40,
   136
Wright, Frank Lloyd, 39
"writer's block," xv, 160. *See
      also* art and religion:
      dryness

wu
   as nonbeing, 125, 143, 156
   as Tao, 38, 86
   in Chinese landscape painting,
      39
   wu-fa, 175, 176. *See* method
   wu-wei, 42, 175, 190

Yepes, Diego de, 85

Zen Buddhism, xvi
   and enlightenment, 161
   emptying one's mind, 149
   power of its arts, 7, 9
   sacred as present in every
      artifact, 13
Zen Buddhist painters, 153
Zen Buddhist paintings, 47, 167
Zimmerman, Benedict, 164

CPSIA information can be obtained
at www.ICGtesting.com
Printed in the USA
LVOW12s0020300316

481355LV00001B/4/P